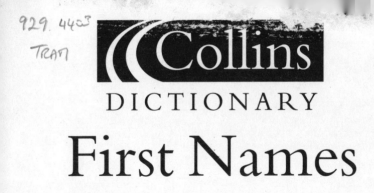

DICTIONARY
First Names

DICTIONARY
First Names

Julia Cresswell

HarperCollins*Publishers*

2469498

HarperCollins Publishers
Westerhill Road, Glasgow G64 2QT

www.collins.co.uk

First published 2003

© Julia Cresswell 2003

Reprint 10 9 8 7 6 5 4 3 2 1 0

ISBN 0 00 716540 4

A catalogue record for this book is available from the British
Library

Text design by Clare Crawford

Printed and bound in Great Britain by Clays Ltd, St Ives plc

The Author

Julia Cresswell is an expert on the history of the English language. She lives in Oxford, with her husband and son, Alexander, where she writes and teaches the history of the language, medieval literature and children's literature. She has written a dozen books, including *Collins Gem Irish First Names*, the *Guinness Book of British Place Names* and the *Penguin Dictionary of Clichés*.

Contents

Introduction   9

Registering your baby's birth   13

A to Z of first names   17

Appendix 1:
  Websites   315

Appendix 2:
  Top 100 boys' and girls' names in England and
    Wales, 2002   317
  Top 100 boys' and girls' names in Scotland, 2002   318
  Top 100 boys' and girls names in the USA, 2001   319

Introduction

Today's parents have an enormous pool of names to choose from, probably more than at any other time in history. The traditional names for English speakers come from three main sources. There are the Hebrew names from the Bible, particularly from the Old Testament. The Latin and Greek names of the classical world are also often from the Bible, this time from the New Testament, for in the cosmopolitan world of the Roman Empire names from all sorts of sources were found mixed together. The classical names of the New Testament made them respectable for Christians in earlier times to use, so that names that we think of as primarily from history or mythology, such as Alexander or Phoebe, were made respectable by having early Christian associations. However, many of the classical names do indeed come from classical mythology and history, and particularly from their use in classical literature. The third group is that of the old Germanic names brought to the UK by both the Anglo-Saxons and the Normans, and, indeed, taken over much of western Europe by the great waves of Dark Age invaders from northwest Europe. Equally old is a smaller, fourth group of names – those from Celtic languages, some of which go back to pre-Roman times. Once mainly restricted to Wales, Ireland and the Highlands and islands of Scotland, many names from the Irish and closely related Gaelic languages have recently become very widely used indeed. Although Wales has an equally rich tradition, and one that is very much alive and growing in Wales itself, many of these names are still restricted to Wales. Only a representative sample of those that have become more generally used have been included in this book. In the last two centuries, which have seen wider travel alongside wider access to books, the range of names used has increased enormously. We now have names from all over the world, both Continental versions of traditional names and names from cultures with which our ancestors had little or no contact. This has led to a change in the attitude to what a 'real' name is, and as a result people now feel free to create a wonderful range of new names, many unique to their children. The danger here, of course, is that the child will have a lifetime of explaining what his or her name is and how it is spelt, but many of these names pass into general circulation, particularly those that are blends; that is, combinations of sounds from other names. In addition, a much wider range of spellings of any given name is used by parents, perhaps to distinguish their child's name from those of other children with the same name. I have tried to include as many of these different spellings as is reasonably possible under the standard or traditional form of the name. I have also included a wide range of short forms. This is not only to show the range available but also so that parents can check that all possible forms of a chosen name go harmoniously with the surname. For however determined a parent might be to use one particular form of a name, someone will at some time use a pet form of the name.

The move to increase the pool of names used is in part because the first name has become so much more important in our culture. Not so long ago, only those close to you would use your first name. The majority of people who spoke to you would address you by title and surname. To most of the world you would be Mr Smith, Mrs Jones, or whatever. Thus a quite small pool of traditional names would serve to distinguish members within a family. Now that first names are used on first meeting, many parents feel an urge to help their children stand out by giving them a memorable first name. Names are also used to mark which group you belong to. For this reason many of our new names, or at least those new to the general fund of names used by English speakers, come from America, with its rich mixture of cultures. There parents have used names drawn from the cultures they or their ancestors brought with them. Now that the USA has a large Spanish-speaking population, Spanish forms of names are noticeable in the published list of popular names. The African-American communities have sometimes chosen names from Africa and have often been responsible for introducing Muslim names to a wider public, and have been particularly rich coiners of new names, often blends of other names. Some have passed into wider circulation, some remained in restricted use. Significant also has been America's dominance of the entertainment world. I hope that those curious about the unusual names they find used by actors and musicians will find the answer here.

I have tried to indicate in this book the relative popularity of names in the major English-speaking countries. 'Popular' means that the name appears in the top ten to twenty names in the published lists of popular names or has come in with high scores over a number of years; 'well used' indicates somewhere lower down the charts; 'fashionable' indicates that a name may not rank particularly high in the charts but is being used by trend-setters or has been rising rapidly through the lower ranks and looks set to rise further. The internet has made a huge difference in accessing such information. The USA has a particularly good site, Popular Baby Names at http://www.ssa.gov/OACT/babynames/index.html. The UK is well served by the Office of National Statistics (http://www.statistics.gov.uk/cci/nugget.asp?id=184), which deals with names in England and Wales and has links to lists for Scotland and Northern Ireland. Detailed links for Ireland are on the Central Statistics Office site at http://www.cso.ie/text/pressreleases/babies 01.html. For Canada and Australia you need to find the relevant State sites. All these sites also contain links on such things as registering births. The internet is full of sites dealing with first names, many of them going for quantity rather than quality of accuracy. Two that I have found better than most – although I do not always agree with them – are Behind the Name (http://www. behindthe name.com/) and Baby Namer (http://www. babynamer.com/). Other website addresses are given in Appendix 1.

Most of the variant names in this book have been cross-referenced to the name you can find it under. But in order to include as many names as possible into the book, if the cross-reference would come next to the headword, then it has been left out. If you cannot find a name, please look for the name you want under alternative spellings, and check under overlapping sounds such as 'C' and 'K', or 'sh' and 'ch'.

I hope that this book will help you find just the right name for your child.

JULIA CRESSWELL, 2003

Registering your baby's birth

If you have your baby in a hospital in England or Wales, there is a good chance that your local registrar's office will have a branch there. It is worth taking advantage of this facility rather than having to cope with a new baby and getting down to the registrar's office later on. If nothing is said at the hospital, ask one of the nurses. Unfortunately, this facility is not available in Scotland where the regulations concerning the registration of births vary slightly from those in England and Wales.

By law, you have to register the birth of your child within 42 days of his or her birth, or within 21 days in Scotland. If you have not used a hospital office, you can go to any registrar's office, although the procedure is slightly simpler if you use your local one, the address of which should be in the phone book. Registration centres on the mother. If the baby's parents are married, either parent can register the birth. If they are not married, they can register the birth together if they go to the registrar together, or else the father must get special forms from the registrar's office in advance which, when filled in, will enable his details to go on the birth certificate. Otherwise, the father's details will be left blank, although it may be possible to fill these in later – talk to the registrar about this. There is no need to take the baby with you to the registrar, but only a parent can register the birth: a friend or relative will not do.

At the registrar's you will be asked to give the following information: the place and date of the baby's birth (in England the time of birth will be needed only if you have twins or more, although in Scotland it is always required); you will also need to state his or her sex, and will be asked for the names you intend to give your child. If the father's details are to go on the form you will need to give his full name, his date and place of birth and his occupation. The mother will be asked to give her full name, her maiden name if she has changed her surname and her place and date of birth. If she wishes, an occupation (current or previous) can be filled in. She has to give her usual address at the time of the birth, and, if she is married to the father, the date of marriage will be asked for. She will also be asked for the number of other children she has had.

All this information will be entered into a register, which you should then check carefully – it will be difficult to correct mistakes later – and then sign. You will then be given a free short birth certificate, which is all you need. You can also get full copies of the information on the register, if you would like to have them, and spare copies of either type of certificate. There is a charge for birth certificates that varies depending on the type you want, but it is always more expensive to get extra copies later than at the time of registration. It is probably worth considering an extra copy so that each parent can have one or so that one can be sent off with something like an application for a passport and you can still have one to hand.

If you still have not decided on a name for your baby by the time the limit for registration is up, you must still register the birth but the name can be left blank. You then have up to one year from registration to make up your minds, although in Scotland any correction to the records after registration is likely to attract a fee. If your baby is baptised, the baptismal certificate can be produced at the registrar's office as evidence of the child's name. (Extra names given at baptism can also be added in this way.) Otherwise, you need to ask the registrar's office for a Certificate of Naming and use this to have the names inserted. You can give your child any forenames or surname that you like. In Scotland the registrar has the power to refuse to record a name if he or she deems it to be potentially offensive, although in practice a name is rarely objected to. In England and Wales the registrar has no right to refuse your choice, although if your choice is too outrageous you may find that you are asked to think of the effect on the child before confirming that it is really what you want. Modern registrars are trained to be friendly and helpful, and you can always phone your local office for any advice you need; alternatively, contact The General Register Office, Smedley Hydro, Trafalgar Road, Birkdale, Southport PR8 2HH (telephone 0870 2437788) or The Registrar General's Office for Scotland, New Register House, Edinburgh (telephone 0131 334 0380).

A

Aakash see AKASH

Aaliyah *f*
Aliyyah (also found as **Aliyah, Aliah, Alia, Alea, Aleah** and **Alya**) is a feminine form of ALI. The name became popular in the USA in the form Aaliyah after the singer Aaliyah Houston (1974–2001) became famous. She regarded this as the Swahili form. The name has become more popular in the UK since her death in a plane crash. There is also a Hebrew girl's name, **Aliyah**, meaning 'to ascend'.

Aamena, Aaminah see AMINA

Aaron *m*
In the Old Testament, Aaron was the brother of MOSES and the first High Priest of Israel. The traditional interpretation links this name to the Hebrew for 'high mountain', but, like Moses, Aaron is probably an Egyptian name of unknown meaning. It is connected with the Arabic names **Harun** and **Haroun**, and has been in use since the Reformation. In the past it was pronounced with a first sound as in 'air' (hence the spelling **Aeron**), but now it is also found with a short 'a', a pronunciation reflected in the spelling **Ar(r)on**. See also ARRAN and ARUN.

Abbie, Abby see ABIGAIL

Abdullah *m*
A Muslim name from the Arabic for 'servant of Allah'. The short form **Abdul** also occurs.

AbdurRahim see RAHIM

Abe, Abie see ABEL, ABRAHAM

Abel *m*
In the Old Testament, Abel was the second son of ADAM and EVE and murdered by his brother Cain. The name may come from a Hebrew word for 'breath', but like so many of the earliest names, its meaning is doubtful. The name has been used in England since before the Norman Conquest. The short forms include **Abe** and **Abie**.

Abelard see ELOISE

Abigail *f*
From the Hebrew, meaning 'father rejoiced'. It was the name of one of King David's wives and was much used in England during the 16th and 17th centuries when many Old Testament names were popular. It was so popular for working-class women that it degenerated into a term for a lady's maid, so becoming unfashionable, but it is now very much back in favour. It is sometimes spelt **Abagail** or **Abigal**. The short forms, also used as independent names, include **Abbie**, **Abbey** (popular in Australia) **Abby** and **Gail**.

Abner *m*
From the Hebrew words for 'father of light'. In the Bible it is the name of King Saul's cousin, who was commander of the army. In England it came into common use, together with other biblical names, after the Reformation in the early 16th century. It is still found occasionally in North America, perhaps kept alive by the fame of Abner Doubleday, popularly supposed to have invented baseball. **Avner** is the Hebrew form of the name.

Abraham *m*
This is the name of the Old Testament patriarch who, for the first 90 years of his life, was called Abram, 'high father', but then was told by God that he should be called Abraham, 'father of many nations'. It was used in England regularly after the Reformation and became popular in North America where the abbreviation **Abe**, as in President Abe Lincoln (1809–65), was widely used and is currently increasing in popularity again. Other short forms are **Abie**, **Ham** and **Bram**. See also IBRAHIM

Absolom see AXEL

Ada *f*
A name that started life as a pet form for ADELA, ADELAIDE and
ADELINE, and so means 'noble'. It was fashionable in Britain in the
late 18th and 19th centuries, and well used in the USA in the first
half of the 20th century, but is now rare. **Adah** is often confused with
Ada, but is in fact derived from the Hebrew word for 'ornament' or
'brightness'. See also ZILLAH.

Adam *m*
From the Hebrew, meaning 'red', possibly referring either to skin
colour or to the clay from which God formed the first man. The
name was adopted by the Irish as early as the 7th century, when St
Adamnan, 'Little Adam', was Abbot of Iona. It was very common in
the 13th century and has been in use ever since, and is currently
well used throughout the English-speaking world. **Adamina** is a
rare feminine form.

Adeel see ADIL

Adela *f*
From the Old German, meaning 'noble'. It was common among the
Normans, who brought it to England. One of William the Conquer-
or's daughters had this name. The name died out but was later
revived and became fashionable in the French form **Adèle**. **Addie** or
Addy is used as a pet form for the names derived from this root (see
also ADELAIDE and ADELINE). Adela can also be spelt **Adella**, which
gives us the name DELLA, now more popular than its source.

Adelaide *f*
Derived from the Old German words meaning 'noble and kind'.
The name was common for centuries on the Continent but only
came to Britain in 1830 when Adelaide of Saxe-Coburg became
queen. Adelaide, the capital city of South Australia, was named
after this popular queen. It can be shortened to ADA, and ALIDA is
a Hungarian pet form. See also HEIDI.

Adeline *f*

Like Adelaide, this name is derived from the Old German for 'noble'. It was first cited in England in the Domesday Book and was common during the Middle Ages. After that it disappeared until the Victorian Gothic revival. It is best known from the song *Sweet Adeline*. ADA is sometimes used as a pet form, and **Alina** and **Aline**, now used as separate names, were also once short forms.

Adelice, Adelise see ALICE

Adil *m*

This is an Arabic name meaning 'just, honest'. It is also spelt **Adeel**, and there is a feminine form, **Adila**.

Adnan *m*

An Arabic name of uncertain meaning but traditionally interpreted to mean 'settler'. According to tradition, Adnan, a descendant of Abraham, was the ancestor of the North Arabians.

Adolph *m*

Use of Adolph, meaning 'noble wolf', and its Latin form **Adolphus**, made famous by Gustavus Adolphus (1594–1632) of Sweden, the warrior king nicknamed the 'Lion of the North', has mainly been restricted to Germanic and Scandinavian peoples or to their descendants, and has been even rarer since it became so firmly associated with the name of Hitler. However, the pet forms **Dolphus** and **Dolph**, as in the actor Dolph Lundgrun, are sometimes found.

Adrian *m*, **Adrienne** *f*

From the Latin meaning 'man from Adria', and a form of the name of the Roman Emperor **Hadrian**, who built the wall across northern England. It has been used since Roman times. Adrian and **Adrien** are now sometimes used as girls' names. **Adriana** is a rare female form, the French **Adrienne** being more popular. **Adria** and **Adrianne** are also found.

Aeneas, Aengus see ANGUS

Aeron see AARON

Afra see APHRA

Agatha *f*
From the Greek for 'good woman', this was the name of a 3rd-century martyr and saint. The short form is **Aggie**.

Agnes *f*
From the Greek meaning 'pure'. There was an early Christian martyr called Agnes, whose symbol is a lamb, since the name also sounds very like the Latin *agnus*, 'lamb'. Old forms still occasionally used include **Annis, Annice** and **Annes. Agneta** is the Swedish form and **Inez** is the anglicised form of the Spanish **Inés**. Agnes was popular in Scotland where it also became **Nessie** and **Nessa**. In Wales it became **Nest** and **Nesta. Aggie** is a short form shared with AGATHA. See also INA.

Ahmad *m*
This Arabic name is often spelt **Ahmed**. It is one of the names applied to the Prophet Mohammed and means 'more praiseworthy'.

Aidan *m*
An ancient Irish name that means 'little fire'. It was the name of a 7th-century Irish missionary who founded the monastery of Lindisfarne in Northumbria. The name was revived during the 19th century and is popular in Scotland, and is becoming more popular outside Celtic areas. It is sometimes anglicised as **Edan**.

Ailbhe see ELVIS

Aileen see EILEEN

Ailis, Ailish see ALICE, EILIS

Ailsa *f*
From the Scottish island, Ailsa Craig. First used in Scotland where it can also be a pet form of ALICE, it has now spread through Britain.

Aimée, Aimee see AMY, ESMÉ

Aine *f*
A popular name in Ireland thst is pronounced something like 'oyn-nyeh', with the stress on the first syllable. The name means 'brightness, splendour' and was the name of a prominent figure in Irish folklore.

Ainsley *m* and *f*
A place and surname used as a first name, this comes from the Old English and probably means 'lonely clearing'. It is also spelt **Ainslie**.

Aisha *f*
From the Arabic meaning 'alive and well' or 'prospering'. A favourite name in the Arab world, originally borne by the third (and favourite) wife of the Prophet Mohammed. In Britain and the USA the name is found in many forms, including **Aiesha**, **Aishah**, **Ayisha**, **Asia**, **Aysh(i)a**, **Ieasha**, **Ieesha**, **Iesha** and **Isha**. H. Rider Haggard used the form **Ayesha** in his novel *She* (1887), where the meaning was given as 'she who must be obeyed'.

Aisling *f*
The commonest form of a name also found as **Aislinn**, **Isleen** and the phonetic **Ashling**. It is an old Irish name meaning 'a dream, vision' and has been popular in Ireland since the 1960s. **Ashlyn(n)**, mainly found in the USA, can be seen as an American form of the name or as a blend of ASHLEY and Lynn.

Ajay, Ajit *m*
Popular Indian names from the Sanskrit for 'invincible'.

Akash *m*
This Indian name is sometimes found as **Aakash**. It is from the Sanskrit and means 'the sky'.

Akeem see HAKEEM

Akhil *m*
An Indian name from the Sanskrit meaning 'whole, complete'.

Akshar *m*
An Indian name from the Sanskrit, meaning 'imperishable'.

Al see ALEXANDER

Alan *m*, **Alana** *f*
An old Celtic name of unknown meaning that has appeared in various forms from early times. In England it first became popular after the Norman Conquest as Alain or Alein, the French forms. These developed into Alleyne, which is preserved as a surname. Alan, **Allan**, **Allen** and **Alun** (strictly speaking, a Welsh river name used as a first name) are in use today. **Alana**, the feminine form, is also spelt **Allana**, **Alanah** and **Alanna**, forms regarded in Ireland as coming from an Irish term of endearment. The USA has developed the form **Alaina** or **Alayna**. The actress **Lana** Turner made the short form well known.

Alastair *m*
Also spelt **Alasdair**, **Alistair** and **Alister**, this is the Gaelic form of ALEXANDER, 'defender of men'. It is shortened to **Al**, **Ali**, **Alli** or **Ally**, **Alec** and **Alick**.

Alban *m*, **Albina** *f*
From the Latin *Albanus*, meaning 'man from Alba' (a Roman town whose name means 'white') and the name of the earliest British saint. The town of St Albans, where he was martyred, is called after him. **Albin** and **Albinus** are variants that appear occasionally, and **Albina** and **Albinia**, 'white', are used as feminine forms.

Alberic see AUBREY

Albert *m*
An Old German name meaning 'noble and bright'. The Old English form was **Ethelbert**, the name of the Kentish king (*c*.552–616) who welcomed Augustine to Canterbury when he came to convert the Anglo-Saxons to Christianity. This was replaced after the Norman Conquest by the French form, Aubert. After the marriage of Queen Victoria to Prince Albert of Saxe-Coburg, Albert became so popular

that it became over-used and so went out of fashion. BERT and BERTIE are short forms. **Alberta**, **Albertina** and **Albertine** are rare forms of the name used for girls.

Albina, Albinia, Albinus see ALBAN

Alby see ELVIS

Aldous *m*
From the Old German **Aldo**, meaning 'old'. It has been used in the eastern counties of England since the 13th century and has given rise to various surnames like Aldhouse and Aldiss. Aldo is still used in North America. The writer Aldous Huxley (1894–1963) is the best-known British bearer of name.

Aldwyn *m*
This Anglo-Saxon personal name, meaning 'old friend', has been revived in modern times. Some parents prefer the spelling **Aldwin**.

Alea, Aleah see AALIYAH

Alec see ALASTAIR, ALEXANDER

Aled *m*
The name of a Welsh river used as a first name. There is a female form, **Aledwen**, 'fair Aled'.

Aleesha see ALICE

Alejandro see ALEXANDER

Alessandra see ALEXANDER, SANDRA

Alethea, Aletia see ALTHEA

Alexander *m*
Currently a popular boys' name, this comes from the Greek meaning 'defender of men'. It was made famous in the 4th century BC by Alexander the Great, and was very popular in England in the Middle Ages. **Sandy** is a pet form, particularly in Scotland. **Alex** is the

most common of the many short forms, others being **Al**, **Alec**, ALI, **Lex**, **Xan** and **Xander** or **Zander**. SACHA is another form of the name, while the Spanish form, **Alejandro**, is well used in the USA.

Alexandra *f*
This is the feminine form of ALEXANDER. SANDRA was originally an Italian form of the name **Alessandra** but has become established as a name in its own right. Alexandra shares pet and short forms with Alexander, and has in addition **Alix** or **Alyx** (also from ALICE) and **Alexa** (see ALEXIS). **Alexandria** (currently enjoying a mild fashion in the USA) and **Alexandrina** are also found.

Alexis *f* and *m*
From the Greek word meaning 'helper' or 'defender', Alexis is the name of one of the great saints of the Orthodox church. Originally a man's name, it is now more frequently used for women. Alternative forms are **Alexie**, **Alexus** and, for girls, **Alexia**, **Alexa** and short forms such as **Lexi(e)** and even **Lexus** (although in the USA this can be a conscious use of name of the prestige car brand, see Portia).

Alfred *m*
From two Old English words, meaning 'elf' (hence 'good') and 'counsel'. It is also a possible development of the Anglo-Saxon name Ealdfrith, meaning 'old peace'. It is sometimes written **Alfrid**. When Alfred was written down in old Latin, the name was spelt **Alured** and developed into **Avery** (now used for both sexes). Pet forms are **Fred**, **Alf** and **Alfie**, which has had something of a revival in the last few years, perhaps helped by the popularity of Shirley Hughes' delightful *Alfie* picture books. There is a feminine form, **Alfreda**, and **Elfrida**, although it technically comes from a slightly different name meaning 'elf-strength', is also used as a female version of Alfred.

Algernon *m*
From a Norman French nickname meaning 'with whiskers'. It was popular in the 19th century but is not much used today. The usual diminutive is **Algie** or **Algy**.

Ali *f* and *m*

When used as a boy's name Ali is a popular Arabic name meaning 'exalted, noble', and as one of the terms used of Allah, invokes God's protection for the child. AALIYAH and its variants is the feminine form. As a western name Ali is a pet form of names such as ALICE, ALISON, ALEXANDER or ALASTAIR.

Alia, Aliah see AALIYAH

Alice *f*

From the Old German word for 'nobility'. It originally had the form **Adelice** or **Adelise**. A number of forms remained popular from the Middle Ages until the 17th century, when it went out of favour. It was revived again in the 19th century together with the variant **Alicia**. Nowadays these have developed additional forms such as **Allice, Allyce** and **Alyssa, Alysia, Alis(s)a, Alisha** (currently increasing in popularity). **Aleesha**, or even **Elis(s)a** or **Elys(s)a** although these are also pet forms of ELIZABETH. ALISON is a variant. **Alys** is the Welsh form, and Irish forms are **Alis, Ailis** or the phonetic **Ailish**. **Ali**, **Allie** and **Alley** are used as pet forms, while **Alix** and **Alyx** can be used either as forms of Alice or ALEXANDRA.

Alick see ALASTAIR

Alida see ADELAIDE

Alina, Aline see ADELINE

Alis, Alisa, Alisha see ALICE

Alison *f*

Originally a diminutive of ALICE that was adopted in the 13th century, this was soon treated as a separate name. It was at one time a particularly Scottish name. Pet forms include those used for Alice and ELSIE. **Allison** and **Al(l)yson** are standard forms in the USA.

Alistair, Alister see ALASTAIR

Alix see ALEXANDRA, ALICE

Aliyah, Aliyyah see AALIYAH

Allan, Allana, Allen see ALAN

Allegra *f*
An Italian word meaning 'cheerful, lively', given by the poet Lord Byron to his daughter and still used occasionally as a result.

Alli, Ally see ALASTAIR

Allice, Allie, Allyce see ALICE, ALISON

Alma *f*
There are many opinions about the origin of this name. It could be derived from the Hebrew word for 'maiden', the Latin for 'kind' or the Italian for 'soul'. Most importantly, the name became very popular after the Battle of Alma during the Crimean War, and is still found occasionally.

Alondra *f*
Alondra is both a pet form of the name Alejandra, the Spanish form of ALEXANDRA, and also the Spanish for 'lark'. In this sense it is a common American place name, but more importantly in the 1990s it was the name of a successful Mexican-made television series, named after its heroine. Its broadcast led to increased use among Spanish-speaking Americans.

Aloysius *m*
This is the Latin form of Aloys, an old Provençal form of Louis (see LEWIS). There was a popular Spanish saint of this name in the 16th century, and Roman Catholics continue to use the name in this country. **Aloys** or **Aloyse** was the female form of the old name and is a possible source of ELOISE.

Althea *f*
From the Greek for 'wholesome', this was the Greek name for the marsh mallow plant, still used as a healing herb. It seems to have been introduced into England with various other classical names

during the Stuart period and appeared in the charming lyric by Richard Lovelace *To Althea from Prison*. The similar-sounding **Alethea** (**Alethia**, **Aletia**) comes from the Greek for 'truth'.

Alun see ALAN

Alured see ALFRED

Alvin *m*
From two Old English names, *Alwine*, 'friend of all' and *Athelwine*, 'noble friend'. **Aylwin**, **Alvan**, **Alvyn** and **Alvy** are alternative forms. There is a rare feminine, **Alvina**. The similar-sounding **Alvar** means 'elf army'.

Alya see AALIYAH

Alys, Alyssa see ALICE

Alyson, Alysson see ALISON

Alyx see Alexandra, Alice

Amabel *f*
From the Latin meaning 'lovable'. It has been in use in England in various forms since the 12th century. The short form, MABEL, became established as an independent name at an early date.

Amalia see AMELIA

Amadea *f*, **Amadeus** *m*
Best known as the middle name of Wolfgang Amadeus Mozart (1756–1791). Amadeus, which means 'love god', is a Latin translation of the Greek **Theophilus**. Mozart's middle name sometimes appears as **Gottlieb**, which is in turn the German translation. Despite the name's close association with Mozart, nowadays it is more likely to be found in the girl's form, **Amadea**.

Amanda *f*
From the Latin for 'deserving love'. It appears first in Restoration plays, where many classical or pseudo-classical names were intro-

duced or created. It has remained in use since then and is still popular. **Mandy** is a pet form also used as a name in its own right. The variant **Amandine** is currently well used in France.

Amaryllis *f*

Originally from Greek, probably meaning 'sparkling', and used by Greek poets as a name for a country girl. It served the same purpose for Latin poets and was introduced to Britain via English poetry in the 17th century.

Amber *f*

The name of the gemstone used as a first name. It was not used before the 20th century.

Ambrin *f*

From the Arabic for 'ambergris', a substance renowned for its sweet odour. It can also be spelt **Ambreen**.

Ambrose *m*

From the Greek for 'divine'. There was a 4th-century St Ambrose who was Bishop of Milan. The name is found in the Domesday Book and has been used occasionally ever since. The Welsh name **Emrys** is derived from the Latin form of the name. There is a rare feminine form, **Ambrosine**.

Ameer, Ameera, Ameir see AMIR

Amelia *f*

From an Old German name, possibly meaning 'work', its Latin-looking form is perhaps influenced by Emilia (see EMILY). **Amalia**, **Amalie**, **Amaline** and **Amalita** are forms of the name. It can be shortened to **Milly** or **Millie**. It has grown steadily in popularity in the last few years, while use of the French form **Amelie**, already popular in France, has increased in the UK since the release of the film of that name in 2001.

Amin *m*, Amina *f*

From the Arabic for 'honest', 'trustworthy' or 'reliable'. Amina, the feminine form, has always been much used by Muslim families, in honour of Amina bint-Wahab, mother of the Prophet Mohammed. It is sometimes spelt **Aamena, Aaminah** or **Amena. Iman,** 'faith, belief', comes from the same root. The fashion model who uses this name has made it widely known, and it sometimes appears as **Imani** or **Imana.**

Aminta see Araminta

Amir *m*, **Amira** *f*
This is principally an Arabic name, from a word meaning 'prince, commander', that is also the origin of the title Emir. The masculine form can also be found as **Ameer, Ameir** and **Amiri,** and is one on the Muslim names adopted by African-Americans. The feminine is also found as **Ameera.** These can also be Jewish names, from a word meaning 'treetop'.

Amit *m*
An Indian name from the Sanskrit for 'without limit'. It is also a simplified pet form of names like **Amitbikram** ('limitless prowess') and **Amitjyoti** ('limitless brightness').

Amitabh *m*
A name of the Buddha, from the Sanskrit meaning 'limitless splendour'. The spelling **Amitav** is also used.

Amos *m*
A Hebrew name, possibly meaning 'he who carries a burden'. It was the name of an Old Testament prophet and was adopted by English Puritans after the Reformation, when saints' names fell out of favour. Popular until the 19th century, it is at present uncommon, although used occasionally in the USA.

Amrit *f* and *m*
In the Vedic epics of the Hindus, this Sanskrit name refers to immortality or that which confers it, such as the 'water of life, soma juice, nectar, [or] ambrosia'. Amrit can be used for both sexes, although the form **Amrita** can also be used for a girl.

Amy *f*
From the French, meaning 'beloved'. Sir Walter Scott's novel *Kenilworth*, about Amy Robsart, the tragic wife of the Earl of Leicester, made the name fashionable in the 19th century, and it has been popular again in recent years in all English-speaking countries. **Aimée** is the French original of this name, which can also be found in forms such as **Aime(e)**, **Ami(e)** and **Amye**.

Amynta see ARAMINTA

Anaïs *f*
A French name that comes from the Greek word for 'fruitful'. There has been a small increase in its use since it became the name of a perfume in the UK, and it is currently well used in France.

Anand *m*, **Ananda** *f*
From the Sanskrit for 'happiness', 'joy' or 'bliss'. It is the name of a god in the Veda, the sacred books of the Hindus. Variants of the girl's form include **Anandamayi** ('full of joy'), **Anandi** and **Anandini** ('joyful').

Anastasia *f*
From the Greek, meaning 'resurrection'. The name of a 4th-century saint and martyr, it became fashionable in England in the 13th century, although it was usually abbreviated to **Anstey** or **Anstice**, which mainly survive today as surnames. It has always been very popular in Russia, and a daughter of the last tsar of Russia, called Anastasia, is said to have escaped from the massacre at Yekaterinburg in which the rest of her family died in 1918. **Tansy** and STACEY started as pet forms of this name, a fact played on by the singer **Anastacia** (real name Stacey Newkirk). **Nastasia** is a Russian pet form, and the emerging name **Tassia** (**Taja**, **Tasia**) is probably a shortening of this.

Andrew *m*, **Andrea** *f*
From the Greek for 'manly', Andrew is the name of the Apostle who is patron saint of Scotland, Russia and Greece. The name first

appears in England in the Domesday Book. Since then it has been used in Britain continuously and has enjoyed particular favour in Scotland. The pet forms include **Andy**, **Dandy** (Scots) and **Drew**, which is also used as an independent name. The Italian form, **Andrea**, is actually a boy's name in Italy but is used as a girl's name elsewhere. The French boy's form, **André**, is likewise sometimes used for girls, although the more correct form, **Andrée**, is also used. Other female forms include **Andrene**, **Andrena** and **Andreana**, while **Andra** is both a traditional Scots form of the boy's name and used for girls. While Andrew is currently moderately popular in the British Isles, Andrea is generally out of favour, except in the Republic of Ireland.

Aneka, Aneke, An(n)ika see ANNE

Aneurin *m*
This name is traditionally interpreted as the Welsh form of Latin *Honorius*, meaning 'honourable', and is one of the oldest names still in use in Britain. It also appears in the form **Aneirin**. Short forms are **Nye** and **Neirin**.

Angela *f*
From the Latin *angelus*, derived from the Greek word meaning 'messenger', the original function of our 'angel'. It is shortened to **Angel** and **Angie**. Other forms of the name include the French **Angelique** and elaborations such as **Angelica**, **Angelia**, **Angeline** and **Angelina** as well as spellings with a 'j' instead of a 'g'. Masculine forms of the name died out at the Reformation, but the Italian boy's name **Angelo** and the Spanish **Angel** are now found in the USA. There, Angel has been steadily climbing in popularity, perhaps helped by the character who originally appeared in the television show *Buffy the Vampire Slayer*.

Angharad *f*
A Welsh name meaning 'much loved'. It is an important name in early Welsh literature and has been in use since at least the 9th century. The stress is on the second syllable.

Angus *m*
From the Gaelic **Aonghas**, meaning 'one choice'. It appears in Irish legend in the form **Aengus** or **Oengus** but is more common in Scotland. The name became associated with the classical myth of **Aeneas** (which is close to the Irish pronunciation) in the 15th century, and this form was also used.

Anil *m*, **Anila** *f*
The name of the wind-god in the Hindu Vedic epics. It is derived from the Sanskrit meaning 'air' or 'wind'. Anil is the driver of Indra's golden chariot, which is pulled by a thousand horses. **Anila**, the feminine form, is used mainly by Hindu families.

Anish *m*, **Anisha** *f*
A Sanskrit name, one of the thousand borne by the Hindu god Vishnu. Its meaning is possibly 'without a master'.

Anita, Ann, Anna see ANNE

Annabel *f*
Together with **Annabelle** or **Annabella**, this is probably from the Latin *amabilis*, meaning 'lovable', a variant of AMABEL. It is found in Scotland earlier than ANNE, so it is unlikely to be a form of that name, although it is now sometimes thought of as a compound of Anna and the Latin *bella*, meaning 'beautiful'. Diminutives include **Bel**, **Belle** and **Bella**.

Anne *f*
From the Hebrew HANNAH, meaning 'God has favoured me'. The French form, Anne or **Ann**, traditionally the name of the mother of the Virgin Mary, was introduced into Britain in the 13th century and the name has enjoyed great popularity since. Anne is currently slightly more popular than Ann, but the form **Anna** is now much more popular than either. Pet forms include **Nan**, **Nanette**, **Nana**, NANCY and **Annie**, as well as the variants **Anita**, **Annette** and **Anona** (although this, with its pet form **Nona**, can be Welsh in origin). Ann(e) has often formed part of compounds such as **Mary Ann(e)** or

Annalise. Anneke is the Dutch pet form, more often spelt **Anneka** in this country to reflect the Dutch pronunciation; **Aneke, Aneka** and **An(n)ika** are also found. **Anya** is from the Spanish pronunciation of the name, and **Anouk** is a Russian form.

Annes see AGNES

Annette, Annie see ANNE

Annice, Annis see AGNES

An(n)ora see HONORIA

Anona, Anouk see ANNE

Anoop see ANUP

Anstice see ANASTASIA

Anthea *f*
From the Greek *antheos*, meaning 'flowery'. This name seems to have been introduced by the pastoral poets of the 17th century and it has been in use ever since, although it was not until the 20th century that it became very widely known.

Ant(h)ony *m*, **Antonia** *f*
A Roman family name. Its most famous member was Marcus Antonius, the Mark Antony of Shakespeare's *Julius Caesar* and *Antony and Cleopatra*. The name was very popular in the Middle Ages as a result of the influence of St Antony the Great and St Antony of Padua. The alternative and more common spelling Anthony was introduced after the Renaissance, when it was incorrectly thought that the name was derived from the Greek *anthos*, meaning 'flower', as in ANTHEA. The usual short form is **Tony**, which is also used for the female forms, **Antonia** and the French **Antoinette**. Feminine short forms **Toni** and **Tonya** are also found, and **Toinette**, **Net** and **Nettie** are pet forms of Antoinette. **Anton**, a Continental form of the name, is now also used for boys. In the USA **Antonio** (shortened to **Tonio**) and **Antoine** (often in phonetic spellings such as **Antwan** or **Antuan**) are often used.

Anup *m*
An Indian name, from the Sanskrit meaning 'without comparison'.
The spelling **Anoop** is also used.

Anusha *f*
The name of a star in Hindu astrology.

Anya see ANNE

Aoife see EVE

Aonghas see ANGUS

Aphra *f*
From the Hebrew word for 'dust'. It is best known from the novelist, playwright and spy Mrs Aphra Behn (1644–89), said to have been the first woman in England to earn her living as a writer. It is also spelt **Afra**.

April see AVRIL

Arabella *f*
A possible variant of AMABEL, although it could be derived from the Latin for 'obliging, listening to prayer'. It used to be a predominantly Scottish name, particularly in the forms **Arabel** and **Arabelle**. Another traditional form is found in Lady **Arbella** Stuart, the niece of Mary Queen of Scots, who was at one time thought of as a possible heir to Queen Elizabeth I of England. It can be shortened to **Bel**, **Belle** and **Bella**.

Araminta *f*
This name appears to have been invented by the English architect and dramatist Sir John Vanbrugh (1644–1726) to use in one of his plays. It may have been influenced by **Aminta** or **Amynta**, an ancient Greek name meaning 'protector'. They all share the short forms **Minta** and **Minty**.

Aran see ARRAN

Archibald *m*
From Old German words meaning 'truly bold'. The Old English form was used in East Anglia before the Norman Conquest. Thereafter it was primarily Scottish and was associated particularly with the Douglas and Campbell families. The short form is **Archie**, which has been growing in popularity in recent years and is now more common than the full form.

Ardal *m*
This is an Irish name of disputed meaning, either 'high valour' or coming from the word for 'bear'.

Aretha *f*.
Aretha or **Areta** is the Greek word for 'virtue'. It is not a usual name but has become widely known through the singer Aretha Franklin.

Arianna *f*
This is an ancient Greek name meaning 'the very holy one', which probably originally belonged to a goddess. In Greek mythology **Ariadne** was the daughter of King Minos of Crete and helped Theseus to escape from the labyrinth. **Arian(n)a** is an Italian form of the name that is now quite popular in the USA. **Ariane**, the French form, is also used.

Ariel *f* and *m*
The name Ariel has two different origins. The masculine form is a Hebrew name, traditionally said to mean 'lion of God', which is popular in Israel and sometimes used in the USA. As a girl's name it has been popular in the USA ever since it was used as the heroine's name in Disney's *Little Mermaid* film and TV series. This name, which is also found in forms such as **Arial** and **Arielle**, presumably owes at least something to Ariel, the airy spirit in Shakespeare's play, *The Tempest*.

Arjun *m*
A Hindu name from the Sanskrit for 'white' or 'bright'. It was the name of a famous Pandava prince, son of the god Indra.

Arlene *f*
Arlene, **Arleen** or **Arline** is a modern name that probably comes from the final sounds of such names as CHARLENE or MARLENE.

Armand, Armando, Armin, Arminel, Arminelle see HERMAN

Arnold *m*
From the Old German *Arnwalt*, meaning 'eagle's power'. It appeared in various forms, both Germanic and French, in the Middle Ages but dropped out of use from the 17th century until the late 19th when it was revived. **Arnie** is used as a short form.

Aroon see ARUN

Arran *m*
In many cases Arran is probably just a variant spelling of AARON, but the name is particularly popular in Scotland, where it is probably used as one of a group of new first names taken from the names of islands and geographical features. See also AILSA, IONA, ISLA, KYLE, SKYE. In the form **Aran** it can also be both an Irish and Welsh place name.

Arron see AARON

Artemis, Artemisia see DIANA

Arthur *m*
The origin of this name is disputed. Possible sources are the Celtic word for 'bear' and the Roman name *Artorius*. Whatever its source, its use comes entirely from the fame of its first known bearer, King Arthur. Victorian interest in things medieval made it popular in the 19th century when Queen Victoria gave the name to one of her sons. Overuse in the late 19th and first quarter of the 20th centuries led to a decline, but there are now signs of a revival in popularity. **Art** or **Arty** is used as a short form, particularly in America.

Arun *m*, **Aruna** *f*
An Indian name from the Sanskrit for 'reddish brown', a colour associated with the dawn. It became the name of the mythical per-

sonification of the dawn, charioteer of the sun. **Aroon** is an alternative spelling for boys, while for girls **Arumina** is also used. Occasionally Arun is a form of the name AARON.

Arwen f
This is an old Welsh name that can also be found as **Arwyn** (also used for men) and **Arwenna**, meaning 'fair and fine', sometimes glossed as 'Muse' – probably though confusion with **Awen** (*m*) **Awena** (*f*), Welsh names with this meaning. Recent use, however, is more likely to be linked with the appearance of the name in J. R. R. Tolkien's *Lord of the Rings*, where Arwen is the name of a beautiful elf princess whose name is said to mean 'noble maiden' in Sindarin, the language of the Grey Elves. Use of the name has increased since the release of the filmed version of the book.

Asa m
From the Hebrew word meaning 'physician'. In the Bible it is the name of a king of Judah, noted for his piety.

Asha f
An Indian name from the Sanskrit for 'hope, desire, aspiration'.

Ashanti f
The name of this Ghanaian people has had a certain popularity among people of African origin wanting to honour their roots. It is often shortened to **Shanti** (**Shante, Shaunti**). The success of the singer Ashanti has let to a distinct rise in use.

Asher m
The name of one of the tribes of Israel. It means 'happy'. Although it is an unusual name, there are signs that its use is on the increase, along with other names from the Bible. It is, of course, also a common surname meaning 'ash tree', and some of its uses may be from this.

Ashish m
A relatively modern Indian name, probably derived from the Sanskrit for 'prayer' or 'benediction'.

Ashley *f* and *m*
A place and surname meaning 'ash field' that has become very popular throughout the English-speaking world. The spelling **Ashleigh** is rather more common for girls, and the variant **Ashlyn(n)** (see also AISLING) is used as a girl's name in the USA. The related surname **Ashton**, meaning 'ash farm', is also found as a first name for both sexes in the USA.

Ashling, Ashlyn(n) see AISLING, ASHLEY

Ashraf *m*
A popular Muslim name, from the Arabic for 'more noble' or 'more honourable'.

Asia see AISHA

Aslam *m*
A Muslim name, from the Arabic meaning 'safer' or 'sounder'.

Asma *f*
A popular Muslim name, from the Arabic for 'more eminent' or 'more prestigious'. Asma was the daughter of the caliph Abu-Bakr. She courageously helped the Prophet and her father escape from Mecca when their lives were threatened.

Astrid *f*
From the Old German words meaning 'god' and 'beauty'. The name of the wife of St Olaf of Norway, it has long been popular in Scandinavia but has been used in Britain only since the 20th century.

Atalanta, Atlanta *f*
In Greek mythology, Atalanta was a beautiful princess who wanted to remain single. Since she was a very fast runner, she responded to pressure to marry by declaring that she would marry only the man who could beat her in a race but that anyone whom she beat would be put to death. Many of her suitors tried and died, but one man, Hippomenes, used cunning. He had three golden

apples made and rolled them one by one in front of her. The delay as she picked each apple up was just enough for him to win the race. The name is said to mean 'unswaying'. The very similar name Atlanta is unrelated but has been used either for those with connections with the city of Altanta, Georgia, or for those born during an Atlantic crossing or who have some other connection with that ocean. **Atlantic** has occasionally been used for boys. Both Atalanta and Atlanta are shortened to **Lanty**.

Athene *f*
This is the name of the Greek goddess of war, crafts and wisdom. In Britain, it has been used occasionally as a girl's name, as has the Latin form of the name, **Athena**. The Roman equivalent, **Minerva**, recently brought to public attention by J. K. Rowling's *Harry Potter* books, is also found.

Athol *f* and *m*
Athol or **Atholl** is the Scottish place name (and surname) used as a first name. The place name means 'New Ireland'.

Atlanta, Atlantic see ATALANTA

Aubrey *m* and *f*
From the Old German meaning 'elf ruler'. In medieval romance the pet form **Auberon** was used and Shakespeare adopted it as **Oberon** in *A Midsummer Night's Dream*. The German form, **Alberic**, developed first into Albery and later into Aubrey. Aubrey is now to be found as a girl's name in the USA, in which case it can have spellings such as **Aubree** or **Aubry**.

Audrey *f*
A shortened form of Etheldreda, Old English for 'noble strength' and one of the sources of ETHEL. St Etheldreda was a 7th-century Anglo-Saxon princess who founded a religious house at Ely in East Anglia that later developed into the cathedral that now stands on the site. She was a popular saint, and many churches are still dedicated to her.

Augusta *f*, Augustus *m*

From the Latin for 'venerable'. Augustus was a title given to the first Roman Emperor, and Augusta is its feminine form. **Augustine**, the name of two important saints, one of whom converted the English to Christianity, is another form of the name. It was so popular in the Middle Ages that it developed the shorter forms **Austin**, **Austyn** or **Austen**, a name that has been popular in North America for some years. **Augustina** is a feminine form of Augustine, and there is an Irish feminine **Augusteen**. **Gus** and **Gussie** are pet forms.

Aurelia *f*

From the Latin *aurelius*. meaning 'golden'. It has been used since the 17th century, and recently a short form, **Auriol**, **Auriel**, **Oriel** or **Oriole**, has shown some popularity. The boy's form is **Aurelius** or, in France, **Aurelian**.

Aurora, Aurore see DAWN

Austen, Austin, Austyn see AUGUSTA

Autumn *f*

This season is growing in popularity as a girl's name in the USA, having been in the top hundred names for at least five years. **Summer** is also well used, but **Spring** is less popular. Not surprisingly, however, winter does not feature in the statistics.

Ava *f*

This name is of obscure origin but probably started life as a pet form of names beginning Av- or as a form of **Eva** (see EVE). It was made famous by the film star Ava Gardner and is more commonly found in the USA than Britain, although well used in the Republic of Ireland.

Aveline see EVELYN

Averil *f* and *m*

Probably from the Old English *eofor* ('boar') and *hild* ('battle'), which appears as **Everild** and **Everilda** in the 7th century. It was regularly in use until the 17th century, since when it has been less common. Averil is often confused with AVRIL, which originally was an entirely different name.

Avery see ALFRED

Avis *f*
Avis or **Avice** is an old Norman name of obscure meaning, although now sometime associated with the Latin *avis*, 'bird'. It was well used up to the 16th century and was revived along with other medieval names in the 19th century. It never became popular, although it is still used occasionally.

Avner see ABNER

Avril *f*
The French for **April**. The name has been popular in the 20th century, mainly for girls born in that month. See also AVERIL.

Awen, Awena see ARWEN

Axel *m*
This is the Scandinavian form of the Old Testament name **Absolom**. Its probable meaning is 'father of peace', which seems an ironic name for King David's rebellious son.. The feminine form of the name is **Axelle**. While both names are uncommon in the UK, they are sometimes found in the USA where they were introduced by Scandinavian immigrants, and both names are currently fashionable in France.

Ayala see AYLA

Ayesha, Ayisha see AISHA

Ayla *f*
This name has recently come into use by fans of Jean Auel's *Clan of the Cave Bear* sagas, where it is the name of her Ice-Age heroine. Ayla can also be a form of **Ayala**, a Hebrew name meaning 'deer, gazelle'.

Aylmer see ELMER

Aylwin see ALVIN

Aysha, Ayshia see AISHA

Azim *m*, **Azima(h)** *f*
This Arabic name means 'determined'.

Aziz *m*
This Arabic name means 'friend'. **Azeez** is a common alternative spelling, and **Aziza** and **Azeeza** are feminine forms.

Bab, Babs see BARBARA

Babette see BARBARA, ELIZABETH

Bailey *f* and *m*
This surname, which comes from the job of steward or bailiff of an estate, has been fashionable for some time as a girl's name in the USA and entered the British charts in 2000. In Australia it has been popular as a boy's name.

Bairre see BARRY

Bala *f* and *m*
An Indian name, from the Sanskrit for 'young child'. The boy's form can also appear as **Balu** and **Balan**.

Balqis *f*
This ancient name, of unknown meaning, is traditionally the name of the fabled Queen of Sheba, who became SOLOMON's consort, winning his heart as much by her wisdom as by her great beauty. It is also found in the forms **Balquis**, **Balkis**, **Belkis** and **Belkys**.

Baptist, Baptiste see JOHN

Barbara *f*
From the Greek *barbaros*, meaning 'strange' or 'foreign', and associated with St Barbara, a 3rd-century martyr. The name was little used after the Reformation, until the 20th century when it became popular again. Abbreviations include **Bab**, **Babs**, **Barbie** and sometimes **Bobbi**. The variant form **Barbra** was publicised by the singer Barbra Streisand. **Babette** is a French form of the name.

Barnabas *m*
From the Hebrew meaning 'son of exhortation or consolation', it is best known as the name of the New Testament companion of St Paul. The pet form, **Barnaby**, is rather fashionable at the moment, more so than the full form. **Barney** is a short form that is also shared with BERNARD.

Barney see BARNABAS, BERNARD

Barry *m*
The English form of a variety of Celtic names, most prominently **Bairre**, a pet form of the Irish **Finbarr** (**Finnbar**, **Fionnbharr**) meaning 'fair-haired'. Barry can also be spelt **Barrie**, the usual spelling in the name's infrequent use for girls.

Bartholomew *m*
From the Hebrew, meaning 'son of Talmai', Talmai meaning 'full of furrows'. It was the surname of the Apostle NATHANIEL and was very popular in the Middle Ages when the cult of St Bartholomew was at its height. St Bartholomew's Hospital in London was founded in the 12th century, and a riotous annual Bartholomew Fair held in the city to provide funds for it was suppressed only in the 19th century. The name is still in use and has the short forms **Bart**, made famous by the cartoon character Bart Simpson, and **Barty**.

Basil *m*
From the Greek *basileios*, meaning 'kingly'. It was probably brought to England by the Crusaders, and it has remained in use ever since. Diminutives include **Bas** or **Baz**, **Basie** and **Bazza**, and there are two feminine forms, **Basilia** and **Basilie**. These were common in the Middle Ages but are hardly ever found today.

Bastian, Bastien see SEBASTIAN

Bathsheba *f*
This name derives from Hebrew words that mean 'daughter of opulence'. In the Old Testament Bathsheba was the beautiful wife

of Uriah and was seduced by King David who arranged to have Uriah die during a battle. Bathsheba married David and became the mother of SOLOMON. The name was formerly used in Cornwall in the form **Bersaba**, and appears also in its pet form **Sheba**. Bathsheba Everdene is a central character in Thomas Hardy's *Far From the Madding Crowd*.

Baz, Bazza see BASIL

Beatrice *f*
From the Latin **Beatrix**, meaning 'bringer of happiness'. It has strong literary associations. Dante's Beatrice is probably best known, but Shakespeare also used the name in *Much Ado About Nothing*. Recently, both forms of the name have shown signs of returning to popularity, no doubt helped by the publicity given to it as the name of one of the Duke and Duchess of York's daughters. Short forms include **Bea** or **Bee**, **Beata**, **Beatty**, **Triss** and **Trixie**. There is also a Welsh variant, **Bettrys**, and a Spanish form, **Beatriz**.

Becky see REBECCA

Bel see ANNABEL, ARABELLA, BELINDA, ISABEL

Belinda *f*
From an Old German name, the latter part of which means 'a snake' (see LINDA). The first part of the name is obscure but is commonly thought of as representing the French 'fair'. Its popular use began in the 18th century when it was used in plays by Congreve and Vanbrugh, and in Alexander Pope's poem *The Rape of the Lock*. Short forms include **Bel** and all forms of Linda.

Bella, Belle see ANNABEL, ARABELLA, ISABEL

Belkis, Belkys see BALQIS

Ben see BENJAMIN

Benedict *m*
From the Latin *benedictus*, meaning 'blessed', and most familiar as the name of St Benedict, founder of the Benedictine Order. It was

common in medieval England in the forms **Bennet** and **Benedick**. The latter is the name of a character in Shakespeare's *Much Ado About Nothing*. There are feminine forms, **Benedicta** and **Benedetta**, and a Spanish-American form, **Benita**.

Benjamin *m*

From the Hebrew, meaning 'son of the south' or 'right hand', which might imply strength and good fortune. The Old Testament story of Benjamin, son of Jacob, gave the name the added implications of a favoured youngest son. The commonest pet forms are **Ben**, **Bennie**, **Benny**, **Benjie** and **Benjy**. It is currently a popular name, well used in all English-speaking areas, both in its full form and in the shortened form Ben.

Bennet see BENEDICT

Berenice *f*

From the Greek *Pherenice*, meaning 'bringer of victory'. It was spread by the imperial conquests of Alexander the Great over Europe and Asia. It was especially popular in Egypt during the period of Macedonian rule, and its use spread also to the family of Herod of Judea. **Bernice** is a modern form of the name, and **Bunny** is sometimes used as a pet form. See also VERONICA.

Bernadette *f*

The commonest female form of BERNARD. Its use has spread because of the fame of St Bernadette of Lourdes, who lived in the mid 19th century and whose visions started the pilgrimages of healing to that town. The Italian **Bernardetta** has been shortened to **Detta**, which can be used as an independent name. **Bernadine** is another form of the name, and **Bernie** a short form for all of them.

Bernard *m*

A Germanic name meaning 'brave as a bear', which was very popular in the Middle Ages. Two important medieval saints bearing the name were St Bernard of Menthon, after whom St Bernard dogs are named, and St Bernard of Clairvaux, who inspired the

Second Crusade. It has remained in use ever since. The most usual short forms are **Bernie** and **Barney**, which are shared with BARNABAS.

Berry see BERTRAM

Bersaba see BATHSHEBA

Bert, Bertie *m*
A pet form of a large number of names, including ALBERT, BERTRAM, BERTRAND, GILBERT, HERBERT, HUBERT, ROBERT. In all these cases, the '-bert' part of the name is a Germanic element meaning 'bright'. The name is sometimes used as a given name, when it may take the form **Burt**.

Bertha *f*
From the Old German word *berht*, meaning 'bright'. The first famous English Bertha was the wife of King Ethelbert of Kent who welcomed St Augustine to England on his mission of conversion. In the Middle Ages both Bertha and **Berta** were popular, and the name has been regularly used ever since, although it is rather uncommon at present.

Bertram *m*
From the Old German meaning 'bright raven', the bird associated with the god Odin. The name has been used in England since the early Middle Ages, and has the short forms **Bert** and **Bertie**, and the less common **Berry**. **Bertrand**, meaning 'bright shield', is often treated as the French form of Bertram and shares with it the short forms BERT and **Bertie**.

Beryl *f*
From the gemstone, the name of which is related to the Arabic for 'crystal'. It appeared in the 19th century, and was popular in the early part of the 20th century.

Bess, Bessie, Beth see ELIZABETH

Betha see BETHIA

Bethan, Bethany *f*
Bethany is a popular name taken from a New Testament place name, the village where Lazarus lived. Its short form, **Bethan**, is used independently and is also a short form of ELIZABETH, which has spread from Wales.

Bethia *f*
Bethia or **Bethea** can be interpreted in three different ways. It can be thought of as a pet form of ELIZABETH, as a use of the Old Testament place name Bethia, or as an English version of a Gaelic name also found as **Betha**, meaning 'life'.

Betsy, Bette, Bettina see ELIZABETH

Bettrys see BEATRICE

Betty see ELIZABETH

Beulah *f*
This is a Hebrew word meaning 'bride, married'. In the Old Testament it is used as a name for Israel, with the explanation 'as the bridegroom rejoices over the bride, so shall your God rejoice over you'. Its use as a first name among Puritans was encouraged when John Bunyan used the name in his *Pilgrim's Progress* (1678) for 'the land of heavenly joy'.

Beverl(e)y *f* and *m*
From an Old English surname meaning 'of the beaver-meadow'. It is shortened to **Bev**, and is now only rarely used for boys.

Bevis *m*
This is a French name, possibly meaning 'bow', introduced into England at the Norman Conquest. It was popular in the Middle Ages and revived again after Richard Jeffries' *Bevis, The Story of a Boy* was published in 1882.

Bharat *m*
This was the name of several famous heroes in the Hindu epics and

derives from the Sanskrit for 'being maintained'. India officially became Bharat when it achieved independence.

Bharati *f*
A Hindu name identified with the goddess of speech and learning.

Bhaskar *m*
A Hindu name from the Sanskrit for 'the sun'. **Bhaskara**, the famous 12th-century Indian astronomer and teacher, shows an earlier form of the name.

Bhavana see BHAVNA

Bhavini *f*
A Hindu name meaning 'illustrious, beautiful', a term for the goddess PARVATI, wife of the god Siva.

Bhavna *f*
An Indian name, from the Sanskrit meaning 'wish', 'desire' or 'thought'. The form **Bhavana** is also used.

Bianca see BLANCHE

Bibi see BRITTANY

Bidelia, Biddy see BRIDGET

Bill see WILLIAM

Billie, Billy *f* and *m*
Bill and Billy are pet forms of the boy's name WILLIAM. Billy has been well used in the UK as an independent boy's name, and it is also sometimes found as a girl's name (particularly in the form Billie), most frequently in America. There it is often used for both sexes in combinations to produce names such as **Billie Jean** or **Billy Joe**.

Birgitta see BRIDGET

Björn *m*
A popular Scandinavian name that means 'bear'. The name has

become widely known in modern times through the Swedish tennis champion Björn Borg.

Blair *f* and *m*
This Scottish surname and place name, meaning 'marshy plain', entered the lists of most popular boys' names in Scotland in 2002. It has been used for some time in the USA, however, primarily as a girl's name, in which case it can be spelt **Blaire** or **Blayre**. Another similar-sounding Scottish surname, **Blaine**, from the Gaelic for 'yellow [haired]', is also used for boys in the USA.

Blaise *m*
From the French, meaning either someone from the Blois region, or derived from the Latin for 'stammerer'. It is also spelt **Blase** or **Blaze** (in which spelling it may represent the vocabulary word). While not common, there has been an increase in use in the USA in recent years.

Blake *m*
A surname, from the Old English meaning 'black, dark-complexioned', used as a first name. It is most likely to be found in the USA or Australia and is occasionally used for girls.

Blanche *f*
This is a French name that was brought to England in the 13th century. It means 'white' or 'fair-skinned'. The Spanish and Italian form **Bianca** was used by Shakespeare and is now rather more popular than the older form.

Blase, Blaze see BLAISE

Blodwen *f*
From the Welsh for 'white flower', this name is rarely found outside Wales. **Blodeuwedd**, 'flower form', is the name of a beautiful but unfaithful woman in Welsh medieval romance, while **Blodyn** or **Blodeyn** is the more simple 'flower'.

Blossom see FLEUR

Bob see ROBERT

Bobbi(e), Bobby *f* and *m*
These pet forms of ROBERT, ROBERTA and BARBARA are used as names in their own right and in combinations such as **Bobby Joe**.

Bonnie, Bonny *f*
A Scots word for 'pretty' used as a name. Like many modern names, it probably owes its spread to its appearance in the novel (1936) and film (1939) of Margaret Mitchell's *Gone with the Wind*.

Boris *m*
From the Russian word for 'fight'. It was used in Britain and North America in the 20th century, possibly because of cultural influences such as Moussorgsky's opera *Boris Godunov*, the film actor Boris Karloff, and the author of *Dr Zhivago*, Boris Pasternak; as well as the large number of Slavic immigrants who have come to the West.

Boyd *m*
From a Gaelic word meaning 'yellow', referring to the colour of the hair. It is the name of a Scottish clan, although the surname can also derive from 'isle of Bute'. Boyd became more widespread outside Scotland after its use in the novel (1936) and film (1939) of Margaret Mitchell's *Gone With the Wind*.

Brad(d) see BRADLEY

Braden *m*
One of a number of similar-sounding Irish names that have grown in use in recent years. This one comes from an Irish surname that in turn comes from the Irish word for 'salmon'. It is better used in the USA than in the UK. It occurs in a number of spellings, such as **Brayden** (particularly popular in Australia), **Bradon** and **Braydon**.

Bradley *m*
A surname from the Old English, meaning 'wide meadow', now popular as a first name. **Brad(d)**, as in the actor Brad Pitt, is a short

form. The name has been popular throughout the English-speaking world in the last decade.

Brady *m*
An Irish surname, possibly meaning 'broad-chested', now found as a first name. It is also found as **Bradie**.

Bram see ABRAHAM

Bran see BRENNA

Brand see BRENDA

Brandan see BRENDAN

Brandi *f*
This name, which seems to come from the vocabulary word 'brandy', has been a well-used girl's name in the USA for some years, although currently declining in use. It is also found spelt **Brandy**, **Brandee** and **Brandie**, and probably serves as a feminine form of Brandon (see BRENDAN).

Brandin, Brandon see BRENDAN

Brannan see BRENNA

Brayden, Braydon see BRADEN

Breanna *f*
This new name, which has developed in the USA, can either be seen as a blend of the names Bree (a pet form of BRIDGET) and Anna, or as a development of Brianna, a feminine form of BRIAN. It is also used in the form **Breanne**, and found in spellings such as **Breeanna** and **Brieanne**.

Bree see BRIDGET

Bren see BRENNA

Brenda *f*
Probably a feminine form of the Norse name Brand, meaning 'a

sword', found in the Shetland islands. It came into general use after it was used by Walter Scott in his 1821 novel *The Pirate*. In practice, however, it has been used more frequently as a feminine form of BRENDAN.

Brendan, Brandon *m*

An Irish name meaning either 'with stinking hair', or, according to one authority, from the Welsh word meaning 'prince'. It is most famously found in the 6th-century Irish St Brendan the Navigator, credited in legend with the discovery of America. The form **Brandan** or **Brandon** – the most popular form in the UK – has a long history as an alternative form of Brendan but can also come from an Old English place and surname meaning 'a hill where broom grows'. The names, which have been popular for some years throughout the English-speaking world, are also found as **Brandin**, **Brandyn**, **Brenden** and **Brendon**.

Brenna *f*, Brennan *m*

Brennan is a pet form of the Irish name **Bren**, which probably means 'tear, sorrow'. Brenna is a modern feminine form. Since the earliest records, Bren and **Bran**, 'raven', and its pet form, **Brannan**, have regularly been confused, and it is not always possible to tell which form of the name has come from which source.

Brent *m*

An English surname with various origins, including one that meant the bearer came from land cleared by fire, which has had a certain popularity as a first name in the USA, particularly in the early 1990s. Its popularity may have been encouraged by Brent Spiner, the actor who played the popular character of Commander Data in *Star Trek – The Next Generation*. The elaboration **Brenton** has also been used.

Bret(t) *m*

From an Old French word meaning 'a Briton' or 'a Breton'. It has been well used in recent years in the USA, usually in the form Brett, but now seems to be declining in popularity. See also BRITTANY.

Brian *m*, **Brianna** *f*
A Celtic name, the origin of which is obscure, although it may be
derived from words meaning 'hill' or 'strength'. It was known
mainly in Celtic areas until the Norman Conquest, when it was
introduced into England. Brian Boru was a famous Irish king of the
11th century who defeated the invading Vikings, and the name has
long been popular there. The name continued to be popular in
England until Tudor times, but after that it disappeared until it was
reintroduced from Ireland in the 18th century. Today the spellings
Bryan, **Brien** and **Brion** are found, and **Bryant** or **Briant**, originally a
surname developed from the name Brian, is also found. At the
moment the name is most likely to be used in Eire or the USA.
Brianna – currently popular in both the USA and Australia –
Bryan(n)a and **Brianne** (**Bryanne**) are used as feminine forms, as is
BRYONY.

Brice *m*
Brice, possibly meaning 'speckled', is an old Gaulish name, the
name of a 5th-century French saint and bishop of Tours that is now
well used in the USA, often in the form **Bryce**. The surname, which
developed from the first name, **Bryson**, is also found used as a first
name.

Bridget *f*
Brigit was the ancient Irish goddess of poetry whose name meant
'strength'. Her name was borne by 5th-century St Brigit of Kildare,
the most revered of the Irish female saints. The Irish name also
appears in the forms **Bri(d)gid** and **Bride** (which reflect the Irish
pronunciation of the name, with a long 'ee' sound and no 'g'), with
the diminutives **Bridie**, **Biddy**, **Bree** (now sometimes **Brea**) and the
older elaboration **Bidelia**. There is also a Swedish saint, **Birgitta** or
Brigitta, whose feast day falls on the same day as St Brigit's, and her
name has influenced the most common English form of the name,
Bridget. **Britt** is a pet form of the Swedish name.

Brien see BRIAN

Brigid, Brigit, Brigitta see BRIDGET

Brin see BRYN

Brion see BRIAN

Briony see BRYONY

Britt see BRIDGET

Brittany *f*
This French place name began to be used as a name for American girls in the 1960s, for reasons that are unclear. The sound of the name – usually pronounced with two syllables in the States – rather than its meaning seems to be important, as it also occurs as **Britanee, Britani, Britney** (made famous by Britney Spears), **Brittney** and at least 50 other spellings. Pet forms include **Bibi** (also used of other names beginning with 'B'), **Bret(t)** and **Brittie**. In the 1980s a sudden surge in popularity saw it climb steadily towards the top of the American name charts, but after peaking in the early 1990s, use has declined. It has also been popular in Australia, and made it to 98th position in England and Wales in 1999, but has not been in the top hundred names since. BRET would be the masculine equivalent.

Brodie *m*
A surname, from the Irish for 'ditch', which has been well used in Australia and is also used in the USA, usually in the form **Brody**.

Bronwen *f*
From the Welsh words meaning 'white breast'. This name has long been popular in Wales where it has strong associations with ancient legend.

Brooke *f* and *m*
The surname meaning 'a brook', used as a first name, made famous by the actress Brooke Shields.

Brooklyn *f* and *m*
The American place name Brooklyn, most famously used in the UK

for a boy, Brooklyn Beckham, is more often used for girls in the USA and is treated as if a blend of BROOKE and LYN in forms such as **Brooklynne**.

Bruce *m*
A French surname that came to Britain at the time of the Norman Conquest. Members of the family moved to Scotland where a descendant of one, Robert Bruce, became King of Scots, and was the ancestor of the Stewart or Stuart Kings. Bruce has been used as a first name only since the 19th century, but it proved so popular in Australia in the mid 20th century that it is almost a nickname for an Australian man. **Brucie** is a pet form.

Bruno *m*
This is a German name meaning 'brown', probably imported to the UK via the USA where it has been established for longer.

Bryan, Bryan(n)a, Bryant see BRIAN

Bryce see BRICE

Bryn *m*
A Welsh name, originally describing where someone lived, meaning 'hill'. It can be found as **Brin**, and **Brynmor** ('large hill') is also used.

Bryony *f*
Bryony, or **Briony**, is the name of the climbing hedgerow plant used as a girl's name. It is a rather insignificant plant, although it has pretty berries, and the name probably owes its popularity to the fact that it can be used as a female equivalent to BRIAN.

Bryson see BRICE

Buddy *m*
This word for a friend is occasionally used as a first name but is usually a nickname. The singer Buddy Holly, for example, was baptised CHARLES.

Buck *m*
This word, in use since the 18th century as a term for a dashing man, is more often used as a nickname, although sometimes used as a given name. It is perhaps best known from the spaceman hero of comic book and screen, Buck Rogers.

Buffy see ELIZABETH

Bunny see BERENICE

Bunty *f*
This was a traditional name for a pet lamb, which came into use for girls after 1911, when it was featured in a very successful play called *Bunty Pulls the Strings*. It has been used more commonly as a nickname, however, than as a given name.

Burhan *m*
An Arabic name meaning 'evidence' or 'proof'. **Burhanuddin** means 'proof of faith'.

Burt see BERT

Byron *m*
A name more frequently used in America than Britain, although it honours the English poet Lord Byron (1784–1824). Byron comes from the word 'byre', which means a cow-shed or barn. The name may have originally indicated someone who lived near a barn.

Caddie, Caddy see CAROLINE

Cadwallader *m*
An ancient name, from the Welsh for 'battle chief'. It is one of a large number of Welsh names containing the element *cad*, 'battle'. These include **Cadfael**, 'battle prince', brought to public attention as the name of the hero of Ellis Peters' medieval whodunits; **Cadell**, 'little battle'; **Cadfan**, 'battle peak', the name of a 6th-century Breton missionary to Wales; and **Cadoc**, a Welsh saint who was martyred by the Saxons.

Cahal see CAROL

Cai see CAIUS

Caitlin *f*
This, like Kathleen, is an Irish form of KATHARINE. It is currently popular in the UK, and it has been one of the most popular names in the USA for some years. The Irish pronounce it with the sound of 'cat' but the American pronunciation is reflected in the spelling **Katelynn**. Forms such as **Caitlyn(n)**, **Kaitlyn** and **Katlin** are also found.

Caius, Gaius *m*
A Roman first name, meaning 'rejoice', which is still used occasionally. The Welsh name **Cai**, **Kai** or **Kay**, well known as the name of Sir Kay, King Arthur's foster-brother, is derived from this. See also KAI.

Caleb *m*
From the Hebrew *kalebh*, meaning 'dog' or 'intrepid'. It first appeared in England in the 16th century and is now coming back into fashion, being well used in the USA and Australia. It is shortened to **Cale** and can be spelt with a 'K'.

Callie *f*

Callie or **Cally** was originally a short form of several names but is now used as a name in its own right. It is an old pet form of CAROLINE, or it can come from any name beginning Cal-, particularly those containing the Greek element for 'beautiful', such as **Calliope**, 'beautiful face', the name of the ancient Greek muse of epic poetry, or **Calista**, 'most beautiful', a name that may become more popular with the success of the actress Calista Flockhart. It is also found spelt **Kally** or **Kalli(e)**.

Callum *m*

Callum comes from the Latin *columba*, 'a dove'. When the Irish St Columba went as a missionary to Scotland in the 6th century, he introduced the name there, and it became a typically Scottish name, along with MALCOLM, which comes from it. It has recently become very popular in the rest of the UK and is well used in Australia but rare in the USA. It is found spelt **Calum** (the commonest spelling in Scotland, although the spelling with -ll- is preferred elsewhere) and **Colum**, while the form **Colm** is particularly Irish. See also COLIN.

Calvin *m*

From the surname of the 16th-century French religious reformer Jean Cauvin or Chauvin, which was latinised to Calvinus and adopted as a first name by Protestants. The surname may mean 'bald'. It is most commonly found in North America and Scotland, and can be shortened to **Cal**.

Cameron *m* and *f*

From the Gaelic meaning 'crooked nose', this is the name of a Scots clan. Its popularity as a boy's name has spread from Scotland, and it is now a popular choice in England, Australia and the USA. Thanks, perhaps, to the actress Cameron Diaz, it is now being used for girls as well, when it can be shortened to **Cami** (see also CAMILLA).

Camilla *f*

A name from Roman legend. Camilla was queen of the Volsci, a great warrior and exceptionally swift runner. The name may be Etruscan and possibly means 'one who helps at sacrifices'. It was recorded in Britain as early as 1205. **Camelia** is a Spanish form, and **Camille** is the French form, which can be used for either sex and is currently very popular for girls in France. **Cami**, **Camia**, **Milla**, **Milly** and **Millie** are used as short forms, and the name is also found spelt with a K-.

Camry see PORTIA

Candice, Candace *f*
This is an ancient title of the queen of Ethiopia. It is also spelt **Candis**; **Candy** is a short form.

Candida *f*
From the Latin meaning 'white'. The name was not used in Britain until the early 20th century, and its introduction probably resulted from G. B. Shaw's 1897 play *Candida*.

Candis, Candy see CANDICE

Caoilfhionn, Caolán see KEELY

Caoimhe *f*
Although little used outside Ireland, this is a popular name in Eire and seems to have caught the fancy of fantasy role-playing gamers as well. It comes from the Gaelic for 'beautiful, precious' and is the feminine equivalent of KEVIN. It is pronounced in Irish 'kweeva' and is anglicised as **Keavy**.

Cara *f*
This Italian word meaning 'dear' came into use as a first name only in the 20th century and is often spelt **Kara** in the USA. Pet forms, used as names in their own right, include **Carissa**, **Carita** and particularly **Carina** or **Karina**. These are found in a number of variant forms such as **Karissa**, **Karena**, **Caryssa** and **Charissa**, and it is not always easy to tell when parents are using forms of Cara, KAREN or CHARIS.

Caradoc *m*
From the Welsh for 'beloved'. It is common in Wales but not in other parts of Britain. In the form *Caratacus*, the name of a Briton who fought against the Romans in the first century, it is one of the earliest recorded British names.

Cari see CERI

Carisma see CHARISMA

Carl, Karl *m*, **Carla, Karla** *f*
These are German forms of CHARLES. The names have been in general use in America for a century and from there spread to Britain. The feminines Carla or Karla, **Carlie** or **Carly** can also be found as forms of the names found under CAROLINE.

Carlo see CHARLES

Carlotta see CHARLOTTE

Carlton, Charlton *m*
These names are both forms of an Old English place name and, later, a surname meaning 'countryman's farm'.

Carlyn see CAROLINE

Carmel *f*
From the Hebrew meaning 'garden' and the name of a mountain famous for its lush vegetation near the city of Haifa in Israel. St Louis founded the church and convent on this mountain, which, as legend has it, the Virgin Mary and infant Jesus often visited. **Carmen** is the Spanish form of the name, **Carmela** the Italian, and **Carmelita** and **Carmelina** pet forms. Carmen is also the Latin word for song, and some people like to think of it in this sense, hence such modern coinages as **Carmina**, the Latin for 'songs'. See also LITA.

Carol *f* and *m*
The female forms of this name, which include **Carole**, **Carola** and **Caryl**, were originally pet forms of CAROLINE or **Carolina** but are now

popular names in their own right. As a boy's name it can be an English form of the Irish **Cathal** or, in its phonetic spelling, **Cahal** ('battle-mighty'). It is also used in central Europe and often spelt **Karol** or **Karel**. In these cases it comes from *Carolus*, the latinised form of CHARLES.

Caroline, Carolyn *f*

These names come from **Carolina**, the feminine form of **Carlo**, the Italian for CHARLES. The name was introduced into Britain from southern Germany by Queen Caroline of Brandenburg-Anspach, wife of George II. Both forms have been used steadily since the 18th century. Derivatives are **Carla** (see CARL), **Carlyn**, CAROL, **Carola**, **Carole**. Abbreviations include **Carrie**, **Caddy**, **Caddie**, **Caro** and LYN.

Caron see KAREN

Carson *m*

This surname of unknown meaning, found mainly in Scotland and Northern Ireland, has been growing in popularity as a boy's name in the USA for a number of years. It is sometimes used for girls and, indeed, the most famous barer of the name, the author Carson McCullers (1917–1967) was female, dropping her given name of Lula and using her middle name for publication.

Carrie see CAROLINE

Carwen, Carwyn see CERI

Cary *m*

A surname that was only rarely used as a first name until it became famous through the film star Cary Grant. Ultimately, it probably goes back to one of a number of Irish surnames, including ones meaning 'battle-king' or 'dark brown'.

Caryl see CAROL

Caryn see KAREN

Carys see CERI

Caryssa see CARA

Casey *f* and *m*
This usually comes from an Irish surname meaning 'vigilant in war', but it can also be a form of the Polish name **Casimir**, 'proclamation of peace'. This has a female form, **Casimira**. The name takes various forms, often spelt with a 'K'.

Caspar see JASPER

Caspian *m*
Although at first this looks like the name of the great Asian inland sea, use of Caspian as a first name comes from the character of Prince Caspian in C. S. Lewis's *Narnia* books, particularly the 1951 volume named after him.

Cassandra *f*
In Greek literature this was the name of a prophetess and princess of Troy who was condemned to tell the truth but never be believed. Despite the fact that Cassandra came to an unpleasant end, the name first became popular in the Middle Ages and has continued in use ever since. It is shortened to **Cassie** and **Cass** and sometimes SANDRA or **Sandy**. The name has been well used in the USA in recent years. Cass also occurs as a masculine name, when it may come from an Irish name meaning 'curly-haired'.

Cassia see KEZIA(H)

Cassidy *f*
This is an Irish surname, of unknown meaning, used as a first name, mainly in the USA. **Cassie**, also used as a name in its own right, is a short form it shares with CASSANDRA. It is occasionally used for boys.

Cathal see CAROL

Cáthan see KANE

Catharine, Catherine, Cathleen, Cathy see KATHARINE

Catriona *f*

A Gaelic form of KATHARINE. It was the title of a book by Robert Louis Stevenson and became very popular in the 19th century as a result of this. **Catrina**, **Katrina** and **Katrine** are other forms of the name, and it becomes **Catrin** in Welsh. **Riona** is an Irish pet form, which can also be a form of **Ríoghnach**, meaning 'queenly' and the name of an early Irish queen.

Cecily see CECILIA

Cecil *m*

From the Latin meaning 'blind'. It was the name of a famous Roman clan and was first adopted into English as a girl's name. The popularity of the name in its masculine form became marked only in the 19th century, probably as one of several aristocratic surnames, which it was then fashionable to use as first names.

Cecilia *f*

The female version of CECIL. It was the name of a 2nd-century martyr and saint, the patroness of music. The name was first introduced into Britain by the Normans. Variant forms are **Cicely**, **Cecily**, **Sisley**, **Cecil** and the French **Cecile** (used for boys and girls in France). The shortened form **Celia** (which can also be derived from another Roman name, *Coelia*) probably came into fashion as a result of the Celia in Shakespeare's play *As You Like It*. Other abbreviated forms are **Sis**, **Ciss** and **Cissy** or **Sissy**. See also SHEILA.

Cedric *m*

This name seems to have been a creation of Sir Walter Scott's for a character in the novel *Ivanhoe* (1819). Scott is said to have used it by mistake for Cerdic, who was the first king of the West Saxons. However, as there is a Welsh name **Cedrych** ('pattern of generosity'), it may well be from this. Cedric became popular with parents as a result of the children's novel *Little Lord Fauntleroy* (1886) by F. H. Burnett whose hero bore that name, and it may well also owe its fall in popularity to its association with the book and its hero's smugly virtuous image. It does, however, show signs of coming back into fashion, particularly in the USA, and in the form **Cédric** currently has a certain popularity in France.

Celeste *f*
From the Latin meaning 'heavenly'. Pet forms, used as names in their own right, are **Celestine**, **Celestina** and **Celesta**.

Celia see CECILIA

Celina, Céline see SELINA

Cenydd see KENNETH

Ceri *f*
A popular Welsh name, sometimes spelt **Keri** to reflect its pronunciation with a hard 'c'. It comes from the Welsh word for 'love', as do the names **Cerian**, **Cerys** or **Carys** and **Cari**. **Carwen** is 'fair love' and has a masculine form, **Carwyn**. Cerys has recently started to be used more often in England, perhaps because the name has been brought to public attention by Cerys Matthews, the singer with the group Catatonia. See also KERRY.

Ceridwen *f*
This name probably comes from the Welsh words for 'poetry' and 'white, blessed'. It was the name of a Celtic goddess who was said to inspire poetry and was the mother of the great poet **Taliesin** ('radiant brow'). It is pronounced with a hard 'c' and is generally confined to Wales.

Cerise see CHERIE

Cerys see CERI

Chad *m*
The name (of uncertain meaning) of a 7th-century saint who was bishop of Lichfield. The name became quite popular in America in the 20th century. A famous holder of the name was the Rev. Chad Varah, founder of The Samaritans.

Chae see CHARLES

Champak *m*
The Hindu name of a god and of a tree bearing yellow flowers.

Chandan *m*
An Indian name from the Sanskrit for 'sandalwood'. The paste derived from sandalwood is important in Hindu religious ceremonies, when it is used to anoint statues of the gods and to make a mark on the foreheads of worshippers. Chandan occurs as a divine personal name in traditional Hindu texts.

Chander see CHANDRA

Chandler *m*
The success of the television series *Friends* has led to an increased use of the name, originally a French surname meaning 'candle maker'.

Chandra *f*, **Chander** *m*
An Indian name from the Sanskrit meaning 'the moon'. In the Hindu religion, the moon is a god rather than a goddess, but the name Chandra is nevertheless a popular one for girls. The variant **Chander** is often used for boys while **Chandrakala**, 'moonbeams', can be used for girls.

Chandrakant *m*, **Chandrakanta** *f*
From the Sanskrit for 'loved by the moon', referring to a mythical jewel mentioned in classical Hindu texts, supposedly formed by the moon's rays. It is also the name of a white water-lily that blossoms at night.

Chanel *f*
The name of this famous French perfume has been taken up as a girl's name in recent years, especially by African-Americans. The perfume was named after the French fashion designer Gabrielle 'Coco' Chanel, whose family name derives from an Old French word meaning 'wine jar', indicating an ancestral connection with the wine trade. Chanel is frequently spelt phonetically, taking such forms as **Shanel, Shanell, Shanelle** and **Shannel**. **Chanelle** is also used.

Chantal *f*

This is a French name that has been in use only since the beginning of the 20th century. It was the surname, meaning 'stone', of the 16th-century saint Jeanne-Françoise de Chantal. It has been popular in the USA, where it has developed forms such as **Chantalle** and **Chantel(l)e**. It is pronounced, and sometimes spelt, with a 'sh' sound at the beginning.

Chardonnay *f*

Chardonnay is the name of a very popular and highly esteemed variety of wine grape. Its name seems to have come from a French village name meaning 'place full of thistles'. It has been used occasionally in the USA as girl's name since at least the mid 1990s, but suddenly became used in the UK, where it had been all but unknown, in 2002 after it was used as the name of a prominent character in the successful television series *Footballers' Wives*. The spelling **Chardonay** already shows sign of establishing itself.

Charis *f*

From the Greek meaning 'grace'. The 'Ch' is pronounced as a 'K' and the name is occasionally spelt **Karis**. It was first used as a name in the 17th century, although in the 16th century the poet Edmund Spenser, in the *Faerie Queen*, used the form **Charissa**. It has been quite popular in the USA. **Chrissa** can be a short form of this or belong under the CHRISTINE group of names. There is some overlap between the names under CERI, CARA and Charis as they are pronounced so similarly.

Charisma *f*

This is one of the more recent vocabulary words that has been adopted by parents, no doubt in the hope that their child will show the attractiveness the name suggests. The word comes from the same Greek word as CHARIS. Although recent, it has already begun to have variants, such as **Karisma** and **Carisma**.

Charissa see CARA, CHARIS

Charisse see CHERIE

Charity *f*
From the Latin *caritas*, meaning 'Christian love'. Translated into English as *charity*, it was adopted when it became the custom for Puritans to name children after the Christian virtues. The name Charity was shortened to **Cherry** and is the source of this name. Another abbreviation is **Chattie**, used also for CHARLOTTE.

Charlene *f*
A 20th-century, feminine form of CHARLES. It may owe something to **Charline**, a Dutch form of CHARLOTTE. **Charleen** and **Sharlene** are also used. See also ARLENE.

Charles *m*
Originally from an Old German word *carl*, meaning 'man', that was latinised as *Carolus* and then changed by the French to Charles. The Normans brought the name to England, but it did not become popular until its use by the Stuart kings of Britain caused it to be taken up by Royalists in the 17th century and Jacobites in the 18th century. Its popularity has continued ever since. The pet form **Charlie** is now common as the given form of the name, indeed more common as a first name in the UK, although not elsewhere. As a feminine name Charlie is a form of CHARLOTTE. **Chas**, originally a written abbreviation, has now come to be used as a short form, and **Chip** is a short form shared with CHRISTOPHER. **Chuck** is also used, and in Scotland **Chae** or **Chay**. **Carlo**, the Spanish and Italian form, is well used in the USA.

Charlotte *f*
The French female form of CHARLES. It was introduced into Britain from France in the early 17th century. Goethe's heroine from the 1774 romantic novel *The Sorrows of Werther* and Princess Charlotte, daughter of George IV, increased its popularity. Abbreviations are **Lottie**, **Lotty**, **Totty**, **Charlie** and **Chattie**, and spellings such as **Sharlott** have been recorded. It has been one of the most popular girls' names in the UK for a number of years. **Carlotta** is the Italian form.

Charline see CHARLENE

Charlton see CARLTON

Charmaine *f*
A 20th century name of rather obscure origin. It may well be a form
of **Charmian**, from the Greek, meaning 'joy'. This was the name of
one of Cleopatra's attendants in Shakespeare's *Antony and Cleopatra*. Strictly speaking, Charmian should be pronounced with a
hard 'c', but the 'sh' pronunciation is also found. Charmaine is
sometimes spelt **Sharmaine**.

Charulata *f*
A Hindu name meaning 'beautiful'.

Chas see CHARLES

Chase *m*
The rise in popularity of this surname, meaning 'hunter', as a first
name in the USA probably owes much to its use for a character in
the 1980s' television series *Falcon Crest*. It is occasionally used for
girls.

Chasity *f*
In 1969 the singer Cher and her then husband, Sonny Bono, named
their daughter **Chastity**. This name seems to have been misinter-
preted, and Chasity developed as a first name in the USA.

Chattie see CHARITY, CHARLOTTE

Chay see CHARLES

Chelsea *f*
This name, which originally indicated a 'landing place (on the
River Thames) for chalk or limestone', of a fashionable part of
London and of New York is also a place name in Australia, where
its use as a girl's name seems to have begun. The name was introduced to America firstly by the actress Chelsea Brown, who was a
member of the cast of *Rowan and Martin's Laugh In*, which ran on

television from 1968, and then by a character in the 1981 film *On Golden Pond*, and its popularity was secured by the widespread publicity it received through Chelsea Clinton, daughter of US President Bill Clinton, who was named after a Joni Mitchell song. It is now well used in Britain. Spelling variants such as **Chelsie**, **Chelsey** and **Chelsi** are also found.

Cher see CHERIE, CHERYL

Cheralyn, Cherilyn see CHERYL

Cherie *f*
The French word for 'darling'. The forms **Cheri**, **Sherry**, **Sheree** and **Sherrie** are phonetic spellings. **Cher** can be the French for 'dear' or a short form of CHERYL. **Cherise**, used in the USA, has been interpreted in a number of different ways. It can be regarded either as a development of Cherie or as a form of **Charisse**, the French form of CHARIS, or as a form of the French name **Cerise**, 'cherry'.

Cherry see CHARITY

Cheryl *f*
This is probably a development of the name Cherry (see CHARITY). Other forms of the name are **Cheralyn**, **Cherilyn**, **Sheril** and **Sheryl**, and **Cher** can be a short form (the singer Cher was originally Cherilyn). See also CHERIE. These names came into general use only in the 1940s but rapidly became popular.

Chester *m*
A surname taken from the English city used as a first name. The word comes from the Latin for 'fort'.

Chetan *m*
A Hindu name meaning 'consciousness' or 'awareness'.

Chevelle see PORTIA

Chevonne see SHEENA

Cheyenne *f*
The name of a famous American Indian nation. It is said to come, via Canadian French, from the DAKOTA name for them, which meant 'unintelligible speakers' since they spoke very different languages. The Cheyenne's own name for themselves, which meant 'our people', had a similar sound. Cheyenne was first launched as a boy's name in a television series of that name in the USA in the late 1950s. Pronunciation of the name as **Shyann**, in which form it is also found, possibly linked it in parents' minds with the name ANNE, suggesting its use for girls, and it is now more common as a girl's name.

Cheyna see SHAINA

Chiara see CLARE

China see CHYNA

Chintana *f*
An Indian name meaning 'meditation'. The form **Chintanika** is also used.

Chip see CHARLES, CHRISTOPHER

Chloe *f*
Chloë comes from the Greek, meaning 'a green shoot', a name given to the goddess Demeter who protected the green fields. It was a popular name in classical literature that was picked up by the Elizabethan poets. It is very popular at the moment in Australia and in the UK, having been the most popular name for girls in England and Wales for the last six years, and its popularity is increasing in the USA. **Chloris**, 'greenish', is another name from Greek myth and is again associated with fertility. It is sometimes spelt **Cloris** to reflect the pronunciation of these names with a hard 'c'.

Chris see CHRISTABEL, CHRISTINE, CHRISTOPHER

Chrissa see CHARIS, CHRISTINE

Chrissie, Chrissy see CHRISTABEL, CHRISTINE

Christabel *f*
This name was first used in Britain in the 16th century, and is thought to be a combination of 'Christ' and the Latin *bella* to mean 'beautiful Christian'. It is not a common name in Britain, although it is sometimes used in memory of the suffragette, Dame Christabel Pankhurst (1880–1958). It is also spelt **Christobel**, and abbreviated forms are **Chris**, **Chrissy**, **Chrissie** or **Christie**.

Christel, Christen see CHRISTINE

Christian *f* and *m*
This name, with its transparent meaning, has been used in Britain since the 13th century. It became more popular after its use by John Bunyan for the hero of *Pilgrim's Progress* (1678) but has never been as common as the feminine form, CHRISTINE, although it is currently enjoying some popularity, particularly in the USA.

Christie see CHRISTABEL, CHRISTOPHER

Christine *f*
The commonest of the many girls' names meaning 'a Christian'. **Christen** is probably the oldest form, followed by **Christiana**. Others are **Christina**; **Christian(n)e**, a feminine form of CHRISTIAN; the Welsh form **Crystin**; and spellings such as **Krystyna**, **Kristina**, **Krista** and **Kristin**. The German form, **Christel**, may have helped the development of the name CRYSTAL. Short forms are **Chrissie**, **Chrissy** and **Chris**, and further variants will be found under the Scottish pet form, KIRSTY. **Chrissa**, **Chryssa** or **Kryssa** can be thought of either as a part of this group or as a short form of Charissa. See CHARIS.

Christmas see NOEL

Christobel see CHRISTABEL

Christopher *m*
From the Greek meaning 'bearing Christ'. As a first name it is used in honour of the saint who was believed to have carried the infant

Christ to safety across a river. Thus St Christopher became the patron saint of travellers. The popularity of the name in Britain has fluctuated since the 13th century when it was first used, but it is presently a popular choice in the UK, USA and Australia. The Scottish equivalent of the name was **Chrystal** or CRYSTAL. Abbreviated forms are **Kester**, **Kit**, **Chris** and occasionally **Chip**, which is also a short form of CHARLES. **Christie** or **Christy** is a pet form particularly used in Ireland.

Chryssa see CHRISTINE

Chrystal see CHRISTOPHER, CRYSTAL

Chuck see CHARLES

Chyna *f*
Based on the place name **China**, the name is particularly associated with the singer **Chynna** Philips, while the form Chyna is associated in the USA with a woman wrestler.

Cian see KEENAN

Ciara, Ciaran see KIERAN

Cicely see CECILIA

Ciera, Cieran see KIERAN, SIERRA

Cilla see PRISCILLA

Cillian see KILLIAN

Cimmie see CYNTHIA

Cindy *f*
A short form of names such as LUCINDA and CYNTHIA, now used as an independent name. It is also spelt **Cindi** and **Cindie**.

Ciss, Cissy see CECILIA

Clare, Claire *f*
From the Latin meaning 'clear, famous'. The religious order of the Sisters of St **Clara**, or 'Poor Clares', founded in the 13th century, was

probably responsible for the rapid spread of the name throughout Europe. The name has been popular for some time. Among the many derivatives are **Claribel** and **Clarinda**, which can be shortened to **Clarrie**. The Italian form, **Chiara**, is sometimes used.

Clarence *m*
In the 14th century Lionel, son of King Edward III of England, married the heiress of the town of Clare in Suffolk. He was later created Duke of Clarence, the name Clarence meaning 'of Clare'. This title seems to have been first used as a name in the early 19th century in Maria Edgeworth's novel *Helen*.

Claribel, Clarinda see CLARE

Clarissa *f*
From the Latin meaning 'brightest, most famous'. It was made popular in the 18th century by Samuel Richardson's novel *Clarissa Harlowe*. **Clarice** is an older form of the name. They share the pet form **Clarrie** with CLARE names.

Clark *m*
The surname, meaning 'a clerk', used as a first name. Famous users were the actor Clark Gable and, in fiction, Clark Kent, the everyday name for Superman. **Clarke** is also found.

Claud *m*, Claudia *f*
From the Roman name **Claudius**, itself derived from the Latin meaning 'lame'. In homage to the Emperor Claudius, who was ruler when Britain was conquered by the Romans, the name was used in what is now England in the 1st and 2nd centuries. Its use soon lapsed in Britain although not in France where it is spelt **Claude** and used for either sex. It was from the French that it was revived in Britain in the 16th century by the Scottish family of Hamilton. A derivative is **Claudian**, and the pet form **Claudie** can be found. The female form, Claudia, is at the moment the more popular. Two French diminutives are also used: **Claudette** and **Claudine**, a name made famous by the novels of Colette.

Clarrie see CLARE, CLARISSA

Claus see NICHOLAS

Clayton *m*
Clayton, from a place name, later a surname, meaning 'settlement on clay', is enjoying some popularity in the USA as a boy's name, as is the shorter **Clay**. Both are also found spelt with a 'K'.

Clement *m*, **Clementina**, **Clementine** *f*
From the Latin, meaning 'mild, merciful'. Clement was the name of an early saint and of several popes. Its abbreviated forms are **Clem** and **Clemmie**, which are shared with the feminine forms Clementina and Clementine. Clementine was originally a German form, fashionable during the 19th century, and is now showing signs of returning to popularity. **Clemency** is also used for girls and **Clémence** found in France.

Cleo *f*
A shortened form of Cleopatra, from the Greek meaning 'glory of her father'. The famous Egyptian queen of this name died in 30 BC, and it did not take long for her name to become a byword for sexual allure and tragic love. The form **Clio** is, strictly speaking, the name of the Greek muse of history.

Cleona, **Clidna** see CLIONA

Clifford *m*
There are several places named Clifford ('ford by the cliff') in Britain, any of which could become a surname. Towards the end of the 19th century the surname came into use as a first name, as one of a group of surnames, such as HOWARD, taken from noble families to use as a first name. It is now most often used in its short form, **Cliff**. **Clifton**, 'settlement by the cliff', is also found.

Clint *m*
A short form of **Clinton**, an aristocratic surname meaning 'farm by the river Glyme', used as a first name. The short form has been given fame by the actor Clint Eastwood.

Clio see CLEO

Cliona *f*
Cliona of the fair hair is one of the most important fairy-women of
Irish legend. The name is mostly restricted to Ireland and can also
be spelt **Cleona**, **Clidna**, **Cliodhna** and **Cliodna**.

Clive *m*
A surname, meaning 'dweller by the cliff', which has come to be
used as a first name, probably in honour of Robert Clive (1725–
1774), known as Clive of India, who was prominent in the British
conquest of India. It is not much used currently.

Clodagh *f*
The name of a river in Ireland. It was introduced in the 20th century
as a first name by the Marquis of Waterford who chose it for his
daughter. It is well used in Ireland, and its use has now spread
beyond that country, perhaps helped by the fame of the Irish singer
Clodagh Rodgers.

Cloris see CHLOE

Clotilda *f*
This is an old Germanic name meaning 'loud battle'. Clotilda was
a queen in France in the 6th century who converted her husband,
King Clovis (see LEWIS) to Christianity. The name is not common
among English speakers, but is more likely to be found in France,
where it appears as **Clothilde**.

Cloudie, Cloudy see STORM

Clover *f*
This is the flower name used as a first name. Its spread may have
been helped by its use for a character in the *Katy* books by Susan
Coolidge. Names such as **Clova** can be interpreted either as a respelling of Clover or as a feminine form of Clovis (see LEWIS).

Clovis see LEWIS

Clyde *m*
Clyde is an ancient Scottish river name meaning 'the washer', possibly from the name of a local goddess and used since before the Roman occupation. It became a surname, then a first name.

Cody *f* and *m*
This is said to be an Irish surname meaning 'descendant of a helpful person'. It has been popular in Australia and in the United States, where it is also a place name and well known as the surname of the Wild West hero Buffalo Bill Cody. **Codey** and spellings with 'K' have also been recorded. **Codi(e)** is the spelling most often used for girls, but all forms are more commonly used for boys .

Coinneach see KENNETH

Colby, Cole *m*
Colby is an English place name and surname, now used as a first name in the USA where it grew steadily in popularity in the early 1990s. The name originally indicated a farmstead owned by a Norseman called Koli. **Colton**, however, comes from a place name meaning 'farm by the River Cole'. Both these can be shortened to **Cole**, a name made famous by the song-writer Cole Porter. Alternatively, Cole, currently the most popular of these names, well used in Canada and the USA, can be from yet another surname, from the Old English for 'black', which could have started out as a nickname for someone with a dark complexion. It can also be from an old pet form of NICHOLAS. When Cole is found used for girls it is usually a pet form of NICOLE.

Colette *f*
From a French diminutive of NICOLA. It was the name of the 15th-century reformer of the Poor Clares' religious order. The name is best known as the pen name of a 20th-century French writer. It is also spelt **Collette**.

Colin *m*
Colin is a name that comes from two different sources. As an Eng-

lish name it has a similar origin to COLETTE, for it was a French pet form of NICHOLAS. As a Celtic name it was interpreted as coming from the Gaelic word *cailean*, which in turn has been interpreted in two ways, either as a word meaning 'puppy' or 'youth', or as a pet form of the name Columba (see CALLUM). It is too early to see if the distinctive pronunciation chosen by the American politician Colin Powell will influence the way most people pronounce the name. There are rare feminine forms, **Colina** and **Colinette**.

Colleen *f*
The Irish word for 'girl' used as a first name. The name is not widely used in Britain but has been fairly common in North America and Australia. **Coline** is a French form.

Collette see COLETTE

Colm, Colum, Columba see CALLUM

Colton see COLBY

Con, Conchobar, Conchobhar see CONNOR

Conan *m*
From the Irish meaning 'hound, wolf'. A famous holder of the name was Sir Arthur Conan Doyle, creator of Sherlock Holmes, but the name is probably best known today from the fictional stories and films of Conan the Barbarian. Although the fictional character's name is pronounced in the American films with the same sound as in 'cone', in Ireland the name has a short 'o'. It shares its short forms with CONNOR.

Conn see CONNOR

Connie see CONSTANCE

Connor *m*
From the ancient Irish name **Conchobar** or **Conchobhar**, meaning 'lover of hounds'. It was the name of one of the great kings in Irish heroic stories and has long been a popular name in Ireland. Connor's popularity has spread to the UK, Australia, Canada and

increasingly in the USA. In all these countries it is usually spelt Connor, but in Ireland **Conor** is preferred. It can be shortened to **Con** or **Conny** and sometimes **Conn**, which is also a separate name, perhaps meaning 'wisdom'.

Conrad *m*

From the Old German words for 'bold counsel'. The name is found mostly in Germany where in the 13th century Duke Conrad was a greatly loved figure. Objection to his public execution by the conquering Charles of Anjou led to a widespread use of this name in German-speaking states. Examples of it have been found in Britain since the 15th century. **Curt** or **Kurt** is a short form used as an independent name, now used rather more frequently than the full form.

Constance *f*

Constance and its Latin form, *Constantia*, mean 'constancy'. It became popular in many parts of Christendom after Constantine the Great ordered the toleration of Christianity in the Roman Empire, AD 313. It was introduced into England at the time of the Norman Conquest. The form **Constancy** was used by the Puritans in the 17th century while **Constantia** became popular in the 18th century. **Constantina** is another form of the name. Constance was popular in the 19th century, but has been out of fashion since the early 20th century, although there has recently been a small increase in its use. Its abbreviation is **Connie. Constantine**, the masculine form, comes from the Latin for 'firm, constant'. Three Scottish kings were named Constantine after a Cornish saint who was believed to have converted their ancestors to Christianity in the 6th century. It became popular in England from the 12th to the 17th centuries and was the origin of the surnames Constantine, Considine, Costain and Costin. It is not widely used in Britain today. The composer **Constant** Lambert (1905–51) shows another form of the name.

Cora see CORINNA

Coral *f*

This name reflects the beauty and value of the substance, and was popular in the early 20th century. A French form that is also in use in Britain is **Coralie**.

Corbin *m*
Corbin comes from a surname based on the Old French word for 'raven'. Its spread owes much to the success of the actor Corbin Bernsen. **Korben**, **Corban** and **Korbyn** are also used.

Cordelia *f*
This name first appeared as Cordeilla in the 16th-century chronicles of Holinshed, from which Shakespeare altered the name to Cordelia for his play *King Lear*. The name is probably a form of **Cordula**, the name of one of the virgins martyred with St Ursula. It probably comes from the Latin word for 'heart'.

Corey *f* and *m*
This is an Irish surname of unknown meaning that has come to be used as a first name. It has been popular in the USA for some years. It is also spelt **Cory**, and in forms such as **Cori** or **Corrie** has been used for girls, especially in combination with other names. Spellings beginning with 'K', particularly Kori for girls, are also found.

Corinna *f*
This name and **Cora** both come from the Greek word *kore*, meaning 'girl' or 'maiden', a name given to the goddess **Persephone**, who was associated with the coming of spring. The appearance of Corinna in Ovid's love poetry probably inspired its use among some 17th-century poets, particularly Herrick. The French form **Corinne** is also used. **Corin**, much used in poetry as the name for a lovesick shepherd, is the male form of the name, although it is occasionally also used for girls.

Corisande *f*
This is a name full of glamour and romance, having been the name of a fair maiden in medieval romance. Later it was a poetic name given to Diane de Poitiers, the beautiful and influential mistress of the 16th-century French king, Henry II of France. Use of this name

was given a boost in the 19th century when Disraeli created the charming Lady Corisande as the heroine of his 1871 novel *Lothaire*.

Cormac *m*

This Irish name is of doubtful meaning, although it is sometimes said to mean 'a charioteer'. It appears frequently in Irish legend, but through its prevalence in early Irish history and the Irish Church the name was accepted as having a Christian character in Ireland, so remained in steady use there although it is not much used elsewhere. A variant is **Cormick**.

Cornelius *m*, Cornelia *f*

From the Latin *cornu*, meaning 'a horn', these were the male and female forms of the name of a famous Roman clan. The male form was used in Ireland as a substitute for the native **Conchobar** (see CONOR). Its abbreviated forms are **Corney**, **Corny** and **Cornie**.

Corrie, Cory see COREY

Cosmo *m*

From the Greek *kosmos*, meaning 'order'. It is the name of one of the two patron saints of Milan and was used by the famous Italian family of Medici in the form **Cosimo** from the 14th century onwards. It was the name of the 3rd Duke of Gordon, who had family connections with Cosimo III, Grand Duke of Tuscany, and the name was thereby introduced into several other Scottish families. **Cosima** is the feminine form.

Courtney *f* and *m*

An aristocratic surname used as a first name. It comes from Courtnay, a French place name, although the name is often interpreted as coming from *court nez*, the French for 'short nose'. It is currently more used for girls than for boys and has been popular in the UK, USA and Australia.

Craig *m*

The place and surname from a Celtic word meaning 'crag', used as a first name. It was popular in many countries in the 1970s but is now most likely to be used in Scotland and Ireland.

Cressida *f*
Cressida comes from a medieval misreading of the name Briseida, 'daughter of Brisis', who appears in Homer's Ancient Greek account of the Trojan War. In the 14th century, the Italian writer Boccaccio used the name, in a work that was adapted by Chaucer in his verse novel *Troilus and Criseyde*, the story of Troilus's undying love for the fair Cressida, set against the background of the Trojan War. Shakespeare changed the name to Cressida for his version of the story. Despite the fictional character's faithlessness in love, the name has recently become quite fashionable in the UK. An abbreviated form is **Cressy**.

Crispin, Crispian *m*
From the Latin *crispus*, meaning 'curled'. The 3rd-century martyrs Crispinus and Crispinianus were the patron saints of shoemakers. Crispin was popular in Britain in the Middle Ages and has recently enjoyed a revival.

Crystal *f*
While this looks like, and is no doubt mainly used as, another jewel name (see also AMBER, JADE), the spread of this name may have been helped by **Christel**, the German form of CHRISTINE. Crystal is also spelt **Chrystal**, and the form **Krystal** has become known through the TV series *Dynasty*. As a man's name it is a pet form of CHRISTOPHER.

Crystin see CHRISTINE

Cudbert, Cuddy see CUTHBERT

Curt see CONRAD

Curtis *m*
A surname from the French, meaning 'courteous', used as a first name. It has been used more frequently in the United States than in Britain.

Cuthbert *m*
From the Old English words *cuth* and *beorht*, meaning 'famous' and 'bright'. It was in common use both before and after the Norman Conquest, and was the name of a 7th-century saint who was Bishop of Lindisfarne in Northumbria. It sometimes appeared as **Cudbert** and had the pet form **Cuddy**. The name fell out of use just after the Reformation until the 19th century, when it was brought back by the Oxford Movement. It was a slang term for someone who avoided military service during the First World War, and it may be partly due to this usage that the name is not popular today. The school 'swot' in the *Beano*'s Bash Street Kids is called Cuthbert Cringeworthy.

Cy see CYRIL, CYRUS

Cybill see SYBIL

Cynan *m*
This is a Welsh name based on the word *cyn*, meaning 'chief' or 'outstanding'. It can also be found spelt **Cynin** or **Cynon**. There are a number of other Welsh names formed from this word, including **Cynyr**, which means 'chief hero'.

Cynthia *f*
One of the titles of the Greek goddess Artemis (see DIANA), Cynthia means 'of Mount Cynthus', reputedly one of her favourite places. It first became known as a name through its use by the Latin poet Propertius, and it was later popular among Elizabethan poets. Mrs Gaskell's character in her novel *Wives and Daughters* brought it back into favour during the late 19th century. Pet forms include CINDY, **Cindi** or **Cindie** and the rarer **Cimmie**. It is most likely to be used in the USA.

Cyprian *m*
From the Latin *Cyprianus*, meaning 'from Cyprus'. It was the name of a Christian martyr of the 3rd century.

Cyra see CYRUS

Cyril *m*

From the Greek *kyrios*, meaning 'lord'. There were two saints of this name in the 4th and 5th centuries, and it was a 9th-century Saint Cyril who took Christianity to the Slavs and devised the Russian Cyrillic alphabet. The name was first used in England in the 17th century but did not become common until the 19th century. The name shares the abbreviation **Cy** with Cyrus and has been recorded spelt **Syril**. There is a rare feminine form, **Cyrilla**.

Cyrus *m*

A Greek form of the Persian word meaning 'sun' or 'throne'. This is the name of the founder of the Persian Empire in the 6th century BC as well as a number of other Persian kings. It was first used in Britain in the 17th century among Puritans, probably in honour of the fact that the Emperor Cyrus allowed the Jews to return to Palestine from their Babylonian captivity. They took it to North America, where the short forms are **Cy** and **Cyro**. There is a feminine form, **Cyra**.

D

Dáire, Dáiríne see DERRY

Dafydd, Dai see DAVID

Daisy *f*
This probably started out as a 19th-century pet name for MARGARET, a pun on *marguerite*, the French word for daisy. There is no reason, however, why it should not have come into use as a simple flower name, and few people today would use it otherwise. It has been increasingly popular in the UK in the last few years.

Daithi see DAVID

Dakota *f* and *m*
The name of this American Indian people is now being regularly used in the USA. The name means 'friend'. Its use can be compared to that of CHEYENNE.

Dale *f* and *m*
The Old English for 'valley'. At first more common as a girl's name, it is now more frequently used for boys. There are a number of other surnames from place names starting with the same sound, such as **Dalton**, **Dallas** and **Dallin**, that may owe their use as boys' names to the popularity of Dale.

Damaris *f*
The Greek name in the New Testament of an Athenian woman converted to Christianity by St Paul. This led to its adoption by Puritans in the 17th century. It is probably a form of a Greek name meaning 'heifer'.

Damhnait see DEVNET

Damian, Damien *m*
From the Greek, meaning 'tamer'. There have been four saints called by this name. It was little used in the UK before the 20th century but became popular in the 1970s.

Damon *m*
From the Greek, meaning 'to rule' or 'guide'. In Greek legend, Damon and Pythias were inseparable friends, famous for their willingness to die for each other.

Dan see DANIEL

Dana *f* and *m*
As a boy's name this comes from the surname, the Old English word for a Dane, and is sometimes found in the form **Dane**. The female name is either a Scandinavian girl's form of DANIEL or, in Ireland, can be taken from the pagan fertility goddess, Dana or Ana.

Dandy see ANDREW

Daniel *m*, **Danielle** *f*
Daniel and Danielle have both been popular in recent years, with Daniel in the top ten names for boys in most countries. Meaning 'God has judged', Daniel is the Hebrew name of an Old Testament prophet. It was found in England before the Norman Conquest but only among priests and monks. It became more widespread in the 13th and 14th centuries. In Ireland and Wales it is often found as a version of the Irish **Domhnall** (see DONALD) and the Welsh **Deiniol**, meaning 'attractive, charming'. Its shortened forms are **Dan** and **Danny**. For girls, Danielle is the most common form, but **Daniel(l)a** and **Danette** are also used, all shortened to **Danny** or **Dani(e)**.

Dante see DONTE

Daphne *f*
From the Greek for 'bay tree, laurel'. In classical mythology, it was the name of a nymph who was loved by the god Apollo. She called

on the other gods for help to escape his attentions and was changed by them into a laurel. The name was a traditional name for dogs until the end of the 19th century, when it became quite common as a girl's name.

Dara *m* and *f*
This is an Irish name, a shortened form of Mac Dara, 'son of the oak', the name of a popular Connemara saint. It is also spelt **Darragh** and **Daragh**. The name is so popular in Ireland that all these spellings get into the top 100 names there, with Darragh the most popular. Although traditionally a masculine name, Dara is now also used for girls.

Darcy *f* and *m*
Darcy can be either from a French surname meaning someone from a place called Arcy, hence the form **d'Arcy** or **D'Arcy**, or an Irish surname meaning 'descendant of the dark one'. For girls it often takes the form **Darcey** or **Darci(e)**.

Dareen see DERRY

Daria *f*, **Darius** *m*
Darius was the name of the 6th-century BC king of the Persians who was defeated by the Athenians at Marathon. The name means 'protector'. **Daria** is the feminine form.

Darian, Darien see DORIAN

Darina see DERRY

Darlene *f*
This appears to be a relatively modern invention, made up of the first syllable of one of the names beginning 'Dar-', or perhaps from 'darling', with the -ene ending that is popular with newly created names such as CHARLENE and **Raelene**.

Darrel(l) *f* and *m*
Also spelt **Dar(r)yl**, this is another surname used as a first name. In this case the surname comes from a French village, the village name

meaning 'courtyard, open space'. Originally mainly a boy's name, its spread as a girl's name may owe something to Enid Blyton's use of her second husband's surname, Darrell, for the heroine of her *Malory Towers* school stories.

Darren *m*
A surname of unknown meaning used as a first name. It seems to have been introduced in the 1950s and become popular in the 1960s. At the moment it is quite popular in Scotland and Ireland but not much used elsewhere. **Darran** is also found.

Darshan *m*
An Indian name from the Sanskrit meaning 'to see'. Darshan refers to being in the presence of, or being near enough to touch and see with one's own eyes, a holy or revered person. It is thought to bestow spiritual enrichment on the observer.

Dary see DERRY

Dash(i)a, Dasia see DEJA

David *m*
The Hebrew name of the second king of Israel in the Old Testament, meaning 'beloved'. This name absorbed the Celtic **Daithi**, meaning 'nimbleness' (the 'th' is pronounced 'h') and became very popular in Wales and Scotland. The patron saint of Wales is a 6th-century David. There were Scottish kings of this name in the 10th and 14th centuries. The name did not appear in England before the Norman Conquest, but it was a common medieval surname in the variant forms Davy, Davit and Deakin. Short forms are **Dave**, **Davy**, **Davie**, and in Wales **Dafydd** becomes **Dai** or **Taffy**, the latter being an English nickname for a Welshman. David is currently a popular choice.

Davida, Davina *f*
These Scottish female forms of DAVID are found from the 17th century but were not much used until the 20th century, when they started to become more popular. They are sometimes shortened to **Vida** and **Vina**, and **Davita** and **Davinia** are also found.

Davie, Davy see DAVID

DaVon see DEVON

Dawn *f*
This name came into use in the late 19th century. **Aurora**, the name of the Greek goddess of dawn, had been in vogue slightly earlier and the English translation was probably a literary invention. **Aurore** is currently popular in France.

Deaglán see DECLAN

Dean *m*
A surname, meaning 'valley', adopted as a first name. It seems to have become popular in the United States first but has been widely used in the UK since the 1960s. **Deana** or **Dena** is a feminine.

DeAndre *m*
One of the names that was highly fashionable among African-American families throughout the 1980s. The prefix 'De-' was regularly attached to other names, leading to new forms such as **DeAngelo, DeJuan, DeMarco** or **DeMarcus, DeMario, DeShawn** and **DeWayne**. For the meanings of these names, look under the entries for the names that follow the 'De-' prefix.

Deanna, Deanne see DIANA

Dearbhail see DERVLA

Deb, Debdan see DEV

Deborah *f*
A Hebrew name meaning 'bee', and the name of a prophetess and poet in the Old Testament. It was first used by Puritans in the 17th century. **Debbie** or **Debby** is a common abbreviation that is sometimes used independently. **Debra** is a modern spelling of the name.

Declan *m*
The name of an 5th-century Irish saint associated with Ardmore. It has long been popular with Irish parents and has now spread to

general use in the UK. The Irish spelling is **Deaglán**. **Dec** is used as a pet form.

Dee *f* and *m*
This is usually a nickname, given to anyone with a name beginning with the letter 'D' but is occasionally found as a given name. Compounds such as **Deedee** also occur.

Deepak *m*, **Deepika** *f*
An Indian name from the Sanskrit meaning 'little lamp'. It is one of the descriptive names applied to Kama, god of love. The spelling **Dipak** is also used for boys.

Deiniol see DANIEL

Deirbhaile see DERVLA

Deirdre *f*
The Irish name of a character in Irish and Scottish legend, possibly meaning 'raging' or 'sorrowful'. The name became popular after the late 19th-century Celtic revival. It often takes the form **Deidra** in the USA.

Deja *f*
This new name is something of a mystery. It has been linked to the French word *déjà*, 'already', as in *déjà vu*, but this seems unlikely. It can also be seen as a short form of **Dejanira**, the Spanish form of **Deianeira**, the wife of Heracles in Greek mythology, whose name means 'destroyer of men'; but in this case the 'j' is pronounced with a 'y' sound. A more likely source is the character of Dejah Thoris, the beautiful princess in Edgar Rice Burroughs' Barsoom novels. Spellings include **Dejah**, **Dash(i)a** and **Dasia**.

DeJuan see DEANDRE

Del, Dell see DELBERT, DEREK, DELYTH

Delbert *m*
This name has been in use since at least the beginning of the 20th

century. It is probably formed on the pattern of several surnames such as **Delroy** ('of the king') and **Delmar** ('of the sea'), which are also used as first names, particularly in the USA, keeping the 'Del-' part and adding '-bert' from the many Germanic names that end in this suffix. The short forms **Del** or **Dell** are also used as first names and can be pet forms of DEREK.

Delia *f*

This name is derived from Delos, the legendary birthplace of the Greek moon goddess Artemis (see DIANA), and was a name sometimes given to her. It was popular with pastoral poets in the 17th and 18th centuries, but in the UK has now become so strongly associated with the cookery expert Delia Smith that the name has actually entered the dictionaries as a term for her reliable cooking style.

Delilah *f*

This is the name borne by the well-known biblical character who betrayed Samson to the Philistines. It derives from a Hebrew name meaning 'coquette' or 'flirt'. It was also the title of a song popularised by Tom Jones, but this failed to persuade many parents to make use of it.

Della *f*

Originally a short form of ADELA, this is now well established as a name in its own right.

Delmar, Delroy see DELBERT

Delorean see PORTIA

Delyth *f*

Delyth is a Welsh name, means 'pretty' and comes from the word *Del*, 'pretty'. Other names based on the word are **Delun**, 'pretty one', **Delwen**, 'pretty and fair or blessed', and **Delwyn**, originally the masculine form of Delwen but now used for both sexes.

DeMarco, DeMarcus, DeMario see DEANDRE

Demelza *f*
A place name, meaning 'the hill-fort of Maeldaf', used as a first name in Cornwall. It became more widely known through its use by the novelist Winston Graham in his *Poldark* books and the TV series based on them.

Demetrius *m*, **Demi** *f*
Demetrius is an ancient Greek name that means 'follower, devotee of Demeter', the Greek pagan goddess of corn and agriculture whose name in turn means 'earth mother'. It was the name of a highly successful general who died in 286 BC. In the form **Demetrios**, it is the name of a Greek saint, and as **Demitrus** it is found in the Bible. **Dimitri** or **Dmitri** is the form the name takes in Russia, where it has been long established. **Demetra** or **Demitria**, which can be shortened to **Demi**, as in the actress Demi Moore, is the commonest form for girls. Demetrius was a name little used by English speakers until fairly recently, when it became more used in the United States among African-American families because it began with the fashionable 'De-' prefix. See DEANDRE.

Den see DENIS

Dena see DEAN

Denholm *m*
A place name, meaning 'island valley', used as a first name. The similar **Denham**, 'home in a valley', is also used.

Denis *m*, **Denise** *f*
A development of the name of **Dionysos**, the Greek god of wine and revelry. Denis or **Dennis** is the French form and the name of the patron saint of France. It occurs in England from the 12th century on. In Ireland it has long been used as a substitute for the Irish **Donnchadh** (see DUNCAN). **Den** and **Denny** are short forms. Denise, the female form, is also from French. **Dion** or **Deon** (*m*) and **Dionne** (*f*) can either come from Dionysos or be a separate name from the same root, connected with the word for 'a god', while **Dione** can be

thought of either as a variant of Dionne or as the name of another character from Greek mythology whose name means 'divine queen'. **Denisha** (*f*) is a further development of the name. See also DWIGHT.

Denzil *m*
In the form **Denzell**, this is an old Cornish surname derived from a place name of obscure meaning.

Deo see DEV

Deodan see DEVDAN

Deon see DENIS

Derek, Derrick *m*
This is from the Old German **Theodoric**, meaning 'people's ruler'. Derek occurs in the 15th century but became popular only in the 20th century. Its fall from favour between these two periods is attributed to a notorious 17th-century hangman of that name. Variants recently revived are **Deryk, Deric** and the Dutch form **Dirk**, popularised by the actor Dirk Bogarde. Pet forms are **Derry, Rick, Rickie** and **Del** or **Dell**. **Thierry**, popular in France, is the French form of the name. See also TERRY.

Dermot *m*
This is the anglicised spelling of **Diarmuid, Diarm(a)it** or **Diarm(a)id**, the Irish name possibly meaning 'free from envy' or 'free man'. The legendary character who bore this name eloped with GRAINNE, who was betrothed to FINN. Finn pursued the lovers for a long time and finally brought about Dermot's death.

Derrick, Derry see DEREK

Derry *m*
Derry can be a form of a number of different boy's names. It can be from Irish **Dáire**, meaning 'the fruitful one' and possibly once a name given to a pagan god. This is also anglicised **Dary** and has

feminine forms **Dáiríne, Darina** or **Dareen**. Or it can be pet forms of names such as DEREK or DERMOT.

Dervla *f*
This is the phonetic form of **Deirbhaile**, an old Irish name that means 'daughter of the poet'. It is best known through the travel writer Dervla Murphy. It also occurs as **Dervila**, reflecting the Irish pronunciation. The similar-looking **Dearbhail**, which can be anglicised **Derval** or **Dervilia**, means 'daughter of Fal' (a figure in Irish legend).

Deryk see DEREK

Des see DESMOND

DeShawn see DEANDRE

Desi see DESMOND

Désirée *f*
A French name meaning 'desired'. It has been in use since the beginning of the Christian era in the Latin form **Desideria**, originally for a long-awaited, much desired child. The French boy's name **Didier**, 'longing', shortened to **Didi**, would be the male equivalent.

Desmond *m*
From the Irish *Deas-Mumhain*, meaning '(man) of Desmond', an old name for Munster. It was originally used as a surname in Ireland. Later it became a first name, and came to England in the late 19th century. **Des** and **Desi, Desy** or **Dezi** are short forms.

Destiny *f*
This vocabulary word has become increasingly popular as a girl's name in the USA and is now among the most frequently chosen.

Detta see BERNADETTE

Dev *m*
An Indian name from the Sanskrit meaning 'god'. Deva is also the term used to address royalty, Brahmins and priests. Dev becomes **Deb** or **Deo** in different parts of India. **Devdan** means 'gift of the

gods'. The forms **Debdan** and **Deodan** are also used. Dev was one of the names of the founder of Sikhism, the Guru Nanak Dev Ji, so is popular with his followers. **Ji** is an element added to show respect and is sometimes run on to a name, giving forms such as **Devji** or **Deviji**.

Devin see DEVON

Devnet *f*
This is the anglicised spelling of the Irish name **Damhnait**, the name of an early Irish martyr meaning 'fawn, little deer'. An older form is **Dymp(h)na**.

Devon *f* and *m*
This name appears to be the name of the English county, and it is often used in this way; but American parents sometimes stress it on the second syllable. This use was probably suggested when 'De-' became a fashionable prefix for names among African-American families, as in DEANDRE. The alternative spelling **Devin** is frequent (although this can also be linked to an Irish name, the masculine form of DEVNET), and forms such as **DaVon** are also found.

DeWayne see DEANDRE, DUANE

Dexter *m*
This is a surname, originally given to a dyer, now used as a first name.

Dezi see DESMOND

Dhanishta *f*
An Indian name that derives from the Sanskrit for 'star'.

Di see DIANA

Diamond *f* and *m*
Although not one of the commonest jewel names, use of Diamond as a first name is growing, particularly for girls. The name of this most precious gem, famous for its hardness, comes from a Latin

word *adamentem*, which was originally used for a very hard metal, then transferred to the gem and which is also the origin of the word 'adamant'. Diamond is sometimes found as **Dymond** or **Dyamond**, and elaborations such as **Diamenta** have also been recorded.

Diana *f*
The Latin name of the Roman goddess, equivalent to the Greek **Artemis**. She was associated with the moon and virginity. She was also the goddess of hunting and protector of wild animals. **Artemesia** means 'follower of Artemis'. Use of Diana as a first name dates from the Renaissance, when the French form **Diane** is also first found. **Di** is the commonest short form, as seen in the popular nickname for the late Princess of Wales. Despite her immense popularity the name is not very widely used, although it was given to rather more babies than usual in the months following her death in 1997. The actress **Deanna** Durbin introduced a different form of the name, and the form **Deanne** is also found, while Diane has developed forms such as **Dianne** and **Dyan(ne)**. DINAH is a separate name.

Diarm(a)id, Diarm(a)it, Diarmuid see DERMOT

Dick, Dickie, Dickon see RICHARD

Didi, Didier see DÉSIRÉE

Diego *m*
This popular Spanish name is well used in the USA. It is a form of JAMES, through the intermediary forms *Tiego* and *Tiago*, from Sant *Iago*, 'Saint James'.

Dieudonné(e) see DONATA

Digby *m*
A place and surname, meaning 'the settlement by the dike', used as a first name.

Diggory *m*
In the Middle Ages the Romance of Sir Degaré or Degoré was an

immensely popular story. It told of an English prince lost at birth
– the name comes from the Old French *L'égaré*, 'the lost one' – and
his valiant adventures before he gains his rightful place in life. The
name passed into popular use as Diggory or **Digory**. By the 18th
century the name had declined from its chivalric beginnings to
become that of a typical yokel, perhaps because of the associations
of the word 'dig', but returned to respectability in the 1950s when
the medieval scholar C. S. Lewis created the character of Professor
Digory Kirke in his *Narnia* books.

Dilip *m*
The name of several kings in the Hindu epics. It probably comes
from the Sanskrit words meaning 'protecting Delhi'. An alternative form of the name is **Duleep**.

Dillon see DYLAN

Dilys *f*
From the Welsh, meaning 'perfect, genuine'. The name became
current in Wales in the 19th century and is now no longer confined
to Wales. **Dilly** is a short form. **Dilwen** (*f*) and **Dilwyn** (*m*) come from
the same word combined with the word for 'fair, blessed'.

Dimitri see DEMETRIUS

Dinah *f*
From the Hebrew, meaning 'lawsuit' or 'judged'. It was the name
of one of Jacob's daughters in the Old Testament. It came into use
in the 17th century and was a favourite name in the 19th century,
when it was often confused with DIANA. Nowadays it is often spelt
Dina.

Dinsdale *m*
A place and surname used as a first name. It means 'settlement
surrounded by a moat'.

Dion, Dione, Dionne, Dionysos see DENIS

Dipak see DEEPAK

Dirk see DEREK

Divya *f*
An Indian name from the Sanskrit for 'divine lustre'.

Djamila see JAMILA

Dmitri see DEMETRIUS

Dodie, Dodo, Doll, Dolly see DOROTHY

Doireann see DOREEN

Dolores *f*
This name was originally a short form of the Spanish Maria de los Dolores, or 'Mary of the Sorrows', after the feast of the 'Seven Sorrows of Our Lady'. Spain uses other names from titles of the Virgin: **Mercedes** (Our Lady of the Mercies) and **Montserrat**, from Our Lady of Montserrat, a famous monastery. Dolores became popular in North America about 1930. Pet forms are LOLA, **Lolita** and **Lo**. Our Lady of Guadalupe has led to the name **Guadalupe**, which is particularly well used in Mexico, as she is the patron saint of the country. This name is shortened to **Lupe** and **Lupita**. See also LOURDES.

Dolph, Dolphus see ADOLPH

Domhnall see DANIEL, DONALD

Dominic *m*, **Dominique** *f*
From the Latin *dominicus*, meaning 'of the Lord'. It probably became more widespread on account of St Dominic, founder of the Order of Preachers known as the Black Friars early in the 13th century. Until the 20th century it was almost exclusively a Roman Catholic name but is now widely used. **Dominick** is also found, and the name can be shortened to **Dom** and **Nic**. **Dominique**, from the French, is now the most popular form for girls, although **Dominica**, the original Latin feminine form, is sometimes used. These are shortened to **Nici** or **Nicky**. Dominique can be used for both sexes in France, which might explain the name of the French-born Ameri-

can basketball star Dominique Wilkins. His influence has spread the use of Dominique as a masculine name in the USA, along with the pet form used of him, **Nique**.

Donald *m*
From the Irish **Domhnall** or **Donal(l)** (the second reflecting the pronunciation, with a long 'o' as in 'doe'), meaning 'world mighty'. It was the name of a number of medieval Irish kings. The name became Donald in Gaelic. Common short forms are **Don** and **Donny**. Various forms of the name were coined in the Highlands to turn Donald into a girl's name, of which **Donalda** and **Donella** have been the commonest.

Donata *f*
This name is far more often used than its male equivalent, **Donatus** or **Donat**, both Latin for 'given (by God)'. The Old French equivalent was **Dieudonné(e)**, which is also a surname in France and still very occasionally found as a first name.

Donella see DONALD

Donna *f*
This is the Italian word for 'lady'. It became popular as a first name in the 20th century, particularly in North America. **Madonna**, 'My Lady', used of the Virgin Mary, in use in the USA by the 1930s, comes from the same word.

Donnchadh see DENIS, DUNCAN

Donny see DONALD

Donovan *m*
An Irish surname, meaning 'dark brown', used as a first name. It gained publicity as the name of a popular singer from the 1960s.

Donte *m*
The Italian name **Durrante**, meaning 'steadfast', developed the shortened form Donte, and **Dante**, famous as the name of the me-

dieval poet. Donte (pronounced with two syllables) has been current in the USA in recent years.

Dora *f*
Originally this name was a short form of DOROTHY and THEODORA, but it is now a name in its own right. It came into use at the beginning of the 19th century. A pet form is **Dorrie**, shared with other names like DOREEN and DORIS. **Dorinda** was an 18th-century elaboration of the name.

Dorcas see TABITHA

Doreen *f*
From the Irish **Doireann**, a name sometimes found in English spelling as **Dorren**. Its origin is rather obscure, but in Irish mythology it is the name of at least two supernatural beings. A short form is **Dorrie** (see also DORA), and the name can also be spelt **Dorinne**.

Dorian *f* and *m*
The ancient Greek people known as Dorians came from Doris in the north but later dominated southern Greece. The best-known group of Dorians were the Spartans. The word was introduced as a first name in Oscar Wilde's *The Picture of Dorian Gray* (1891). Like so many boy's names, it is now used as a girl's name as well. It is also spelt **Dorien** or **Dorrien** and for girls **Dorianne** and **Doriana**. Forms such as **Darian** and **Darien** can be seen as either a form of this name or a blend of such names as DARIUS and DARREN.

Dorinda see DORA

Dorinne see DOREEN

Doris *f*
The name of a sea nymph in Greek mythology, possibly meaning 'bountiful', and also a term for a woman member of the DORIAN people of Greece. In classical literature it was used as a poetic name for a lovely woman. It came into common use at the end of the 19th century and was popular into the 1930s. A short form is **Dorrie**.

Dorothy, Dorothea *f*

From the Greek meaning 'gift of God'. The name is found in Britain from the end of the 15th century and has been in use ever since. In the 16th century, it was abbreviated to **Doll(y)** and was so popular that the toy became known as a doll, Doll being such a likely name for a baby. In Scottish dialect, a doll is sometimes called a **Dorrity**. Later short forms are DORA, **Dot, Dottie, Dodo, Dodie** and **Thea** (see also THEODORA).

Dorren see DOREEN

Dorrie see DORA, DOREEN, DORIS

Dorrien see DORIAN

Dorrity, Dot, Dottie see DOROTHY

Dougal, Dugal(d) *m*

From the Irish *dubh ghall*, meaning 'dark stranger', a name given to the Danish Vikings. It was a common first name in the Scottish Highlands, and while it still has strong Scottish associations, it now has a more general use.

Douglas *m*

From the Gaelic *dubh glas*, meaning 'black stream'. It was first a Celtic river name, then the surname of a powerful Scottish family famous for its strength and bravery in fighting, and then, from about the late 16th century, a first name for both girls and boys. It is now overwhelmingly restricted to boys. **Duggie** and **Doug(ie)** are pet forms.

Drew *m* and *f*

From the Old German **Drogo**, meaning 'to carry' or 'to bear', a name that was brought to Britain by the Normans and later, as Drew, became a surname. This surname, which, like any other, can also be used as a first name, may also come from two other sources: as a short form of ANDREW, probably the commonest form of Drew as a first name, and from an old French word for 'lover'. Parents wishing to use this name may take their choice. It has recently been used occasionally for girls.

Drusilla *f*
A feminine form of the Latin **Drusus**, a Roman family name, possibly meaning 'firm'. It occurs in the New Testament and was adopted in the 17th century by the Puritans. It is still used occasionally, mainly in North America.

Duane, Dwayne *m*
An Irish surname, probably meaning 'black', used as a first name. Pop star Duane Eddy made the name better known in the 1950s. More recently it has developed exotic variants such as **DeWayne** or **Du'aine**.

Dudley *m*
Originally a surname from the place name in Worcestershire. Robert Dudley, Earl of Leicester, was the favourite of Queen Elizabeth for many years. Like other aristocratic names, Dudley came into general use as a first name in the 19th century. **Dud** is a short form.

Dugal(d) see DOUGAL

Duggie see DOUGLAS

Duke see MARMADUKE

Dulcie *f*
Dulcie is a name coined in the 19th century from the Latin *dulcis*, meaning 'sweet'. There was an earlier name, **Dulcibella** ('fair and sweet'). Dulcie was very popular in the early years of the 20th century but now has an old-fashioned ring to it.

Duleep see DILIP

Duncan *m*
The Scots form of the Irish **Donnchadh** (pronounced don-ne-ha, the 'h' ideally the sound in Scottish 'loch'), meaning 'brown'. It was the

name of two Scottish kings and at one time was almost entirely confined to Scotland, although this is no longer the case.

Dunstan *m*
From the Old English words *dun*, meaning 'hill' and *stan*, meaning 'stone'. It was the name of a famous 10th-century archbishop of Canterbury. It appears from time to time before the Reformation and was revived by the Oxford Movement in the 19th century.

Durga *f*
The name of the Hindu goddess, the wife of Shiva, when depicted in her terrifying form. Durga is from a Sanskrit word for 'inaccessible'.

Durrante see DONTE

Dustin *m*
Best known from the actor Dustin Hoffman, this name has recently been popular in the USA. It may be from a place name meaning 'dusty' or could be a form of **Thurstan**, a Norse name meaning 'Thor's stone', i.e. an altar dedicated to the thunder god Thor.

Dwayne see DUANE

Dwight *m*
Originally an English surname that may go back to the same source as DENIS. The use of this name as a first name in the United States probably arose from respect for Timothy Dwight, President of Yale University (1795–1817). US President Dwight D. Eisenhower gave a wider circulation to the name.

Dyamond, Dymond see DIAMOND

Dyan, Dyanne see DIANA

Dylan *m*
This is the name of a legendary Welsh hero, son of the sea god, whose name possibly means 'son of the wave'. It was once rare outside Wales, but the Welsh poet Dylan Thomas (1914–1953)

made it more familiar to the general public. This was further boosted by the singer Bob Dylan, often referred to by his second name, who has said that he took his stage name from the poet, although an alternative version says it came from the fictional character of Marshal Matt **Dillon**, hero of the television series *Gunsmoke* that ran from 1955 until 1975. Dylan is currently a popular choice throughout the English-speaking world.

Dymp(h)na see DEVNET

E

Eachan see HECTOR

Eadan see ETAIN

Eamon(n) see EDMUND

Earl *m*
From the title, in Old English meaning 'nobleman' or 'chief'. It has been used as a first name for about a century, mainly in North America. **Erle** is a variant spelling, as in the author Erle Stanley Gardiner.

Earnest see ERNEST

Eartha *f*
From the Old English *eorthe*, meaning 'earth'. A famous modern example is the singer and actress Eartha Kitt, but the name is rare outside the southern USA, where the forms **Ertha** and **Erthel** are also found.

Ebenezer *m*
From the Hebrew meaning 'stone of help'. In the Old Testament it is the name of a stone monument set up by Samuel in memory of the triumph of the Jews over the Philistine army and in thanks for God's help. It was first used as a first name in the 17th century among the Puritans. It is now used mainly in North America, with the shortened form **Eben**.

Ebony *f*
The name of an intensely black wood that symbolises blackness, Ebony began to be used by African-American parents in the 1970s. It reached a peak of popularity in the 1980s after the song *Ebony and Ivory* by Paul McCartney and Stevie Wonder, but then began to

fade. Its other spellings include **Ebbony, Eboney, Eboni, Ebonie** and **Ebonnee**.

Ed, Eddie see EDGAR, EDMUND, EDWARD

Edan, Edana see AIDAN, EDNA

Edgar *m*
From the Old English meaning 'fortunate spear'. Owing to the popularity of King Edgar, King Alfred's grandson, the name continued in use after the Norman Conquest, but it faded out at the end of the 13th century. It was then used by Shakespeare in *King Lear* and was revived with other Old English names by 18th-century writers of fiction. Its popularity in the 19th century probably stems from its use for the hero of Scott's novel *The Bride of Lammermoor*. It is shortened to **Ed** or **Eddie**.

Edina see EDNA

Edith *f*
From the Old English name *Eadgyth*, meaning 'fortunate war'. There were at least two English saints of that name in the 10th century. The name survived the Norman Conquest and was probably adopted by the Normans and used to replace several English names. Edith was in use throughout the Middle Ages, after which it became rather rare, but it returned to favour in the 19th and early 20th centuries. Often shortened to **Edie**, it has a rare form, **Editha**.

Edmund *m*
From the Old English *Eadmund*, meaning 'happy protection'. It was the name of two kings of England and of two saints. **Edmond** is a French form that was used from the late Middle Ages. **Eamon(n)** is the Irish form. It was well used in the 19th century, then went rather out of fashion but is now in use again. Shortened forms are **Ed**, **Eddie**, **Ted** and **Teddy**.

Edna *f*
One source of this name may be **Edana**, a feminine form of the Irish

name **Edan**, meaning 'fire' (see AIDAN). It has also been connected with a shortened form of **Edwina** (see EDWIN) via **Edina**. In addition, the name occurs twice in the Apocrypha and its Hebrew meaning is probably 'rejuvenation'. The modern use of it may stem from the popularity of the novelist Edna Lyall in the late 19th century.

Edward *m*
From the Old English meaning 'fortunate guardian'. Edward the Confessor established its popularity in England and ensured its survival after the Norman Conquest. It was further strengthened by the accession of Edward I in 1272, after which there was an Edward on the English throne for over a hundred years. It has remained in use ever since. The short forms **Ned** and **Ted**, together with **Neddy** or **Teddy**, have been used since the 14th century, but **Ed** and **Eddie** are the more common abbreviated forms found today.

Edwin *m*, **Edwina** *f*
From the Old English meaning 'fortunate friend'. Edwin was the first Christian king of Northumbria in the 7th century. The name survived the Norman Conquest and became popular in the 18th century. Edwina is a 19th-century female form. See also EDNA.

Effie see EUPHEMIA

Egbert *m*
From the Old English meaning 'bright sword'. This was the name of the first king of a united England and of a 7th-century Northumbrian saint. It enjoyed some degree of popularity in the 19th century but is now rarely found.

Eibhlin see EVELYN

Eileen *f*
An Irish development of EVELYN. Like other Irish names, it spread throughout Britain at the beginning of the 20th century. **Eily** is a short form. It is not uncommon to find it spelt **Aileen**.

Eilidh see HELEN

Eilis, Ailis *f*
In theory **Eilis**, sometimes spelt **Eil(l)ish** to reflect its pronunciation, is an Irish form of ELIZABETH, and **Ailis** (**Ailish**) an Irish form of Alice, but in practice many users do not distinguish between the two.

Eimear see EMER

Eireann see ERIN

Eithne *f*
A name prominent in Irish legend and history, being used by a goddess, a number of queens and no fewer than nine saints. It means 'kernel', which in old Irish poetry is a term of praise. Modern variants include **Ethne**, **Ethna** and **Enya**, which reflect one pronunciation of the name, the other being ENA.

Ekata *f*
An Indian name from the Sanskrit meaning 'unity'.

Ekaterina see KATYA

Elaine *f*
An Old French form of HELEN that occurs in medieval literature. It came into general use through the popularity of Tennyson's *Idylls of the King* (1859), which is based on Malory's *Morte d'Arthur* and which includes the story of Lancelot and Elaine. There is also a Welsh name **Elain**, meaning 'fawn'.

Eleanor *f*
Eleanor and **Elinor** are French forms of HELEN that have been used in the UK since the Middle Ages. **Eleanora**, the Italian form that gives us LEONORA, is also found, as is **Elena**. Eleanor is shortened to **Elli(e)** (currently, like Eleanor, very popular as a given name in the UK), ELLA, ELLEN, NELL and NORA.

Elena see ELEANOR, HELEN

Elfrida see ALFRED

Eli *m*

From the Hebrew meaning 'elevated'. It was the name of the high priest in the Old Testament who looked after the prophet Samuel when he was given to the Temple as a baby. It was used as a first name in the 17th century. Eli is also a shortened form of a number of names beginning with the sound, including ELIAS, **Eliza** (see ELIZABETH) and **Elihu**, which means 'God is the Lord'. Eli is increasing in popularity in the USA

Elias, Elijah *m*

From the Hebrew meaning 'Jehovah is God'. Both forms were very common in the Middle Ages, along with the pet forms **Ellis** and **Eliot(t)** or **Elliot**, which became surnames and are now used as first names. **Elijah** has been growing steadily in popularity in the USA for the last decade. **Elisha**, 'god is', is often thought of as a variant of this name, although it is also found, particularly in the USA, as a girl's name, when it can be interpreted either as a form of **Alisha** (see ALICE) or as a blend of Alisha and ELISE.

Eligius see ELOY

Elijah see ELIAS

Elinor see ELEANOR

Eliot(t) see ELIAS

Elise, Elissa *m*

Elise is one of the many pet forms of ELIZABETH, which has recently come into fashion in the UK. **Elissa** is a name by which Dido, Queen of Carthage, was also known, but in modern use it too is probably a pet form of Elizabeth. The Austrian-Italian film actress Elissa Landi (whose full name was Elizabeth Zanardi-Landi) was well known in the 1930s. See also ALICE.

Elizabeth, Elisabeth *f*

From the Hebrew **Elisheba**, meaning 'oath of God' or 'God has sworn'. The present form developed from the Greek **Elisabet** through the Latin **Elisabetha** to Elizabeth. In Britain the 'z' form is usual, on the Continent the 's' is used. In the Authorised Version of the New Testament, the name is spelt Elisabeth. The name was first used by members of the Eastern Church, then found its way across Europe to France, where it developed the form ISABEL(LE). This was also the usual medieval form in England. Elizabeth became common about the end of the 15th century, and its later popularity in England stemmed from the long reign of Elizabeth I. Among the many pet forms are: **Bess(ie)**, **Betsy**, **Bette**, **Betty**, **Beth** (with **Bethan** in Wales, see BETHANY), **Buffy**, **Eliza**, **Lizzy**, **Liz**, **Liza**, **Libby** and the Scottish **Elspeth**, **Elspie** and **Elsie**, which are now used independently. The German ELSA, ELISSA (see also ALICE), **Ilse** (sometimes found as **Ilsa**), **Lisa**, **Liese** or **Liesel**, the Italian **Bettina**, and the French ELISE, **Lisette** and **Babette**, are also used outside their countries of origin.

Elke *f*
A German pet form of the name ALICE. It is found in a slightly different form used by the singer **Elkie** Brooks.

Ella, Elle *f*
A name used by the Normans, probably derived from the Old German **Alia**, meaning 'all'. It can also be a pet form of **Isabella** (see ISABEL), ELLEN or ELEANOR and is currently an increasingly popular choice for parents (see also LUELLA). The real name of the Australian model Elle Macpherson, who has brought this form of the name to popular attention, is Eleanor. Both Ella, and to a lesser extent Elle, are popular in the UK at the moment.

Ellen *f*
An older English form of HELEN, now used independently, and also a short form of ELEANOR. In the past it has been especially popular in Scotland and Ireland but is now widely popular.

Elli(e) see ELEANOR

Elliot(t), Ellis see ELIAS

Elmer *m*

This is a surname that comes from both the Old English Ethelmer, 'noble and famous', and Ethelward, 'noble guard'. It became a first name in the USA in honour of two brothers with the surname Elmer who were prominent in the American War of Independence. **Aylmer** is another form of the name. While **Elma** is actually a short form of Wilhelmina, a German feminine of WILLIAM, it can also be used as a female form of Elmer.

Elodia *f*

This is one of the names taken by the Goths to Spain and naturalised there. It is formed from the elements *ali*, 'foreign, other', and *od*, 'riches, wealth'. St Elodia, a 9th-century Spanish martyr, made the name widely known in Spain, and from there it was taken by Spanish speakers to the USA. **Élodie** is the form of the name used in France.

Eloi see ELOY

Eloise *f*

Currently, the more popular version of the name known to history as **Heloise**. **Abelard** ('noble strength') and Heloise were two famous and tragic French 12th-century lovers, and Heloise was renowned for her beauty, intellect and faithfulness in love. The name can be spelt **Heloïse** or **Eloïse** and sometimes occurs as **Eloisa**. Experts do not agree on its origins: some say it is an Old German name perhaps meaning 'helmet power'; others say it comes from the same source as LEWIS by way of an old southern French name **Aloys** or **Aloyse** (see ALOYSIUS).

Eloy *m*

St **Eloy** or **Eloi** (also known as **Eligius** and **Loy**) was a 7th-century French goldsmith, popular with his patrons as much for his remarkable economy with his material as for the skill of his design. After he became a priest he rose to be bishop and personal counsellor to the queen-regent. She was an ex-slave, and they worked together to improve conditions for slaves. He is the patron saint of metalworkers. The name comes from the Latin word *elegere,* 'to chose', and is not uncommon in the USA

Elroy *m*
This mainly American name is formed on the same pattern as LEROY and Delroy (see DELBERT), being the Spanish rather than the French for the word 'the' combined with an old form of the word for 'king'.

Elsa, Elsie *f*
One source of **Elsa** is the Old German for 'noble one', but both names are also used as abbreviations of ELIZABETH, and **Elsie** is sometimes a short form of ALISON. Elsie was originally Scottish and is the more common form in Britain. Elsa is the name of the heroine in Wagner's opera *Lohengrin,* which made the name popular in the 19th century.

Elspeth, Elspie see ELIZABETH

Elton *m*
A surname, probably meaning 'Ella's settlement', used as a first name. The singer Elton John effectively began its first-name use.

Eluned see LYNETTE

Elvira *f*
A Spanish name, probably introduced by the conquering Visigoths in the Dark Ages. Its meaning is not clear. It has been used occasionally since the beginning of the 19th century. It is perhaps best known as the name of the ghost in Noël Coward's play *Blithe Spirit* and from the 1967 film *Elvira Madigan.*

Elvis *m*
A name that was almost unknown until given world fame by Elvis Presley. It is probably a version of the name of the Irish saint **Alby** or **Ailbhe** (a name that in Irish can be used for either sex and is pronounced 'alva'), which is found in Wales in the form St Elvis. Although Presley was not the first member of his family to bear the name, modern uses come from him.

Emanuel *m*
From the Hebrew, meaning 'God with us'. It was the name given to the promised Messiah by the prophet Isaiah in the Old Testament. It was introduced as a first name by the Greeks in the form **Manuel**. This is also the Spanish form. **Manny** is used as a pet form, and there is a feminine, **Em(m)anuelle**.

Emer *f*
Emer (pronounced with a long 'ee' at the beginning) is currently one of the more popular Celtic names in Ireland, used both in this form and, at the moment, most frequently in the Irish spelling **Eimear**. In legend it was the name of the woman loved by Cuchulainn, the great hero of the Ulster cycle of legends. She is described as having the following six desirable gifts: those of beauty, voice, sweet speech, skill with the needle, wisdom and chastity. It is occasionally found as **Emir**.

Emerald see ESMERALDA

Emily *f*
From the Latin *Aemilius*, the name of a Roman family. Boccaccio, the 14th-century Italian writer, used **Emilia**, popularising this form in the Middle Ages, and Chaucer borrowed it in the form **Emelye** when he translated Boccaccio's story as *The Knight's Tale*. The name has been used since then. In the 19th century it was sometimes shortened to EMMA. Nowadays, these two names are among the most popular girls' names throughout the English-speaking world. Emily has been the top name for girls in the USA for at least six years. **Milly** is a pet form. **Emmeline** is an old French pet form, and **Emil(e)** can be used for boys.

Emir see EMER

Emlyn *m*
A common Welsh name, possibly derived from the Latin *Aemilius*, also the source of EMILY, but which is more likely to be from a Welsh place name.

Emma *f*

A shortened form of Old German compound names beginning *ermen*, meaning 'universal', as in the name **Ermyntrude**, 'universal strength'. It was introduced into England by Emma, daughter of Richard I, Duke of Normandy. The English form was **Em(m)**, and this was used until the mid 18th century, when the original form was revived. Jane Austen's novel *Emma* (1816) has also been influential. Today, Emma is one of the commonest girls' names. **Emmy** is a pet form, and Emma is also used as a short form of EMILY.

Emmanuelle see EMANUEL

Emmeline see EMILY

Emrys see AMBROSE

Emyr *m*

St Emyr was a 6th-century Breton who went as a missionary to Wales. The name comes from the Welsh for 'ruler, lord'.

Ena *f*

This name can come from a number of sources. It can be a short form of any name ending with '-ina' or '-ena', or an English form of EITHNE, but its popularity in the 19th century came from affection for Queen Victoria's daughter, Princess Ena, who became Queen of Spain. Her name came from neither of these sources but was the result of a misreading of her intended name, 'Eva', at her christening, when the priest mistakenly read out the handwritten 'v' as an 'n'.

Enid *f*

This is a Welsh name, meaning 'life, soul', that came into use in England in the 19th century through Tennyson's Arthurian poem, 'Geraint and Enid' in *Idylls of the King* (1859).

Enoch *m*

From the Hebrew, meaning 'trained, skilled' or 'dedicated'. It was the name of an Old Testament patriarch and was adopted in the

17th century by the Puritans. It is now rare, although a well-known modern example is the politician, Enoch Powell (1912–98).

Enola *f*
This is a 20th-century coinage, probably from the USA, of no known meaning. The name gained worldwide publicity in 1945 as the name, in the form Enola Gay, painted on the side of the plane that dropped an atom bomb on Hiroshima. Enola Gay was the name of the pilot's mother.

Enya see EITHNE

Eoan, Eoghan see EUGENE, EVAN

Eoin see EUGENE, JOHN

Ephraim *m*
From the Hebrew meaning 'fruitful', an Old Testament name that was revived in the 17th century by the Puritans. It is seldom used in England but is still found in North America. **Eph** is a short form.

Eppie see EUPHEMIA

Eric *m*, **Erica** *f*
An name that came originally from Scandinavia; the second syllable means 'ruler', the first is doubtful but may mean 'ever'. The name was brought to Britain by the Danes about the 9th century. Possibly Dean Farrar's book *Eric or Little by Little* was responsible for its popularity with 19th-century parents. It is currently most popular with American parents. **Erica**, the feminine form, is now sometimes identified with the Latin botanical name for heather. Both forms are sometimes spelt with a 'k' instead of 'c'. Short forms are **Rick, Rickie** or **Ricky**.

Erin *f*
From the Gaelic **Eireann**, a poetical name for Ireland. It is a modern name, initially popular in the USA and Australia, but now gaining ground in the UK and Ireland, and particularly well used at the moment in Scotland.

Erle see EARL

Ermyntrude see EMMA

Ernest *m*
From the Old German, meaning 'vigour' or 'earnestness'. It is sometimes spelt **Earnest**. It was introduced by the Hanoverians in the late 18th century and was common in the 19th century. Oscar Wilde's play *The Importance of Being Earnest* (1899) increased its popularity. Neither **Ernestine**, the female form, nor Ernest, is popular today. Shortened forms are **Ern** and **Ernie**.

Errol *m*
Probably a surname used as a first name, although it is not certain whether the surname is a development of Eral, a medieval form of HAROLD, or whether it is a variant of EARL.

Erskine *m*
This is a place name near Glasgow, used as a surname and first name. The meaning of the place name is unclear, but 'prominent hill' or 'green hill' have been suggested. The name was given publicity by the political activist and novelist Erskine Childers (1870–1922).

Ertha, Erthel see EARTHA

Erwin *m*
Erwin is a well-used German name, found occasionally elsewhere, which comes from the Germanic elements *eber*, 'wild boar', and *win*, 'friend'. The most famous bearer is probably the charismatic German fieldmarshal Erwin Rommel (1891–1944), but it was also the name of Erwin Schrodinger (1887–1961), an Austrian physicist who won the Nobel prize for his work on quantum theory but whose name is most strongly linked to the conundrum of Schrodinger's cat. **Irwin** is the surname, sometimes used as a first name, that comes from the Old English form of the same name, and Erwin is sometimes found as a variant form of both Irwin and IRVING.

Esmé *f* and *m*

Probably from the French for 'esteemed', this is now usually treated as a form of the French **Aimée**, meaning 'beloved' (see AMY). It passed from France to Scotland in the 16th century, and then much later to England. It is sometimes found in the form **Esme**, without the accent. It is now more often used as a girl's name, in which case it can also take the forms **Esmée** and **Esma**.

Esmeralda *f*

The Spanish for 'emerald'. The 19th-century French writer Victor Hugo introduced it when he used it for the heroine in his novel *The Hunchback of Notre Dame*. The English form **Emerald** is also found, as is the form **Esmeraldah**.

Esmond *m*

From the Old English *east* and *mund*, meaning 'grace' and 'protection'. This name was never particularly common and fell out of use in the 14th century. Its modern use probably dates from Thackeray's novel *The History of Henry Esmond* (1852). It is nowadays rather rare.

Es(sa) see VANESSA

Ess, Essie, Essy see ESTHER

Essylt see ISOLDA

Estella see STELLA

Esther *f*

In the Old Testament, this name is the Persian equivalent of a Hebrew word meaning 'myrtle'. It was frequently used in the form **Hester** and appears in England in the 17th century, adopted by the Puritans. It can also be spelt **Ester**. Shortened forms of this include **Essy**, **Essie** and **Ess**, with Hester becoming **Hetty**.

Etain *f*

In Irish legend, *The Wooing of Etain* is the story of the love of the fairy Princess Etain of the Fair Hair for a mortal man. This tale was retold in an opera called *The Immortal Hour*, first performed in 1914. The opera was a great success at the time and led to a use of the name outside Ireland. In Ireland the name is usually **Etan** or **Eadan** and pronounced 'ad-an'.

Ethan *m*

This is a Hebrew name meaning 'firmness', which occurs several times in the Old Testament. It has recently been one of the most popular choices for boys in the English-speaking world.

Ethel *f*

Not originally an independent name, this developed in the 19th century as a shortening of various Anglo-Saxon names beginning with the root 'Ethel-', from *aethel*, meaning 'noble'. See AUDREY.

Ethelbert see ALBERT

Etheldreda see AUDREY

Ethna, Ethne see EITHNE

Etta, Ettie see HENRIETTA

Euan see EUGENE

Eufemia see EUPHEMIA

Eugene *m*, Eugenie *f*

From the Greek meaning 'well-born'. In North America the masculine form is usually abbreviated to **Gene**. The Celtic names **Eoghan** (pronounced 'eoh-un' – well used in Ireland) or **Eoan** ('ohn'), and their Scots form **Ewan** – widely popular at the moment – **Ewen** or **Euan** – currently popular in Scotland – have traditionally been interpreted as forms of Eugene, although sometimes confused with **Eoin**, a form of JOHN. Some would claim, however, that they are a native Celtic name meaning 'born of the yew'. Eugenie, the French feminine form, came into use from the French Empress **Eugénie** (1826–1920) who spent the last 50 years of her life in England. **Eugenia** is also used for girls.

Eunice *f*
From the Greek, meaning 'happy victory'. The name is mentioned in the New Testament and was adopted by the Puritans in the 17th century. In Greek it is pronounced as three syllables, with a hard 'c' and the final 'e' sounded, but modern users soften the 'c' if they use the three-syllable pronunciation or more often use the pronunciation indicated by the phonetic spelling **Unice**.

Euphemia *f*
From the Greek, meaning 'fair speech' or, by implication, 'silence'. It occurs as **Eufemia** and **Euphemie** from the 12th century. Later it became confined to Scotland, where it is still found, usually abbreviated to **Effie** (very popular at the beginning of the 20th century), **Eppie** or, occasionally, Fay or Phoebe.

Eustace *m*
From the Greek meaning 'rich in corn' and hence 'fruitful' generally. Because of the two saints Eustachius, this name was in use in Britain before the Norman Conquest and was popular from the 12th to the 16th centuries. **Eustacia**, the female form, was used in the 18th and 19th centuries but is now rare. A short form, Stacey (or Stacy), is now a name in its own right.

Eva see Eve

Evadne *f*
This is a Greek name of uncertain meaning. In Greek myth she was a faithful wife who was so distraught at her husband's death that she threw herself on to his funeral pyre. The name is quite rare now, but it was in use in the early part of the 20th century, which is probably why it was chosen for the character of that 1930s' grand dame of music Dr Evadne Hinge, performed by George Logan, in the British comic duo Hinge and Brackett.

Evaline see Evelyn

Evan *m*
This is a Welsh form of John, the anglicised form of the Welsh spelt

variously **Iefan, Ifan** or **Ieuan**. In Scotland and Ireland, where it is well used, it is also an anglicised form of the Irish **Eoghan** (see EUGENE).

Evangeline *f*
From the Greek meaning 'bringer of good news', the same word that gives us 'evangelist'. It was first introduced by Longfellow for his poem *Evangeline* (1847) and still tends to have a rather literary flavour. **Evangelina** is also found.

Eve *f*
This comes from the Hebrew for 'life', and in the Old Testament this is the name of the first woman. **Eva** is the Latin form, Eve the English. It was in use in Britain in the Middle Ages, when Old Testament names were not generally popular. In Ireland it was used as a substitute for the earlier Gaelic **Aoife** (pronounced 'ee-fa, ee-fur'), meaning 'radiant', currently a very popular name. This may explain why Eva is well used in Ireland at the moment and Eve more popular in the rest of the British Isles. The pet form of Eve is **Evie**, growing in popularity in England, and **Evita** is a Spanish pet form. See also ZOE.

Evelyn *f* and *m*
When the Normans conquered Ireland they brought with them a girl's name **Aveline**, meaning 'wished for (child)'. It was adopted by the Irish in the form **Eibhlin** (pronounced either with the 'bh' as a 'v', or silent, giving EILEEN), which in turn was anglicised as **Eveline** or **Eveleen** and later developed forms such as **Evaline, Evelena** and **Evelina**. It was also adopted as a surname, usually spelt Evelyn, and around the 17th century the surname started to be used as a first name for boys. The boy's form is usually spelt Evelyn; all spellings are used for girls.

Everard *m*
From the Old German for 'brave boar'. The name was brought to Britain by the Normans and was fairly common in England in the 12th and 13th centuries and has been used occasionally ever since.

In Scotland, it became **Ewart**. The surname **Everett** comes from Everard and is also used as a first name.

Everild, Everilda see AVERIL

Evie, Evita see EVE

Ewan, Ewen see EUGENE

Ewart see EVERARD

Ezekiel *m*
From the Hebrew, meaning 'may God strengthen'. It is the name of an Old Testament prophet and was used from the 17th century in Britain. It is still current in North America and is beginning to re-appear in the UK. **Zeke** is the usual short form.

Ezra *m*
From the Hebrew, meaning 'help', Ezra is the name of the author of one of the books of the Old Testament. It was adopted as a first name by the Puritans in the 17th century. The name is no longer common but a well-known example from the 20th century is the American poet Ezra Pound (1885–1972).

F

Fabian *m*
From the Latin family name *Fabianus*, possibly meaning 'bean-grower'. There was a pope of this name and a St Fabian in the 3rd century, and there is a record of the name's use by a 13th-century sub-prior of St Albans. There is little other evidence of it until the 16th century, but its use as a surname shows that it was known previously. The Roman general Fabius, known as the 'delayer' for his tactics of awaiting the right moment to achieve his ends, was the inspiration for the socialist Fabian Society, founded in 1884. A female form, **Fabienne**, comes from the French **Fabien**. Spanish forms are **Fabio** and **Fabiola** for girls.

Fadil *m*, **Fadila** *f*
Fadil means 'virtuous, generous, distinguished' in Arabic. The feminine form from the same word, **Fadila**, means 'generosity, moral excellence'.

Fae see FAITH

Fahimah *f*
A Muslim name from the Arabic for 'discerning' or 'intelligent'.

Faisal see FAYSAL

Faith *f*
One of the Christian virtues used as names after the Reformation. It was formerly used for both sexes but is now a girl's name. FAY(E) or **Fae** is a short form.

Fallon *f*
This is an English form of the Irish surname 'O Fallamhain', or 'leader'. It was made known as a first name by a character in the TV

series *Dynasty* and came into limited use in the USA and Britain as a result.

Fanny see FRANCES, MYFANWY

Farah *f*
From the Arabic, meaning 'joy, cheerfulness'. **Farrah** is also found while **Farhanah** is from the Arabic for 'joyful'.

Farall, Farrell see FERGAL

Farid *m*, **Farida** *f*
These names come from the Arabic for 'unique, unrivalled', which can also be used of a pearl or gem. In the Indian sub-continent the names are usually found in the form of **Fareed** and **Fareeda** or **Faridah**. The 13th-century Persian mystic and poet Farid ud-Din, 'pearl of the faith', is a famous bearer of the name.

Farrah see FARAH

Fatima *f*
This is an Arabic name that means either 'chaste' or 'motherly'. It was the name of the Prophet Mohammed's favourite daughter, the only one of his children to have children of her own. It has been popular in the USA with African-American Muslims. It is also occasionally used in a Christian context in honour of Our Lady of Fatima, Portugal.

Faustine *f*
Fausta and **Faustus** were names given to his twin children by the ancient Roman dictator Sulla. The names mean 'fortunate', and Sulla had always considered himself particularly blessed with good luck, taking the nickname FELIX. **Faustine** is the French form of Fausta. Although the two girls' names are sometimes used, the legend of Dr Faustus, who sells his soul to the Devil, has made it difficult to use the boy's name.

Fawn *f*
The word for a young deer used as a first name.

Fay *f*
A short form of both FAITH and EUPHEMIA, and also an old form of
the word 'faith'. In addition it is an old version of the French word
for 'fairy' found in the name of the Arthurian enchantress Morgana
le Fay. It was in use by 1872, at least in fiction. It is also spelt **Faye**.

Fayruz *f*
This comes from the Arabic word for a turquoise. Once used for
both sexes, it is now restricted to girls.

Faysal *m*
This Arabic name indicates one who decides between right and
wrong, a decision-maker or a judge. This has been a royal name in
modern times, borne by kings of Iraq and Saudi Arabia. The name
is also found as **Faisal** and **Feisal**.

Feargus see FERGUS

Fedelm, Feidhelm see FIDELMA

Feisal see FAYSAL

Felice, Felicia see FELIX

Felicity *f*
From the Latin *felicitas*, meaning 'happiness'. It was the name of
two saints and was used by the Puritans in the 17th century.

Felix *m*, **Felicia** *f*
From the Latin, meaning 'happy, lucky'. **Felix** was widely used in
the Middle Ages and had a fairly strong hold in Ireland, where it
was used to replace the Irish **Phelim** or **Felim**. It is currently enjoying
a small revival in popularity. The female form, **Felicia**, has a long
history of use and was also very popular in the Middle Ages. **Felice**
was a variant form.

Fenella *f*
A Gaelic name meaning 'white-shouldered'. The name became
known in Britain in the 19th century through Sir Walter Scott's

novel *Peveril of the Peak*. The Irish form of the name is **Finola** or **Fionnuala** (pronounced 'Fin-noola'), which can be shortened to **Nola** or **Nuala**, a popular choice in Ireland in recent years.

Ferdinand *m*
From the Old German for 'brave journey'. Never a popular name in Germany, it was common in Spain, especially in the forms **Fernando** and **Hernando**. Short forms are **Ferd, Ferdie** and occasionally **Nandy**.

Fergal *m*
This is an Irish name meaning 'valorous'. The surnames **Farrell** and **Farall**, which come from it, reflect the Irish pronunciation.

Fergus *m*
Fergus or **Feargus** comes from the Irish words for 'man' and 'strength'. It is a fairly common first name in both Scotland and Ireland and is also used in the North of England. **Fergie** is a short form.

Fern *f*
The plant name used as a first name. It was quite well used in the USA in the first half of the 20th century and is used regularly in the UK at the moment.

Feroz, Feroze see FIROZ

Ffion *f*
Ffion is the Welsh word for the foxglove flower and a word used in poetry to describe the cheek of a beautiful girl. It is occasionally found as **Fionn**.

Fi see FIONA

Fidelma *f*
The more usual form of the Irish name **Fedelm** or **Feidhelm** (in modern Irish pronounced 'fed-elm'). Its meaning is not clear, but several of the early women who bore the name were famous for their beauty.

Fifi see JOSEPHINE

Finbar, Finnbar, Fionnbharr see BARRY

Finch see RAVEN

Findlay see FINLAY

Fingal *m*
This is the name given to the Scottish legendary hero (the equivalent of the Irish FINN) who figures in the 18th-century Ossianic poetry. He was a mighty warrior, a defender of the underdog and righter of wrongs. Fingal's Cave is named after him. The name means 'blond stranger' and was a term used of the Vikings.

Finian see FINN

Finlay *m*
This is a Scottish name meaning 'fair hero'. It is also found as **Finley** and **Findlay**. Finlay is the form most used in Scotland; both Finlay and Finley have recently come into general use in England.

Finn *m*
Finn, **Fynn** or **Fionn** is an Irish name meaning 'white, fair' or can also be used as a pet form of **Finbar** (see BARRY). Finn Mac Coul (Finn mac Cumaill) is a great hero of Irish mythology and folklore. He was chosen to lead the Fenians (an elite armed troop) because of his truthfulness, wisdom and generosity, but he was also of great physical strength. All these qualities were not enough, however, to prevent Finn's fiancée, GRAINNE, from running away with his companion, DERMOT. **Finnian** or **Finian** comes from the same root and was the name of a 6th-century British saint; **Fintan** means either 'white ancient one' or 'white fire'.

Finola see FENELLA

Fintan see FINN

Fiona *f*
From Gaelic, meaning 'fair, white'. It was first used in the 19th

century by William Sharp as a pen name (Fiona Macleod). He modelled it on the Irish man's name **Fionn** or FINN. It was long thought of as a particularly Scottish name but is now used throughout the English-speaking world, although still most popular in Scotland and Ireland. **Fi** is the short form.

Fionn see FFION, FINN

Fionnuala see FENELLA

Firoz *m*
This comes from the Arabic for 'victorious, successful, prosperous' and passed into the stock of Muslim names as it was the name of one of the Prophet's notable companions. It is also found as **Firuz**, **Feroz** and **Feroze**.

Flann *m*
This is an Irish name, meaning 'red', that would have started life as a nickname. **Flannan** started as a pet form of this.

Flavia *f*
A Roman family name that probably meant something like 'golden or tawny-haired'. **Fulvia** has much the same meaning.

Fleur *f*
The French word for 'flower'. It was first used as a name in the 20th century, in John Galsworthy's series of novels, *The Forsyte Saga*. The English equivalents **Flower** and **Blossom** are also found. See also FLORA.

Flip see PHILIP

Flo see FLORENCE

Flora *f*
From the Latin, meaning 'flower'. Flora was the Roman goddess of flowers and the spring. The male equivalent names **Florent** and **Florian** are now little used in Britain outside fairytales but are found in continental Europe and are currently popular in France.

Florence *f*

From the Latin name *Florentius*, derived from the word meaning 'blooming'. In the Middle Ages, Florence was used as often for men as for women, but thereafter the name dies out. Florence Nightingale was named after the town in Italy where she was born, and her fame popularised the name in the 19th century. Abbreviated forms are **Florrie**, **Flossie**, **Floy** and **Flo**.

Florent, Florian see FLORA

Florrie, Flossie see FLORENCE

Flower see FLEUR

Floy see FLORENCE

Floyd see LLOYD

Forbes *m*

Forbes is a Scottish surname now used as a first name. It comes from a place near Aberdeen, meaning 'field, district'.

Forrest *m*

This is the word 'forest' in its surname form. It was originally used as a first name in the southern US in the late 19th century, when it was fashionable to name boys after Confederate generals – in this case, General Nathan Bedford Forrest. The name continues to be used sporadically in Britain as well as the USA. It is sometimes found as **Forest**.

Frances, Francesca *f*

Frances is the English form of Francesca, the feminine form of the Italian **Francesco** (see FRANCIS). It was first used in Italy in the 13th century, about the same time as the French form **Françoise** began to appear. **Francine** is another French form. Frances was not used in Britain until the 15th century, and it became popular with the English aristocracy at the time of the Tudors. The short forms are **Fanny**, **Fran**, **Francie** and **Frankie**. Francesca is currently popular in England and Wales.

Francesca see FRANCES

Francis *m*
From the Italian, meaning 'little Frenchman'. The name became popular in Europe in the 13th century because of St Francis of Assisi. The Italian word *Francesco* was the saint's nickname, his Christian name being Giovanni, the Italian form of JOHN. He was teasingly called 'the little Frenchman' in his worldly youth because of his love of fashionable French things. The name was first used in Britain in the 15th century. **Fran** is a short form along with **Frank** and **Frankie**. Frank can be used as an independent name. See also FRANKLIN.

Françoise see FRANCES

Frank, Frankie see FRANCES, FRANCIS

Franklin *m*
From a medieval English word meaning 'free'. A franklin was a man who owned land in his own right but was not a noble. The name came into use in America in honour of Benjamin Franklin (1706–90), statesman, writer and inventor. A famous holder of the name was Franklin D. Roosevelt (1882–1945), 32nd US President. The name shares **Frank** as a short form with FRANCIS.

Fraser, Frazer *m*
A Scottish surname of unknown meaning, used as a first name. **Frasier** is another form of the name. Fraser is currently well used in Scotland but not much used elsewhere.

Frea see FREYA

Fred, Freddie, Freddy see ALFRED, FREDERICK

Freda see FREDERICK, WINIFRED

Frederick *m*, Frederica *f*
From the Old German, meaning 'peaceful ruler'. It is also found with such spellings as **Frederic** and **Frederik**. Common abbrevia-

tions are **Fred, Freddie** and **Freddy**, also used as independent names. The female form is **Frederica**, the origin of the names **Freda, Frida** or **Frieda** (the last two influenced by the German form, **Friede**).

Freya *f*
The name of the ancient Norse goddess of beauty, love and fertility. It can also be found as **Frea** or spelt the Swedish way, **Freja**. The name became better known through the indomitable travel writer Freya Stark (1893–1993).

Frida, Frieda see FREDERICK

Fulvia see FLAVIA

G

Gabriel *m*, **Gabrielle** *f*
A name from Hebrew, containing the elements 'God', 'man' and 'strength', and possibly implying the phrase 'strong man of God' or 'God is my strength'. In St Luke's Gospel, **Gabriel** is the Archangel who announces to Mary that she is to bear the baby Jesus. Use as a first name used to be restricted to Ireland, where it can be shortened to **Gay**, but it is now increasingly fashionable elsewhere. **Gabrielle**, a French form, or the Italian **Gabriella**, the female forms, are much more common, with Gabrielle being used increasingly, perhaps because of the popularity of the singer. A short form is **Gaby**.

Gaenor see JENNIFER

Gaia *f*
In Greek myth **Gaea** or Gaia is the earth goddess, the universal mother, probably once the most important divinity. Her name is occasionally found used as a first name, usually with 'green' or feminist overtones.

Gail *f*
Originally a pet form of ABIGAIL, now widely used as a name in its own right. The spellings **Gale** and **Gayle** are also found.

Gaius see CAIUS

Galal, Galil, Galila see JALAL

Gale see GAIL

Galen *m*
In the 2nd century AD the Greek physician Galen was probably the most prominent doctor in the world. He was personal physician to

the Emperor, and passed on his knowledge in over 100 books, which were influential up to the dawn of modern medicine. Galen is used as a first name, particularly in the United States, in his honour. Appropriately for a doctor the name means 'soothing, calm'. It is sometimes spelt **Gaelan**, is **Galeno** in Spanish, and there is a feminine form, **Galyn**.

Ganesh *m*
A title of the Hindu god SHIVA, and the name of his elder son, derived from the Sanskrit for 'lord of the hosts'. It is customary to appease Ganesh at the beginning of Hindu ceremonies.

Gareth *m*
From the Welsh, meaning 'gentle'. This name was used for one of King Arthur's knights by the 15th-century writer Malory in his *Morte d'Arthur*, and later by Alfred Tennyson, the 19th-century poet, in his version of Malory's story, 'Gareth and Lynnette', published as part of his *Idylls of the King*. It was because of the latter that the name was revived in the 20th century. **Garth** and GARY or **Garry** can be used as short forms.

Garfield *m*
A surname meaning 'spearfield' in Old English, used as a first name, probably after J. A. Garfield (1831–81), 20th president of the USA. The cricketer Sir Garfield (**Gary**) Sobers is a well-known holder of the name and also shows its short form.

Garret, Garrett see GERARD

Garth, Garry see GARETH

Gary *m*
While this can be used as a short form of both GARETH and GARFIELD, its use as an independent name owes much to the film star Gary Cooper (1901–1961). He was born Frank James Cooper, and chose his stage name from the American town of Gary. **Garry** is also found, reflecting the usual pronunciation, although Gary Cooper pronounced his name to rhyme with 'airy'.

Gaspar, Gaspard see JASPER

Gaston *m*
A French name, originally spelt Gascon and meaning a man from the region of Gascony. It is a common French first name that has been used occasionally in Britain.

Gauri *f*
This name is from the Sanskrit for 'white' and was applied to the wife of the Hindu god SHIVA when she had acquired a fair complexion after meditating in the snows of the Himalayas.

Gavin *m*
The name of Sir **Gawain**, King Arthur's famous nephew, was Gauvin in Old French and from France was adopted in Scotland as Gavin. Originally confined to Scotland, the name is now found throughout the English-speaking world.

Gay(e) *f*
This name is simply the adjective meaning happy and lively, and its use dates from the 20th century. Since the adoption of the word 'gay' by the homosexual community, few parents have used the name. In Ireland Gay is a short form of the boy's name GABRIEL.

Gayle see GAIL

Gaynor see JENNIFER

Geena see GINA

Geeta see GITA

Gemma *f*
The Italian word for 'gem'. Its modern use is probably due in part to the Italian saint Gemma Galgani (1875–1903), canonised in 1940. Rare before the 1980s, it then became one of the most popular names in the UK, but is hardly used in the USA. It is also spelt **Jemma**.

Gene see EUGENE

Genevieve *f*

A French name possibly meaning 'lady of the people'. It is found in Latin records as **Genovera** and **Genoveva**. St Genevieve is the patron saint of Paris; she saved the city from the Huns in the 5th century by cool thinking, courage and prayer. The name has been used in Britain since the 19th century. French pet forms are GINA, **Ginette** and **Veva**. **Geneva** may be a form of this name rather than from the Swiss city.

Geoffrey, Jeffrey *m*

From the Old German *Gaufrid*, the second half of which means 'peace', but the meaning of the first half is unclear. Geoffrey or Jeffrey was popular between the 12th and 15th centuries in England, resulting in many surnames, e.g. Jeffries, Jeeves, Jepson. It fell from favour from the 15th until the 19th centuries, when it was revived. **Geoff** and **Jeff** are common abbreviations.

George *m*

From the Greek for 'farmer'. The famous St George is said to have been a Roman soldier who was martyred in Palestine in AD 303. In early Christian art many saints were represented as trampling on dragons as a symbol of good conquering evil. This may be an explanation of how the legend of St George and the dragon originated. In the Middle Ages, St George was closely associated with knighthood and chivalry, and after 1349, when Edward III of England founded the Order of the Garter and put it under St George's protection, he became the patron saint of England. Despite this, the name was not much used until the Hanoverian succession in 1714 brought a line of four Georges to the throne. It is currently popular with parents. **Geordie** is a Scottish and North Country pet form that is used as a nickname for Tynesiders; **Georgie** is more common elsewhere. **Goran**, pronounced with a 'y' sound at the beginning, is a well-used Swedish form of the name and is nowadays familiar to anyone with the least familiarity with English football through the name of the Swedish-born coach of the England national team, Sven Goran Eriksson.

Georgia, Georgina *f*

Georgina and Georgia, the most common female forms of GEORGE, are both a popular choice at the moment. They were first used in Britain in the 18th century, when George became popular. The commonest form then was **Georgiana**, which is still sometimes used. Other feminine forms of George are **Georgette** and **Georgine**.

Ger, Gerry see GERALD, GERARD

Geraint *m*

This is a very old Welsh name, a variant form of the Latin *Gerontius*, which is in turn derived from a Greek word meaning 'old'. The 19th-century poet Alfred Tennyson used the old Welsh story of 'Geraint and Enid' in his *Idylls of the King*, and it was from this that the name's modern use has stemmed. The real-life hero on which the fictional character is based died in battle about AD 530.

Gerald *m*

From the Old German, meaning 'spear rule'. It was used in England from the 11th to the 12th century and was probably introduced by the Normans. The name flourished in Ireland because of the influence of the Fitzgerald ('Sons of Gerald') family, the powerful rulers of Kildare. It was probably from Ireland that the name returned to England in the late 19th century. Shortened forms are **Ger, Gerry** and **Jerry**.

Geraldine *f*

Geraldine started life as a poetic nickname used by the 16th-century Earl of Surrey in a poem praising the beauty of Lady Elizabeth Fitzgerald. Geraldine therefore means 'one of the Fitzgeralds'. It shares short forms with GERALD.

Gerard *m*

From the Old German, meaning 'spear-brave'. It was brought to Britain by Norman settlers and was very common in the Middle Ages. The surnames **Gerrard** and **Garret(t)** are derived from it, and these were the most common medieval pronunciations of the name, although it is not always possible to distinguish between forms of Gerard and GERALD. **Ger**, **Gerry** and **Jerry** are its short forms.

Germaine *f*
Several early saints bore this name, which probably indicated someone who came from Germany, in the way that FRANCIS indicated a Frenchman. Germaine is little used in English-speaking countries but has been made well known by the writer and academic Germaine Greer. There are several masculine forms. **Jermain(e)** is a form of the French **Germain**, which is quite popular in the USA and is also found as **Jermyn**.

Gerry see GERALD, GERALDINE, GERARD

Gertrude *f*
From the Old German for 'strong spear'. The name came to Britain in the Middle Ages from the Netherlands, where a saint of that name was popular. It was much used in the 19th and earlier 20th centuries but is not often chosen by parents now. Pet forms are **Gert** or **Gertie** and **Tru**; **Trudi**, **Trudie** or **Trudy** come from a German pet form of the name.

Gervais, Gervase *m*
From the Old German, meaning 'spear vassal' or 'armour bearer'. The name was first used among English churchmen of the 12th century in honour of the 1st-century martyr St Gervase. It spread to the general public, giving rise to the surname **Jarvis**. Gervais is the French spelling.

Geunor see JENNIFER

Ghislaine *f*
This is an Old French name, related to GISELLE and meaning 'pledge, hostage'. It has come to be used in Britain only comparatively recently. It is also found in the forms **Ghislane** and **Ghislain**, although in France this last form is used for boys. It is pronounced with a hard 'g' and the 's' is silent.

Gianna *f*

A short form of the Italian name **Giovanna**, feminine of **Giovanni**, or JOHN. Use of Gianna is currently increasing in the USA. Other short forms of Giovanna include GINA, **Giannina** and **Vanna**.

Gib see GILBERT

Gideon *m*

From the Hebrew, now generally thought to mean 'having a stump for a hand', although the traditional translation was 'a hewer'. It is the name of an Old Testament Israelite leader who put the forces of the Midianites to flight. The name was adopted at the Reformation and was a favourite among the Puritans, who took it to North America where it is still in use, although by no means common.

Gigi *f*

This name became well known in 1958, when the novel *Gigi* by the French writer Colette was made into a successful musical film. In the book Gigi is the pet form of **Gilberte**, the French feminine form of GILBERT.

Gilbert *m*

From the Old German, meaning 'bright hostage'. The Normans brought the name to England and it was common in medieval times when St Gilbert of Sempringham (died 1189) was much admired. Shortened forms are **Gib**, **Gil**, **Gilly**, BERT and **Bertie**.

Giles *m*

According to legend, St Giles was an Athenian who took his name, Aegidius, from the goatskin that he wore. He left Greece in order to escape the fame that his miracles had brought him and became a hermit in France. There the name became **Gilles**. The name is first recorded in England in the 12th century, but it was not popular. It has been suggested that this may be because of St Giles's association with beggars and cripples, of whom he is the patron saint. However, recent years have seen an increase in its popularity. It is sometimes spelt **Gyles**.

Gillian *f*
This name, which is an English rendering of the Latin name
JULIANA, was so common in the Middle Ages that its short form, **Gill**,
was used as a general term for a girl, as Jack was for a man. It was
revived in the 20th century and once again became very popular,
although it is quite quietly used at the moment. A variant form is
Jillian, and **Jill**, the abbreviated form, is now given as an independent name. **Jilly** is also found.

Gilly see GILBERT

Gina *f*
A short form of such names as GEORGINA and Regina (see QUEENIE),
now used as an independent name. In France, Gina and **Ginette** are
pet forms of GENEVIEVE, and it is also a short form of the Italian
GIANNA. **Geena** is also found.

Ginette see GENEVIEVE, GINA

Gini, Ginny see VIRGINIA

Giovanna, Giovanni see GIANNA

Giselle *f*
From the Old German, meaning a 'pledge' or 'hostage'. **Gisèle** has
for a long time been a common French name, and the English form,
Giselle, and the latinised **Gisela** have been used in Britain (see also
GHISLAINE). The name became widely known after the success of
Adolphe Adam's 1841 ballet *Giselle*.

Gita *f*
An Indian name from the Sanskrit meaning 'song'. **Geeta** is a popular alternative spelling.

Giulia, Giulietta see JULIA

Gladys *f*
This is the anglicised form of **Gwladys**, which means 'ruler'. It is
recorded in Wales as early as the 5th century but moved into the

mainstream of names only in the 19th century. In the earlier part of the 20th century it was very popular, but in recent decades it has become less fashionable. It is often shortened to **Glad**.

Glen(n), Glyn(n) *f* and *m*
These are both forms of Celtic words for 'a valley'. In the last forty years they have become popular names throughout the English-speaking world. **Glenna** and **Glenne** are also found for girls.

Glenda *f*
This is a Welsh name meaning 'holy and good'.

Glenys *f*
From the Welsh, meaning 'holy'. It is spelt in a variety of ways, including **Glen(n)is**, **Glennys** and **Glenice**. See also GLYNIS.

Glinys see GLYNIS

Gloria *f*
This is Latin for 'glory' or 'fame'. The name seems to have been coined by George Bernard Shaw for his (1889) play *You Never Can Tell*. It was very common in the first half of the 20th century.

Glyn(n) see GLEN

Glynis *f*
From the Welsh for 'a little valley' and thus related to GLEN and Glyn. It can be spelt **Glinys** and is often confused with GLENYS.

Gobind see GOVIND

Godfrey *m*
From the Old German, meaning 'God's peace'. It was brought to Britain by the Normans, was well used in the 19th and early 20th centuries but is not much used now.

Gopal *m*
This Indian name can be taken to mean 'a devotee of Krishna'. It derives from the Sanskrit words meaning 'cow-protector', indicating a cowherd, but the name was applied to KRISHNA in medieval

devotional texts. In southern India the name is sometimes given as **Gopalkrishna**.

Goran see GEORGE

Gordon *m*
Originally a Scottish place name from which the local lords took their name, it then became the name of a large and famous clan. It was rarely used as a first name until 1885, when the dramatic death of General Gordon at Khartoum gave the name immense popularity.

Gottlieb see AMADEA

Govind *m*, **Govindi** *f*
This Indian name is similar to GOPAL, deriving from the Sanskrit words which mean 'cow-finding', a reference to a cowherd, but the 12th-century *Song of Govind* associated the name firmly with KRISHNA. Sikhs often make use of the form **Gobind** for boys.

Grace *f*
The vocabulary word, originally used in its religious sense. This name existed as Gracia, the Latin form, in the Middle Ages but did not become common until the Puritans adopted Grace along with other Christian qualities as a name. The pet form **Gracie** is sometimes given as a separate name, and forms from other languages, such as **Gracia**, **Graciela**, **Gratia** and **Grazia** are also found. Grace is currently popular in the UK, Ireland, Australia, Canada and the USA.

Graham *m*
Like GORDON, this was originally a place name that developed into a family name, particularly on the Scottish/English border. At first restricted to this area, it gradually came into general use as a first name. **Graeme** and **Grahame** are also found.

Grainne, Grania *f*
In Irish and Scottish legend, Grainne was a princess betrothed to FINN, the famous chieftain. However, Grainne preferred DERMOT

and eloped with him. The story of Finn's pursuit of the couple and Grainne's suicide after Finn brought about Dermot's death is an important subject in Irish literature. Grania is the anglicised form of the name, reflecting the pronunciation 'grahn-ya'. The name is currently quite a popular choice in Ireland.

Grania see GRAINNE

Grant *m*
A surname from the French for 'tall, large' used as a first name. It seems to have come into general use from the USA, where its use may have been connected with the popularity of General Ulysses Grant (1822–85), the 18th President. But as it is a common Scots surname there is no reason why the name would not have developed independently in the UK, and it is currently more likely to be used in Scotland than elsewhere.

Gregory *m*
From the Greek, meaning 'watchman'. The name first came to Britain through St Gregory the Great, the pope who sent St Augustine to England. It was in common use from the Norman Conquest, when most Latin names were introduced, until the Reformation when, because of its association with the papacy, it fell out of favour. **Gregour** was the usual medieval form, which is still found as **Gregor**, recently a popular choice, in Scotland. This gives us the surname MacGregor. The most common shortened form is **Greg**.

Greta *f*
A Swedish abbreviation of MARGARET. It was rare in England until the 20th century, when the fame of the film actress Greta Garbo led to some parents using it. **Gretel** and **Gretchen** are German pet forms.

Griffith *m*
From the Welsh name **Gruffud** or **Gruffydd**, meaning 'lord' or 'strong warrior'. It has always been fairly popular in Wales and was the name of several Welsh princes. **Griff** is a pet form.

Griselda *f*

The meaning of this old Germanic name is disputed, but it may mean 'grey battle-maiden'. Chaucer told the story of 'Patient Griselda' in the *Canterbury Tales*, which, in the past, encouraged its use by parents who wanted meek and virtuous daughters. **Grizel** is an old Scots form that is little used nowadays, and **Zelda** started as a short form.

Gruffud, Gruffydd see GRIFFITH

Guadalupe see DOLORES

Guendolen see GWENDOLYN

Guenevere, Guinevere see JENNIFER

Gulab *f*

A Hindu flower name, from the Sanskrit for 'rose'.

Gus, Gussie see AUGUSTA

Gustav *m*

An Old Norse name that probably means 'staff (i.e. support) of the Goths'. Gustav was the name of several Swedish kings and is still used by American families of Swedish descent. The best-known English bearer of the name, the composer Gustav Holst (1874–1934) was in fact christened **Gustavus** after his grandfather, whose own father had emigrated to England from Scandinavia. The French form of the name, **Gustave**, is occasionally used by English speakers.

Guy *m*

From the Old German *Wido*, the meaning of which is uncertain, possibly 'wide' or 'wood'. Wido became Guido in Latin records, and Guy was the French form introduced into Britain by the Normans. Medieval clergy identified the name with the Latin **Vitus**, meaning 'lively', hence the disease St Vitus' Dance, which is known in France as *la danse de Saint Guy*. St Vitus was a Sicilian martyr who was invoked for the cure of nervous ailments. Guy fell

out of use after Guy Fawkes' gunpowder plot of 1605. It was revived in the 19th century with the help of Walter Scott's novel *Guy
Mannering*.

Gwen *f*
The pet form of several names, such as GWENDOLYN, which come
from the Welsh word meaning 'white'. Gwen and **Gwenda** (a pet
form, which can also mean 'fair and good') are now used as separate names and have spread to the rest of Britain.

Gwendolyn, Gwendolen, Guendolen *f*
From the Welsh, meaning 'white circle', probably a reference to the
ancient moon goddess. The name occurs frequently in Welsh legend. Its wide range of spellings also include **Gwendoline** and
Gwendolyne. It was a popular name at the beginning of the 20th
century but is not much used now.

Gwenfrewi see WINIFRED

Gwenhwyfar see JENNIFER

Gwill, Gwilym see WILLIAM

Gwladys see GLADYS

Gwyn *m*
From the Welsh, meaning 'white' or 'blessed'. This name has been
anglicised as **Wyn** or **Wynne**. Its use is mainly confined to the Welsh.
Gwynfor or **Wynfor** is Gwyn with the word for 'great' added to the
end.

Gwyneth *f*
From the Welsh meaning either 'fair maiden' or 'happiness'. **Gwyn**
is the pet form.

Gyles see GILES

Hadrian see ADRIAN

Haidee see HEIDI

Hailee, Hailey see HAYLEY

Hakeem *m*
Hakeem or **Hakim** is an Arabic name, meaning 'wise, intelligent one', one of the titles, in Islam, of God. It is one of the Muslim names current in the USA, in large part thanks to the fame of the Nigerian-born, 7-foot-tall basketball player Hakeem (previously **Akeem**) Olajuwon.

Hal see HENRY

Haley see HAYLEY

Halle *f*
The British-born American actress Halle Barry got her name from the Hallé Orchestra, Britain's longest-established professional symphony orchestra, which was founded in Manchester by the pianist and conductor Charles Hallé in the mid-19th century.

Ham see ABRAHAM

Hamish *m*
The anglicised form of **Seumas** (see SEAMAS), the Gaelic form of JAMES. This name became popular in the second half of the 19th century and is still used, mostly in Scotland.

Hamzah *m*
The name of the Prophet Mohammed's uncle, probably from the Arabic for 'lion'. It is also spelt **Hamza**.

Hana *f*, **Hani** *m*

Hana is from the Arabic for 'bliss' or 'happiness'. **Hani** (*m*) and **Haniyya** (*f*), meaning 'joyful, delighted', and **Hanan** (*f*), 'tenderness, affection', come from the same root.

Hank see HENRY

Hannah *f*

From the Hebrew, meaning 'God has favoured me'. In the Old Testament it was the name of Samuel's mother. The Greek form of this, **Anna** (see ANNE), was used at first. Hannah was not adopted in England until after the Reformation. It is currently one of the most popular girls' names in all English-speaking areas.

Hans *m*

This is a form of JOHN found in northern Europe, including Germany, the Netherlands and Sweden. The Latin form of the name was Johanes, which can give either Hans or the more formal **Johan(n)**, as in the great composer Johann Sebastian Bach (1685–1750).

Hari *m*

This Indian name occurs frequently in classic Hindu texts and is often applied to Vishnu or KRISHNA. It derives from a Sanskrit word that indicates a yellowy-brown colour.

Harley *f* and *m*

Harley (sometimes **Harleigh**, **Harli(e)** or **Harlee**, particularly for girls) is an English aristocratic surname, but its use as a first name probably owes much to the glamour of the Harley Davidson motorbike. Use of the similar-sounding **Harlan**, although found in the 19th century, was encouraged by respect for Judge John Marshall Harlan (1899–1971).

Harmony see MELODY

Harold *m*

From the Old Norse, meaning 'army-power'; **Harald** is the original

Scandinavian form. It was used in the Middle Ages but went out of fashion until it became popular again in the 18th century. It is not much used at the moment. It shares the abbreviation **Harry** with the name HENRY.

Haroun see AARON

Harriet *f*
A female form of HENRY, derived from **Harry**, which was the usual form of the name Henry in the Middle Ages. The name was very popular in the 18th and 19th centuries and again in the 20th century. Short forms are **Hattie** or **Hatty**.

Harrison see HENRY

Harry see HAROLD, HARRIET, HENRY

Harsha *f*
A Hindu name derived from the Sanskrit for 'happiness'.

Harun see AARON

Harvey *m*
From the French, meaning 'battle-worthy'. It was common until the 14th century and had a slight revival in the 19th. Its modern use as a first name may be the result in part of its widespread use as a surname. While use of the name is in decline in the USA, it is steadily increasing in the UK.

Hasan *m*
One of the most popular Muslim names, derived from the Arabic for 'handsome' or 'good'. Al-Hasan was the Prophet's grandson. Similar names derived from the same Arabic word are **Hasin**, **Hassan**, **Husayn**, **Husni**, **Hussain** and **Hussein**.

Hattie, Hatty see HARRIET

Hayden *m* and *f*
This appears to be a form of **Haydn**, a name used in honour of the Austrian composer Franz Josef Haydn. As a first name, it is also

spelt **Haydon**. The surname Haydn in its turn derives from the Old German word for 'heathen'. Once restricted to boys and used mainly in Wales, it has been well used in the USA for some years, and its popularity is spreading.

Hayley *f*
This name came into use in the 1960s, after the success of the film actress, Hayley Mills, who was given her mother's maiden name as a first name. The surname means 'hay field'. It has since become very popular. It is spelt in many different ways, including **Hailey** (preferred in Canada and USA), **Hailee, Haley** (a spelling that comes a close second in the USA) and **Haylie** and is occasionally used for boys.

Hazel *f*
One of the plant names adopted as a girl's name in the 19th century.

Heather *f*
This is one of several plant names first used in the 19th century. Since heather is a feature of northern Britain, the name became especially popular in Scotland and is now popular in the USA. **Heath**, another name for the same plant, is also used for both sexes.

Hector *m*
From the Greek, meaning 'hold fast'. It was the name of the Trojan hero who was killed by the Greek Achilles. The name took quite a strong hold in Scotland, where it was used as an equivalent for the quite unconnected Gaelic name **Eachan**, which means 'a horseman'.

Hedwig *f*
This ancient German name, formed from elements meaning 'strife', came into use in German-speaking areas through reverence for the Blessed Hedwig, a 9th-century abbess. It is little used in English-speaking countries – although now famous as the name of Harry Potter's owl – but the Austrian-born American filmstar **Hedy** Lamarr was originally named Hedwig Kiesler

Heena see HINA

Heidi *f*
This name is a pet form of the German version of ADELAIDE. It has
come into use in the English-speaking world thanks to the popularity of Johanna Spyri's *Heidi* stories. **Haidee** is not a variant, but a
separate name created by Lord Byron for his poem *Don Juan* (1819–
24). The delightful descriptions in the poem of this innocent and
beautiful child of nature have led a few parents to choose the name
for their daughter. Byron probably based it on the Greek word for
'modest'.

Heinze *m*
This is a medieval pet form of **Heinrich**, the German form of HENRY,
now used as a name in its own right.

Helen *f*
From the Greek, meaning 'the bright one'. The popularity of this
name in Britain was because originally of the 4th-century St **Helena**.
She was the mother of Constantine the Great and was traditionally
supposed to have been the daughter of the ruler of Colchester, the
Old King Cole of nursery rhyme. When she was over 80 she made
a pilgrimage to the Holy Land where she was believed to have
found the true cross of Christ. The name is first found as **Elena** and
then ELAINE and ELLEN. The 'H' was not used until the Renaissance,
when the study of classical literature brought Homer's story of the
Trojan war and the beautiful Greek queen Helen to public notice.
Lena is a contraction and NELL is a pet form. **Ilona** is a Hungarian
form. **Eilidh** (pronounced ail-ee) is the Gaelic form, currently poular
in Scotland.

Helga *f*
From the Norse, meaning 'holy'. It has occasionally been used in
Britain but is more common in North America, where it was intro-
duced by Scandinavian immigrants. See also OLGA.

Heloise, Heloïse see ELOISE

Hema *f*

An Indian name that derives from the Sanskrit for 'golden'.

Henrietta *f*

The female form of HENRY. It was introduced into England in the 17th century by Henriette Marie, Charles I's French wife. The full form gave way to the abbreviated HARRIET but was revived in the 19th century. Abbreviations are **Etta, Ettie** and **Hetty**.

Henry *m*

From the Old German, meaning 'home ruler'. The Latin Henricus became Henri in France. **Harry**, reflecting the French pronunciation, was the original English form of Henri, used until the 17th century and often abbreviated to **Hal**. Today, Harry is used as the pet form of Henry and increasingly as a name in its own right. Indeed, in the UK in recent years Harry has regularly outranked Henry in the statistics, having long been among the top ten most popular names for boys. **Hank** is a pet form more common in the United States. **Harrison**, 'son of Harry', has become well known through the actor Harrison Ford, and it is now popular in many countries. Its use as a first name is influenced by the fact that it was the surname of two US Presidents, William Harrison (1773–1841) and his grandson, Benjamin Harrison (1833–1901).

Herbert *m*

From the Old German for 'bright army'. It seldom appears before the Norman Conquest, after which it became quite common. It was revived at the start of the 19th century and became quite popular again towards the century's end, the result in part of the fashion for using aristocratic surnames as first names. **Herb, Herbie** and BERT or **Bertie** are short forms.

Herman *m*

A Germanic name meaning 'soldier'. The French form of the name is **Armand** (**Armando** in Italian and Spanish), and the old English form is **Armin** or **Arminel**, which, along with **Arminelle**, can also be used as a feminine name.

Hermione *f*

Hermione (pronounced with four syllables) has recently come to public attention as the name of a major character in J. K. Rowling's *Harry Potter* books. It comes from the Greek, meaning 'daughter of Hermes'. In Greek mythology Hermione was the daughter of the Greek king Menelaus and HELEN. Shakespeare's use of the name in *A Winter's Tale* gave rise to its use in modern times. He used another form, **Hermia**, in *A Midsummer Night's Dream*, and this too has been used occasionally.

Hernando see FERDINAND

Hester see ESTHER

Hetty see ESTHER, HENRIETTA

Hew see HUGH

Hilary, Hillary *f* and *m*

From the Latin, meaning 'cheerful'. The original Latin forms **Hilaria** and **Hilarius** are very occasionally found, and the writer **Hilaire** Belloc used the French form. It was once quite usual as a boy's name but is now rarely used except for girls. Hillary is the usual spelling in the USA, Hilary that in the UK.

Hilda *f*

From the Old English word for 'battle'. There was an Anglo-Saxon St Hilda, a woman of outstanding ability who founded an abbey at Whitby in the 7th century. When the names of Anglo-Saxon saints were revived in the 19th century Hilda became popular but is now often felt to be rather old-fashioned. It is sometimes found with the spelling **Hylda**. There are many other Germanic names containing the element *hild*, 'battle', of which the best known are probably **Hildegard** (*f*), a name formed from *hild* plus a word meaning 'enclosure', and **Hildebrand** (*m*), *hild* plus 'sword'.

Hina *f*

A Hindu name meaning 'henna', the dye used to colour the hair and fingernails. It is also found as **Heena** and **Henna**.

Hiram *m*

From the Hebrew, meaning 'brother of the high one', and the name of an Old Testament king of Tyre. It was a favourite 17th-century name and was taken at that time to North America where it is still found.

Holly *f*

A plant name used as a first name, currently popular on both sides of the Atlantic. **Hollie** is also well used. Because of the plant's association with Christmas, the name is sometimes chosen for a child born at that time of year (compare NOEL, NATALIE).

Homer *m*

The name of the famous ancient Greek author, 'the father of literature' and author of the *Iliad* and *Odyssey*, which means 'pledge, hostage', has been used as a first name, particularly in the USA. Nowadays, it is most strongly associated with the dysfunctional father in the cartoon series *The Simpsons* and is not much used.

Honoria *f*

From the Latin, meaning 'reputation' or 'honour'. The Latin forms **Honora**, Honoria and **An(n)ora** were predominant until the Reformation, when the Puritans adopted the abstract virtue names and used **Honour** and **Honor**. They were then used both as masculine and feminine names. In the 19th century the Latin forms were revived. See also NORA, ANEURIN.

Hope *f*

This Christian virtue was adopted as a first name in the 17th century, in the same way as FAITH and CHARITY. It was especially popular among Puritans at this time, who used it for both sexes. It is now used only for girls.

Horace, Horatio *m*

From the Roman clan named Horatius, borne by a great hero of early Roman history and by the Latin poet Horace. Horatio seems to have come from Italy to England in the 16th century and has been kept alive by the fame of Nelson (see NIGEL), although Horace is the form more likely to be found today. **Horatia** is a rare feminine form, coined for Nelson's daughter.

Howard *m*
Like other aristocratic family names, this one was adopted as a first name by the general public in the 19th century. The origin of the surname is disputed. It may be from the Old German, meaning 'heart-protection', or the French for a 'worker with a hoe', or even from the medieval title of the official, the 'hogwarden', who super-intended the pigs of a particular district. **Howie** can be used as a short form.

Hubert *m*
From the Old German, meaning 'bright mind'. This name was popular in the Middle Ages, probably as a result of the fame of St Hubert of Liège, the patron saint of huntsmen. It was not much used from the 16th to the 18th centuries, after which it was revived to some extent, but it has since gone out of fashion again. BERT is the short form.

Hugh, Hugo *m*
From the Old German, meaning 'heart' or 'soul'. It appears fre-quently in the Domesday Book. It was further strengthened by the popularity of St Hugh, Bishop of Lincoln, in the 14th century. Hugo is the Latin form. **Hew** and **Huw** are Welsh forms of the name; **Hughie** and **Huey** are used as pet forms.

Humayra *f*
This name was given by the Prophet Mohammed to his wife AISHA. Its meaning is unclear.

Humphrey *m*
From the Old German, meaning 'peace'. This name was originally spelt with an 'f', the 'ph' coming in when it was equated with the name of the obscure Egyptian saint Onuphrios in order to Chris-tianise it.

Hunter *m* and *f*
The Old English vocabulary word used as a first name, this is another surname that has come to be used as a boy's name. It is currently popular in the USA. Its increasing use as a girl's name in the USA may be inspired by the actress Hunter Tylo, who appears in *The Bold and the Beautiful* soap opera.

Husayn, Husni, Hussain, Hussein see HASAN

Huw see HUGH

Hylda see HILDA

Hywel *m*
A Welsh name meaning 'eminent'. It has become well known through the actor Hywel Bennett.

Iain, Ian see JOHN

Ianthe *f*
This is an ancient Greek name meaning 'violet flower'. It has a strong literary flavour, having been used by a number of poets, including Byron and Shelley. It is still quietly but steadily used.

Ibrahim *m*
The Arabic form of ABRAHAM.

Ida *f*
From the Old German, meaning 'hard work'. The name was introduced by the Normans and lasted until about the middle of the 14th century. In the late 19th century it was revived by Tennyson for the name of the heroine of his poem *The Princess*, which Gilbert and Sullivan subsequently took as a basis for the operetta *Princess Ida*. These uses led to a revival of the name at the end of the 19th century. In Ireland it is sometimes used as a substitute for **Ide** or **Ita**, meaning 'thirst', the name of one of the earliest Irish women saints.

Idris *m*
This is a Welsh name meaning 'fiery lord'. In Welsh legend, Idris the Giant was an astronomer and magician who had his observatory on the mountain of Cader Idris.

Ieasha, Ieesha, Iesha see AISHA

Iefan, Ieuan, Ifan see EVAN

Ifor see IVOR

Ignatius *m*
Ignatius or **Inigo** is a Latin name, derived originally from a Greek name of obscure origin, possibly meaning 'fiery'. It took root

mainly in Russia and Spain and was carried farther afield by the Jesuits whose founder was Inigo Lopez de Recalde, better known as St Ignatius of Loyola.

Ike see ISAAC

Ilona see HELEN

Ilsa, Ilse see ELIZABETH

Iman, Imana, Imani see AMIN

Imelda *f*
Imelda is probably the Italian form of the Germanic name Irmhilde, 'universal battle'. It is the name of a rather obscure saint and had a certain popularity in Ireland in the middle of the 20th century.

Imogen *f*
First appearing in Shakespeare's *Cymbeline*, this name is thought to be a misprint of the name Innogen, which appears in Shakespeare's source for the story. It may be derived from the Greek, meaning 'beloved child'. It is a popular choice at the moment in the UK.

Ina *f*
This name can come from three different sources. It is an Irish form of AGNES, a form of the name ENA, and can also be from the pet form of first names ending '-ina', such as Christina and GEORGINA.

Inderjit *m*
An Indian name from the Sanskrit, meaning 'conqueror of the god Indra'. The spelling **Indrajeet** is also used.

India *f*
This was the name of a character in Margaret Mitchell's 1936 novel, *Gone with the Wind*, but its popularity is more likely to be due to the interest, particularly since the 1970s, in Indian culture and religion. A well-known bearer is the model India Hicks, given the name as the granddaughter of Lord Mountbatten, last viceroy of India.

Indira *f*
An Indian name associated with the goddess LAKSHMI, wife of the
god Vishnu. It is usually derived from a Sanskrit word meaning
'beauty' but is possibly connected with **Indra**, the name of the god
of the sky and rain in the Hindu tradition. The meaning of the name
is uncertain, but it may be connected with the Sanskrit for 'rain-
drop'.

Indrajeet see INDERJIT

Inés, Inez see AGNES

Ingrid *f*
From the Old Norse, meaning 'Ing's ride'. In Norse mythology Ing
was the god of fertility and crops who rode a golden-bristled boar.
It is a common name in Scandinavia and was made famous in this
country by the Swedish film star Ingrid Bergman (1915–82).
Ingeborg ('Ing's fortress') and **Inga**, the short form of these two
names, are also found occasionally.

Inigo see IGNATIUS

Iola *f*
The Latin form of a Greek name meaning 'dawn cloud'. In Greek
mythology Heracles fell in love with a princess **Iole**. The name is
rare.

Iolanthe see YOLANDA

Iona *f*
This is the name of the Scottish Hebridean island used as a first
name. The island seems originally to have been called Ioua, 'yew-
tree island', but at some point the 'u' was misread as 'n' and so the
island got its present name. The name's popularity has been increasing in recent years, particularly, as might be expected, in Scotland. **Ione** ('eye-oh-nee') is not the same name but a Greek name
connected with the word 'violet' and therefore related to IANTHE.

Ior see IVOR

Ira *m*
A name from the Old Testament meaning 'watchful'. The name was used by the Puritans, who took it over to America where it is now much more common than in Britain. The song-writer Ira Gershwin (1896–1983) was a famous bearer of the name.

Irene *f*
The name of the goddess of peace and also of one of the seasons in ancient Greece. Although the name was used earlier in other parts of Europe, it did not appear in England until the late 19th century. The abbreviation **Renie** is sometimes used, and it can also be found in the form **Irena**. Irene is pronounced in two different ways: in the Greek way with three syllables and the final 'e' pronounced, and the usual modern way with only two syllables.

Iris *f*
Although this name is usually associated with the flower, it comes from the Greek word for 'rainbow', after which the flower was named because of its bright colours. In Greek mythology Iris carried messages from the gods to men, across the rainbow that was her bridge. It was not used in England before the 19th century.

Irma *f*
This was originally a German name meaning 'universal'.

Irving *m*
Irving or **Irvine** are Scottish place names that were used first as surnames and then as first names.

Irwin see Erwin

Isa see Isabel

Isaac *m*
From the Hebrew, meaning 'laughter'. It was the name given by Sarah, wife of Abraham, to the son born in her old age, traditionally because she laughed when she was told that she would conceive. The name appears in Britain in the Middle Ages and came to be

regarded as a specifically Jewish name. It came into general use in
the 16th and 17th centuries when it was spelt with a 'z', as in **Izaak**
Walton, the author of *The Compleat Angler*. In the mid-17th century
the 's' spelling came into fashion, as in Sir **Isaac** Newton, the great
scientist. It is an increasingly popular choice in many countries. **Zak**
or **Ike** are used as pet forms.

Isabel(le), Isobel *f*

These are forms of ELIZABETH that developed in medieval France.
Elizabeth became Ilsabeth and then Isabeau, and finally Isabelle.
Up to at least the end of the 17th century, the forms Isabel(le) in
England, Isobel in Scotland and the Gaelic **Iseabail**, sometimes spelt
phonetically as **Ishbel**, were interchangeable with Elizabeth. **Isa** and
Bel or **Belle** were the common short forms. The Latin **Isabella** and
Bella were used from the 18th century, while spellings such as
Izabela and **Ysabel** can be found today. At the moment Isabel,
Isabelle, Isobel and Isabella are all popular with English-speakers,
with the last the most frequent choice.

Isadora see ISIDORE

Isaiah *m*

From the Hebrew, meaning 'Jehovah is salvation', and the name of
the great Old Testament prophet. It was first used by the 17th-cen-
tury Puritans. It is currently well used in the USA and increasingly
frequent in the UK.

Iseabail see ISABEL

Iseult see ISOLDA

Isha see AISHA

Ishbel see ISABEL

Ishmael see ISMAIL

Isidore *m*, Isidora *f*

From the Greek, possibly meaning 'gift of Isis'. There were two

Spanish saints called Isidore. The scandal caused by the private life and dancing style of Isadora Duncan (1878–1927) made the feminine form of the name well known.

Isla *f*
A Scots island name, used as a girl's name in Scotland since about the 1950s. It has now spread to other parts of Britain but is still most frequent in Scotland. The 's' is silent, as in 'island'.

Isleen see AISLING

Ismail *m*
This is the Arabic form of **Ishmael**. Arabs are sometimes known as Ismailites, 'descendants of Ismail', from their descent from Ishmael, son of Abraham.

Isobel see ISABEL

Isolda *f*
From Old Welsh **Essylt**, probably meaning 'fair one'. It was a common name in medieval times because of its place in the tragic legend of TRISTAN and Isolda. **Iseult** was the Norman form, which became Isolda in Latin, Isot(t) in Middle English. Isolda or **Isolde** had a brief revival in the 19th century owing to the popularity of Wagner's 1865 opera *Tristan and Isolde*. It is also spelt **Yseult(e)** and **Ysolde**.

Israel *f*
From Hebrew, although its meaning is disputed; the most likely translation is 'may God prevail'. In the Old Testament Jacob was named Israel after his struggle with the angel of God. The name was first adopted by Christians after the Reformation.

Ita see IDA

Ivan *m*
The Russian form of JOHN, found occasionally in Britain, more frequently in the USA.

Ivo *m*
From the Old German, meaning 'yew'. It was common in Brittany in the form **Yves** and was brought to Britain at the time of the Norman Conquest. It has been used occasionally since.

Ivor, Ifor *m*
Ifor is a Welsh name that means 'lord', and Ivor is the anglicised spelling. It originally had the form **Ior** but was probably influenced by Yves (see Ivo).

Ivy *f*
This is a plant name that came into use in the 19th century. Because ivy clings so firmly, the name may have been used to indicate faithfulness.

Izaak see Isaac

Izabel see Isobel

Jacey, Jacie see JAY

Jack *m*
Originally the pet form of JOHN, this is now a very popular name in its own right, particularly in Australia and the UK. It has been the most popular name for boys in England and Wales for the past eight years. In the Middle Ages **Jan** evolved from John, and then developed the pet form Jankin, later shortened to Jack. **Jock** is a traditionally Scottish form. Jack shares the pet form **Jake**, now a name in its own right, with JACOB. **Jackson**, a surname meaning 'son of Jack', is also found as a first name.

Jacob *m*
The meaning of this Hebrew name is uncertain. In the Old Testament, it was the name of ISAAC's younger son, who tricked his brother Esau out of his inheritance. This explains the popular interpretation of the name as 'he supplanted'. There were two forms of the name used in the Latin translation of the Bible, *Jacobus* and *Jacomus*. Jacob came from the former and JAMES from the latter. Jacob has survived as a first name because translators of the Bible into English kept this form for the Old Testament Patriarch, although they called the two New Testament apostles James. **Jacoba**, **Jacobine** and **Jacobina** are rare feminine forms. **Jake** is an abbreviation shared with JACK and now a popular choice as a name in its own right.

Jacqueline *f*
Jacqueline and **Jacquetta** are French feminines of b, the French equivalent of JAMES and JACOB. Both were introduced into Britain in the 13th century and have been in use ever since. Jacqueline, with

its pet forms **Jacky**, **Jacki(e)** or **Jacqui**, is found in a very wide range of spellings, which include **Jackalyn**, **Jacaline**, **Jacquelyn** and **Jaqueline**.

Jade *f*
The name of the precious stone used as a first name. Although the names of precious stones have been in use as girls' names since the 19th century, this one seems to have come into general use only in the 1970s and has been popular again recently. **Jada (Jayda)** and **Jaden** can be seen as developments of either Jade or JAY.

Jaelin, Jai see JAY

Janhangir see PARVAIS

Jaimal see JAMILA

Jake see JACK, JACOB

Jalal *m*, Jalila *f*
Arabic names that mean 'glory' or 'greatness'. A similar name is **Jalil**, meaning 'honoured' or 'revered'. Jalila is the feminine form of both. The names are also found as **Galal**, **Galil** and **Galila**.

Jaleesa *f*
Also spelt **Jalisa**, this is an apparently newly formed name, blending the 'Ja-' of names like JANE, JANET and JACQUELINE with the sound of Lisa. It was introduced into the USA in 1988 through a character in the TV comedy show *A Different World*. African-American parents immediately responded to the name with enthusiasm.

Jalen *m*
The African-American basketball star Jalen Rose had his name coined for him by combining his father JAMES' name with that of his uncle LEONARD. Parents started to use his name for their sons as early as 1993 when Rose was still a college player.

Jalil, Jalila see JALAL

Jalisa see JALEESA

Jamaal, Jamal, Jamar see JAMILA

Jamee see JAMIE

James *m*
This name has the same root as JACOB. It became established in Britain in the 12th century when pilgrims started to visit the shrine of St James at Compostella in Spain. At that time the name was more common in Scotland. With the accession of James VI as the first king of both Scotland and England in 1603, the name became more popular in England. It was unfashionable in the 19th century but is now one of the most used boy's name. The pet forms are **Jim**, **Jimmy** and JAMIE, and it is one of the sources of JAY. The Irish form is SEAMAS and the Scots HAMISH.

Jamie *f* and *m*
This was originally a Scottish pet form of JAMES, but it has since spread throughout the English-speaking world and become popular in its own right. Since at least the 1950s it has also been used as a girl's name, particularly in the United States, in which case it may take forms such as **Jami**, **Jamee** or **Jaymie**.

Jamila *f*, **Ja(i)mal** *m*
An Arabic name meaning 'beautiful'. The name is popular in both the male and female forms in the Arab world and with African-American Muslims in the USA, where it is also spelt **Jamil**, **Jamaal** and **Jamel** and has a variant, **Jamar**. Jamila is also used in France, where it can be found as **Djamila**.

Jan see JANET, JACK

Jane *f*
This is now the commonest female form of JOHN. It comes from the Old French form Jehane. It was very rare before the 16th century, the medieval female forms of John being JOAN and JOANNA. An early example was Jane Seymour, third wife of King Henry VIII of England and mother of Edward V. Since Tudor times the name has been in and out of fashion. At the moment it is freely used as a second

name but rarely as a first unless in some combination like Sarah Jane. It can also be spelt **Jayne**. The commonest pet forms are **Jenny** and **Janey** or **Janie** (see also JANET). **Jancis** seems to be a combination of Jane with FRANCES or Cicely. Other elaborations include **Janice** or **Janis; Jana**, a form found in a variety of other languages; **Janae** and **Janelle**. See also SHEENA, SIAN.

Janet *f*
This was originally derived from **Jeanette**, the French pet form of JEAN. It was first used in Scotland. **Janette** and **Janetta** are also found, and sometimes **Jinette**, while **Net**, **Nettie**, **Netta** and **Jan** are pet names. A Scottish pet form is **Jessie**, with **Jinty** an unusual alternative. See also SHEENA.

Janey, Janice, Janie, Janis see JANE

Janine *f*
Like JANET, this name comes from a pet form of **Jeanne**, the French form of JEAN. It is also spelt **Jannine** and **Janene**, and the latinised **Janina** is also used.

Jaqueline see JACQUELINE

Jared *m*
A biblical name meaning 'to descend' and connected with JORDAN. It was used in the past by the Puritans but had become very rare until the mid-1960s when it became popular in the United States and Australia. It is also found in the forms **Jarred**, **Jarod** and **Jarrod**, although some of these forms may be influenced by similar surnames. **Jareth** and **Jaron** are also used.

Jarvis see GERVAIS

Jasmine *f*
A flower name also found in its normal botanical form, **Jasmin**. The word comes from Persian, and the name is also used in the Persian form **Yasmin**, with variants such as **Yasmine** and **Yasmina**. It is currently popular.

Jason *m*

This name was adopted in the 17th century when biblical names became popular, because it is the traditional name for the author of Ecclesiasticus. It has been a popular name in recent years, when parents probably associated it more with the Greek hero Jason, who won the Golden Fleece. A short form, **Jace**, is sometimes used.

Jasper *m*

Gaspar or **Caspar** (**Kaspar**) is the traditional name of one of the three kings or wise men of the Christmas story. It may mean 'keeper' or 'bringer of treasure'. **Gaspard** is the French form, which became Jasper in English.

Jawahir *f*

An Arabic name that means 'jewels'.

Jay *f* and *m*

As an Indian name for boys, Jay comes from a Sanskrit word for 'victory' and can also be spelt **Jai**. Otherwise it comes from a short form of any name beginning with a 'J', or from a surname, originally a nickname for someone who chattered like the bird. It is sometimes spelt **Jaye**. There are a number of elaborations such as **Jaelyn** or **Jaylin** (*f*); **Jac(e)y** (*m* and *f*) and its variants; **Jayla** (*f*); **Jaden** or **Jayden** (*f* and *m*), **Jayden** being particularly well used for boys in Australia.

Jaymie see JAMIE

Jayne see JANE

Jean *f*

This name started as a Scottish form of JANE or JOAN derived from the Old French Jehane. The diminutive **Jeanette** is also found (see JANET). The commonest pet forms are **Jeanie** and **Jenny**.

Jeb *m*

James Ewell Brown Stuart – known from his initials as Jeb Stuart – was a dashing Confederate cavalry officer in the American Civil

War, famous for his gallantry. Not surprisingly, the name, which can also be a short form of JACOB, has strong associations with the southern USA and all that that stands for.

Jed *m*
A short form of the biblical name **Jedidiah**, which means 'beloved of the Lord' and according to the prophet NATHAN was the name of the second child of DAVID and BATHSEHBA. It is more common in the United States than in the UK.

Jeff, Jeffrey see GEOFFREY

Jem see JEREMY

Jemima *f*
From the Hebrew, meaning either 'dove' or 'handsome as the day', and the name of one of Job's daughters in the Old Testament. First used in the 17th century by Puritans, it was very popular in the 19th century and is still used today. **Mima** is a pet form.

Jemma see GEMMA

Jennifer *f*
An old Cornish form of **Guenevere**, from the Welsh, meaning 'white ghost', and the name of King Arthur's wife. It was practically obsolete until its 20th-century revival. It spread rapidly, and was very popular in the 1950s and 60s in the UK and has been popular for many years in the United States. **Jenny** or **Jenni** is the pet form, shared with JANE and JEAN. **Gaenor**, **Geunor** and **Gaynor** are other forms of Guenevere, which is also spelt **Guinevere** and, in Wales, **Gwenhwyfar**. **Jenna**, another Cornish version, has recently become popular, particularly in the USA and Scotland, and can also be a Muslim name, from the Arabic for 'Paradise'.

Jeremy *m*
From the Hebrew, meaning 'may Jehovah exalt'. Jeremiah was the Old Testament prophet who wrote the Book of Lamentations. The traditional English form is Jeremy, which appears from the 13th

century onwards, although during the 17th century, the two forms **Jeremias** and **Jeremiah** were more common. The name is said to have been popularised in the 1920s by a series of school stories by Hugh Walpole that had a hero called Jeremy. **Jerry** is a short form, which is shared with GERALD, and **Jem** and **Jez** are also used. **Jer(r)ell** is a recent variant.

Jermain(e), Jermyn see GERMAINE

Jerome *m*
From the Greek **Hieronymos**, meaning 'holy name'. This name is pre-Christian in origin but soon became popular with the early Church. St Jerome translated the Bible into Latin in the 4th century and was an important religious influence in the Middle Ages. The name appears in England in the 12th century as **Geronimus**, which gradually gave way to the French form, Jerome.

Jerrell see JEREMY

Jerry see GERALD, GERALDINE, GERARD, JEREMY

Jesse *m*
From the Hebrew, meaning 'God exists', and in the Old Testament, the name of King David's father. It was adopted in the 17th century by the Puritans who took it to America where it has been commoner than in the UK. Jesse James, the outlaw, and the politician Jesse Jackson are probably the best known examples. The name is moderately well used in the USA. **Jess** is a short form. The name is sometimes spelt **Jessie**. See also JESSICA.

Jessica *f*
The source of this name is much debated, but it was probably invented by Shakespeare, based on the Hebrew name JESSE, for his play *The Merchant of Venice* in which Shylock's daughter is called Jessica. It is shortened to **Jess** or **Jessie** (also a Scottish pet form of JANET), which is sometimes spelt **Jessye**. It is very popular at the moment throughout the English-speaking world.

Jesus see JOSHUA

Jethro *m*
From the Hebrew, meaning 'abundance' or 'excellence'. In the Bible it is the name of MOSES' father-in-law. It has been used as a first name since the Reformation.

Jez see JEREMY

Ji see DEV

Jill, Jillian, Jilly see GILLIAN, JULIANA

Jim, Jimmy see JAMES

Jinette see JANET

Jinny see VIRGINIA

Jinty see JANET

Jo see JOSEPH, JOSEPHINE

Joan, Joanna *f*
This is the oldest female form of JOHN and is a contraction of **Johanna**, the feminine form of the Latin Johannes. The name came over from France as Jhone and Johan in the second half of the 12th century, but by the 14th century Joan was the established form. By the mid 16th century it was so common that it became unfashionable and JANE superseded it. It was revived at the beginning of the 20th century. **Joanne** was a development of the name, and **Jo(e)** and **Joni(e)** are pet forms. Sometimes **Jodi(e)** is also used as a pet form, although this is usually a form of Judith. **Juanita** is the Spanish pet form, which can be shortened to **Nita**.

Job *m*
From the Hebrew, meaning 'hated' or 'persecuted'. **Jobey, Jobie** or **Joby** are pet forms of the name.

Jocasta *f*
In Greek mythology Jocasta is the name of the woman who unwit-

tingly marries Oedipus, the son she has not seen since his birth. Despite this unfortunate story, the name, the meaning of which has been lost, is occasionally used, most notably by the writer and broadcaster Jocasta Innes.

Jocelyn, Jo(s)celin *f* and *m*
These names seem to be derived from several different names that have come together over a period of time to form one name. The most important source is probably from the Latin, meaning 'cheerful, sportive'. There is also a possibility that it is derived from an Old German name meaning 'little Goth'. A further derivation has been traced from the name **Josse**, 'champion', a form of **Jodoc**, the name of an early Breton saint which also gave us JOYCE. Jocelyn is the usual form for boys, although the name is now rarely masculine.

Jock see JACK

Jodi(e), Jody see JUDITH

Jodoc see JOCELYN

Joe see JOAN, JOSEPH, JOSEPHINE

Joel *m*
From the Hebrew, meaning 'Jehovah is God' and the name of one of the minor Old Testament prophets. It was adopted by the Puritans, like many other biblical names, after the Reformation. The name is currently enjoying wide popularity. **Joelle** is a form of the name for girls.

Johan(n) see HANS, JOHN

John *m*
From the Hebrew, meaning 'the Lord is gracious'. Its earliest form in Europe was the Latin *Johannes*, which was shortened to **Johan** and **Jon** before becoming John. In France, however, the name became **Jean**, and both forms of the name were introduced into the British Isles, which resulted in two groups of names developing. Thus the

Johannes form, where the 'J' was pronounced as an 'I', gives us the Gaelic **Ian** and **Iain**, **Ieuan** and **Evan** in Welsh, and **Eoin** ('oh-n') in Irish, while the Jean form gives SEAN or **Shane** in Irish and **Sion** in Welsh, for the Celtic languages have no 'j' sound. Since the 16th century, John has been one of the commonest boys' names in Britain (see also IVAN, JACK). The popularity of St John the Baptist led to the development of both **St John** and **Baptist**, a first name sometimes used by members of Evangelical churches, while the French form **Baptiste** is a popular choice for boys in France at the moment.

Jolyon see JULIAN

Jon see JOHN, JONATHAN

Jonah, Jonas *m*
From the Hebrew, meaning 'dove'. The Old Testament story of Jonah and the whale was very popular in the Middle Ages and because of this the name was common. It continued to be used occasionally until the 19th century, when it became rare probably because of the association of the name with bad luck, but the name is increasingly used in the USA. Jonas, the Greek form of the name, is also used.

Jonathan *m*
A Hebrew name meaning 'the Lord has given'. In the Old Testament, Jonathan was the son of King Saul, and it was his great friendship with David that gave rise to the expression 'David and Jonathan' to describe two close friends. The name came into use at the time of the Reformation, and it is well used in the UK today. The short form, **Jon**, is often used as a separate name and the name is sometimes spelt **Jonathon**. **Jonty** is a pet form of the name.

Joni see JOAN

Jonty see JONATHAN

Jordan *f* and *m*
Jordan was quite a popular name in the Middle Ages when it was given to children baptised with water from the River Jordan,

brought back by pilgrims to the Holy Land. It was revived as a first name in the later 20th century and has been a popular choice, particularly for boys. The name of the river means 'to descend, flow' and comes from the same word that gives us the name JARED.

Jos see JOSEPH, JOSIAH

Joscelin see JOCELYN

Joseph *m*
From the Hebrew, meaning 'the Lord added' (i.e. to the family). In the Old Testament it was the name of Jacob and Rachel's elder son who was sold into slavery in Egypt. In the New Testament, there are Joseph, the husband of Mary, and Joseph of Arimathea, who is believed to have buried Jesus and whom legend connects with Glastonbury and the Holy Grail. The name was not often used until the 17th century, when Old Testament names were adopted by the Puritans, and Joseph became a favourite. **Joe** and **Jo** are common abbreviations and well used as names in their own right, and **Jos** is also found. The Spanish **José** is well used in the USA

Josephine *f*
Josephine is the French female form of JOSEPH. It was Napoleon's first wife, the Empress Josephine, who started the fashion for the name in Britain and France. **Josepha** and **Josephina** are less common forms of the name. Pet forms are **Jo(e)** and **Josie**, and in France Josephine has the pet form **Fifi**.

Joshua *m*
From the Hebrew, meaning 'the Lord saves'. In the Old Testament Joshua succeeded Moses and finally led the Israelites to the Promised Land. The name was not used in England before the Reformation and is currently popular world wide. **Josh** is a short form also used as a given name. **Jesus** is the Greek form of the name, popular as a first name with Spanish speakers.

Josiah *m*
From the Hebrew, meaning 'may the Lord heal'. The 18th-century

potter Josiah Wedgwood, in whose family the name is still used, is possibly the best-known British bearer of the name. **Josias** is an alternative form of the name, and **Jos** a short form.

Josie see JOSEPHINE

Josse see JOCELYN, JOYCE

Joy *f*
This is the vocabulary word used as a first name. It occurs as early as the 12th century but then disappears, to be revived in the 19th century.

Joyce *f* and *m*
In the Middle Ages, when this name was most common, it usually had the form **Josse**. A 7th-century saint from Brittany, who also gave us the name JOCELYN, was the cause of the name's popularity. One of its French variants was **Joisse**, and it was from this that the name's final form was derived. Joyce was little used after the Middle Ages until the general revival of medieval names in the 19th century. It is now very rare as a man's name.

Juanita see JOAN

Jude *m*
The Hebrew form of this name is **Yehudi**, which was rendered as **Judah** in the Authorised Version of the Old Testament. **Judas** Iscariot bore the Greek form, and because of him Jude was not used by Christians until the Reformation. The name was brought back to public attention by Thomas Hardy's 1895 novel *Jude the Obscure* and the Beatles' song *Hey Jude*. The actor Jude Law is a well-known current user. It means 'praise'. Jude is sometimes a pet form of JUDITH.

Judith *f*
From the Hebrew, meaning 'a Jewess', and in the Apocryphal Book of Judith the name of the resourceful woman who saves the Israelites by letting the enemy general think he was seducing her, and

then cutting off his head with his own sword. The short form **Judy** is often given independently, while the pet forms **Jody** and **Jodi(e)** are now the most common form of the name. JUDE is sometimes used as a short form.

Jules see JULIAN

Julia, Juliet *f*
Julia is the feminine form of **Julius** (see JULIAN), which came to England from Italy as Giulia in the 16th century. It did not become common in Britain until the 18th and 19th centuries. **Julie** is the French form, often used as a pet form of Julia. Julia was popular in the middle of the 20th century, then fell out of favour, but is now coming back into use, particularly in the USA. Shakespeare's heroine in *Romeo and Juliet* gets her name from the Italian pet form Giulietta, which is **Juliette** in French.

Julian *m*
Julianus was a Roman family name that meant 'connected with the family of Julius'. **Julius** probably comes from the same root, which gives the Latin word for 'god', but in Roman times the family believed that it referred to the soft growth of hair that forms a boy's first sign of a beard, as this was the state of development that a founding member of the clan had reached when he first distinguished himself in battle. The most famous of numerous saints called Julian was St Julian the Hospitaller, who devoted himself to helping poor travellers. The name came to Britain in the Latin form, which was anglicised as **Julyan**, and in the North of England as **Jolyon**, a name brought to public attention in the 1920s by Galsworthy's *Forsyte Saga*, televised to great acclaim in 1967. **Jules**, the French form of Julius, is also used as a short form of Julian.

Juliana *f*
This is the feminine form of JULIAN. It was a popular name in the Middle Ages, when the name normally took the form Julian, still occasionally used for girls. The variant forms GILLIAN and JILL were among the commonest girls' names from the 12th to the 15th cen-

turies. The name subsequently dropped out of use but was revived in the 18th century. The short form **Julie** is shared with JULIA (see also LIANNE), and **Julianne (Julie-Anne)** is a common variant.

Julius see JULIAN

Junayd *m*
An Arabic name meaning 'warrior'. It also occurs as **Junaid**.

June *f*
This is simply the name of the month, which, like APRIL, has been used as a girl's name since the 20th century.

Juno see UNA

Justin *m*, **Justine** *f*
From the Latin, meaning 'just'. These were uncommon names until the later 20th century when they came back into fashion. **Justina** is an old feminine form, and **Justice** has recently started appearing as a given name for both sexes.

K

Kacey see CASEY

Kadie, Kady see KAY

Kai *f* and *m*
This is a name that has recently come to be used in the USA and increasingly in the UK. It can be interpreted as at least two different names. As a Hawaiian name, pronounced to rhyme with 'sky', it has the meaning 'sea, sea water'. It can also be a form of the name CAIUS, used in Wales and Germanic courntries. It is also an alternative spelling of KAY.

Kaitlyn see CAITLIN

Kale, Kaleb see CALEB

Kalli(e), Kally see CALLIE

Kamal *m*, **Kamala** *f*
In India this name derives from the Sanskrit, where it means 'pale red', but it is specifically associated with the lotus flower. Kamala, the feminine form, is one of the goddess Lakshmi's names in classical Hindu texts, where it is also a name of SHIVA's wife. In the Arab world Kamal is from an Arabic word that means 'perfection' (see below).

Kamil *m*, **Kamila** *f*
From the Arabic, meaning 'completion' or 'perfection'. Kamil can also be spelt **Kamal** (see above), and Kamila also appears as **Kamilah, Kamilla, Kamla** and **Kamel(l)a**.

Kamilla see CAMILLA

Kane *m*
The Irish name **Cathán** comes from the Gaelic *cath*, 'battle', and means something like 'fighter'. This becomes Kane in English, a name that has been used quietly in the USA for some time and in recent years in the UK, although it is not particularly popular in Ireland itself.

Kanisha *f*
A modern variation of TANISHA, much used in the early 1990s by African-American parents, with whom names beginning with a 'k' sound have been fashionable. It is sometimes spelt **Quanisha**.

Kanta *f*
An Indian name, from the Sanskrit for 'beautiful, desired'.

Kara see CARA

Karan see KAREN

Karena, Karissa see CARA

Karel see CAROL

Kareem see KARIM

Karen *f*
A Scandinavian form of KATHARINE that was introduced into the UK only in the 1920s. Variants include **Karan** and **Karin**, **Karyn**, **Caryn**, **Caron** and **Karyna**, although some of these could be analysed as belonging to CARA. See also KEREN.

Karena see CARA

Karenza see KERENSA

Karim *m*
Karim is an Arabic name meaning 'The Generous One', one of the 99 attributes of God in Islam. The fame of the American basketball player **Kareem** Abdul-Jabbar has encouraged the use of this form of the name among African-Americans

Karina see CARA

Karis see CHARIS

Karisma see CHARISMA

Karissa see CARA

Karl, Karla see CARL

Kasey see CASEY

Kashif *m*
An Arabic name that means 'discoverer'.

Kasia see KEZIA(H)

Kasimir, Kasimira see CASEY

Kaspar see JASPER

Katelyn see CAITLIN

Katharine, Katherine, Catharine, Catherine *f*
A name of unknown meaning but from an early date associated with the Greek *katharos*, meaning 'pure'. The name came to the UK in the early 12th century when crusaders brought back the legend of St Katharine of Alexandria. She was an Egyptian princess who was tortured and put to death in the early 4th century for her learned defence of Christianity. There are a number of further spellings for the name, of which **Kathryn** is one of the most frequent. The most common short forms are **Kate**, **Kitty**, **Katie**, **Cathy** and KAY, all of which are used as independent names. The Irish forms, **Kathleen** and **Cathleen**, are now widely used, while CAITLIN is an older Irish form that has become very popular. **Kathlyn** is a variant of Kathleen. Russian **Katarina**, **Katia** or KATYA and **Katinka** are occasionally found. See also CATRIONA, KAREN, KATYA.

Katinka see KATHERINE, KATYA

Katlin see CAITLIN

Katrina, Katrine see CATRIONA

Katya *f*
Katya is a Russian pet form for **Ekaterina** or **Yekaterina**, the Russian form of KATHARINE. Katya can be further elaborated into **Katinka**, which is also a popular Dutch pet form of Katharine.

Kay *f* and *m*
A pet form of names beginning with a 'K', such as KATHARINE. It has been used as a first name for over a century and can also be spelt **Kai** (see also CAIUS) and **Kaye**. Blends such as **Kaylyn** (**Kaylin, Kaylan**, but see also KEELY), **Kaya** (**Kia**) and **Kady** (perhaps a form of Katie) are also found.

Kayla *f*
This name has been immensely popular in the USA since 1990. It may have started as a pet form of **Michaela** (see MICHAEL), particularly as this often takes the form **Makayla** in the USA, or be a variant of KAYLEIGH, especially in the relaxed pronunciation of rural western states such as Montana, where use of Kayla seems to have begun in the 1970s. The name is also well used in Canada and Scotland.

Kayleigh *f*
This name was brought to public attention as the title of a 1985 hit song by the group Marillion. The song's writer, Derek Dick ('Fish'), wrote it about his former girlfriend whose first two names were KAY and LEE. The fact that both Lee and similar-sounding names such as KYLIE and KELLY were popular at the time probably helped the rapid spread of the name. Spellings such as **Kayley** and **Kaylee** are common.

Kean see KIAN

Keanu *m*
The actor Keanu Reeves has made this Hawaiian name, meaning 'cool breeze over the mountains', widely known. **Kean(n)a** can be seen as a feminine form or as a part of the KIARA group.

Keavy see C<small>AOIMHE</small>

Keely *f*
This increasingly popular name comes from an Irish word meaning 'slender, graceful'. In the case of one early populariser of the
name, the American singer Keely Smith (b. 1932), it was originally
her surname. The name is also spelt **Keeley**. **Keelin**, an anglicised
form of **Caoilfhionn**, 'slender' combined with 'fair' and the name of
several Irish saints, comes from the same root and may be a source
of **Kaylan** (see K<small>AY</small>) as well as of **Keelan** or **Kelan** (Irish **Caolán**) for
boys.

Keenan see K<small>IAN</small>

Keir *m*
Keir is a Scottish surname used as a first name. It came into use out
of respect for James Keir Hardie (1856–1915), who was generally
referred to as Keir Hardie, the first man to be elected to the British
parliament as a Labour MP.

Keiran see K<small>IERAN</small>

Keisha *f*
Another of the names beginning with a 'K' sound that proved so
popular with African-Americans in the 1980s and 90s (see also
L<small>AKEISHA</small>). Keisha is probably a adaptation of A<small>ISHA</small>, or **Iesha** as it is
frequently spelt by American Muslims.

Keith *m*
This is a first name from Scotland that has spread throughout the
rest of the English-speaking world. It was originally a surname that
was taken from a Scottish place name, probably from the Gaelic
meaning either 'wood' or 'windy place'.

Kelan see K<small>EELY</small>

Kelly *f* and *m*
A 20th-century first name that rapidly became very popular. It is an
Irish surname, which means 'warlike', used as a first name. At first

mainly a boy's name, it is now more usual for girls. **Kelley** and **Kellie** are also found. See also KAYLEIGH, KYLIE.

Kelsey *f* and *m*
The surname, which in turn comes from an Old English name meaning 'ship-victory', used as a first name. Despite the success of the American actor Kelsey Grammer, it is more common for girls than boys.

Kelvin *m*
This is the name of a river that flows through Glasgow used as a first name. The river's name possibly means 'narrow water'.

Kendall *f* and *m*
The surname, which can have various sources, used as a first name. Another surname, the similar-sounding **Kendrick**, is also used for boys, and from it a feminine form, **Kendra**, has evolved.

Kenia see KENYA

Kennedy *f* and *m*
Use of this Irish surname as a first name is spreading from the USA to the rest of the English-speaking world. Its choice no doubt owes much to the respect and glamour surrounding the assassinated president John F. Kennedy (1917–63).

Kenneth *m*
This is the English form of the Gaelic **Coinneach**, meaning 'handsome' and equivalent to modern Welsh **Cenydd**. It is basically a Scottish name, most notably of Kenneth MacAlpine, first king of Scotland in the 9th century, who united the Picts and the Scots. It is often shortened to **Ken** or **Kenny**.

Kent *m*
This is the surname, taken from the English county, used as a first name. It first became popular in the United States. The county name is an ancient one, dating from before the Roman conquest of Britain, meaning 'border', from its position on the coast.

Kentigern see MUNGO

Kenton *m*
Kenton is an English surname taken from a common English place name and now used as a first name. The different places get their name from various different sources, the most usual of which means 'royal manor'.

Kenya *f* and *m*
The name of this African country has attracted parents wishing to identify with their African roots. The form **Kenia** is also used.

Kenzie see MACKENZIE

Kera see KYRA

Keren *f*
Although some modern uses of this may be as a form of KAREN, this is an ancient name, a short form of the Old Testament **Kerenhappuch**, one of the beautiful daughters of JOB. The name means 'horn (i.e. container) of kohl'. It has also been found in the form **Kerena** and **Ker(r)yn**.

Kerensa, Kerenza *f*
A Cornish name meaning 'affection, love'. It is also found in the form of **Karenza**.

Keri see CERI

Kerr *m*
An ancient Scottish aristocratic surname, now sometimes used as a first name. The surname originally referred to someone who lived in wet scrubland, although it is traditionally associated with a Gaelic term for 'left-handed'.

Kerry *f* and *m*
The Irish county name used as a given name. It is a fairly modern name, apparently first used in Australia, usually for boys, but it is now in general use mainly for girls. It is also found as **Kerri**. Its

spread may have been helped by the Welsh name CERI, pronounced in the same way.

Ker(r)yn see KEREN

Keshia see KEZIA

Kester see CHRISTOPHER

Ketan *m*, **Ketana** *f*
A Hindu name meaning 'home'.

Kevin *m*
From the Irish, meaning 'handsome birth'. The name was very popular in Ireland on account of St Kevin, a 6th-century hermit and abbot of Glendalough. A few years ago it was widely used throughout the world but has now rather fallen out of fashion except in Ireland and the USA.

Keyanna see KIARA

Kezia(h) *f*
The Hebrew word for the spice cassia and the name of one of JOB's beautiful daughters in the Bible. The form **Keshia** also occurs, with pet forms **Kezie**, **Kizzie** and **Kissie** or **Kissy**. **Cassia** and **Kasia** have also been recorded, with the latter also a Polish pet form of KATHARINE.

Khadija *f*
A Muslim name from the Arabic, meaning 'premature child'. Khadiya bint-Khuwaylid, the first wife of the Prophet Mohammed, was the mother of all his children. The name is also spelt **Khadeeja**, **Khadeejah** and **Khadijah**. Khadija became a popular choice for African-American girls after it became the name of a character played by the rap artist Queen Latifah in the US television series *Living Single*.

Khalil *m*
A popular Arabic name meaning 'friend'. **Khalilah** (**Khalila**, **Kalillah**) can be used for girls.

Kian *m*
The Irish name **Cian**, anglicised as Kian to show the hard 'c', means 'ancient', was the name of the son-in-law of the great fighting king BRIAN Boru, and a leader of the victorious Irish troops against the Vikings in the great battle of Clontarf in 1014. Kian, also found as **Kean** and **Keane**, developed the pet form **Keenan** (**Keenen, Keenon**), well known as a surname and now increasingly used once more as a first name.

Kiara *f*
A name that is currently popular among African-Americans. It probably adapts the word **Tiara**, also used as a first name, making use of the fashionable 'K' sound. **Tiana** and **Kiana** (also found in forms such as **Kean(n)a, Keyanna** and even **Quiana**) are similar coinages; while **Kia** and **Kaya** hover somewhere between this group and KAY.

Kiefer *m*
The American actor Donald Sutherland named his son Kiefer after the writer-director Warren Kiefer, who had been instrumental in furthering his career. The surname means 'barrel maker' in German. The success of Kiefer Sutherland as an actor in his turn brought the name into use.

Kieran *m*, **Kiera** *f*
These are forms of the Irish name **Ciaran**, meaning 'dark-haired'. It was the name of 26 Irish saints, and in the last two or three decades it has become increasingly popular. For boys it is sometimes spelt **Cieran, Keiran** or **Kieron. Ciara** (but see also SIERRA), **Ciera**, KIARA and **Kiera** are used for girls. See also KIRAN.

Killian *m*
Killian, in Irish **Cillian**, was the name of a number of early Irish saints, most notably St Killian, bishop of Wurtzburg, martyred while trying to convert the Germans in about 689. The origin of the name is disputed, being either from Irish *ceallach*, 'strife', or *ceall*, 'church'. The name is well used in Ireland and is also popular in

France, where Celtic names are currently fashionable, both as Killian and in the alternative spelling **Kilian**.

Kim *f* and *m*
Probably from Old English *cynebeald*, meaning 'royally bold', developing through the surname Kimball. Rudyard Kipling's hero in the novel *Kim* (1901) used a shortened form of his true name, Kimball O'Hara, showing the use of the surname as a first name. More recently the name has been commoner for girls. **Kym** is also found.

Kimberl(e)y *f*
Another possible source of the name KIM. Kimberley is a diamond-mining town in South Africa, and the association with jewels seems to have encouraged its use. It spread rapidly after it came into use in the 1940s. There was earlier a brief fashion for Kimberley as a boy's name, about 1900, no doubt commemorating events of the Boer War. **Kimmie** is also used as a short form

Kira see KYRA

Kiran *m*
An Indian name deriving from the Sanskrit for 'ray of light, sunbeam'.

Kirk *m*
A Scandinavian name for 'church', brought to prominence as a first name by the actor, Kirk Douglas. It would originally have been the surname of someone who was connected with the church or lived near one.

Kirsty, Kirsten *f*
Both these are forms of the name CHRISTINE. Kirsty was originally a Scottish pet form, while Kirsten comes from Scandinavia. **Kiersten** or **Kirstin** are also found.

Kishan, Kishen see KRISHNA

Kissie, Kissy see KEZIA(H)

Kistna see KRISHNA

Kit see CHRISTOPHER

Kitty see KATHARINE

Kizzie see KEZIA(H)

Klaus see NICHOLAS

Klay, Klayton see CLAYTON

Kodey, Kody see CODY

Korben, Korbyn see CORBEN

Kori, Korey, Korrie, Kory see COREY

Krishna *m*
The name of a popular Hindu god, a partial incarnation of Vishnu and deriving from a Sanskrit word for 'black'. In northern India it occurs as **Kishen**; other regional forms include **Kishan, Krishan** and **Kistna**.

Krista, Kristin, Kristina, Kryssa see CHRISTINE

Krystal see CRYSTAL

Krystyna see CHRISTINE

Kumar *m*, **Kumari** *f*
The boy's name derives from the Sanskrit for 'boy', but it is usually taken to mean 'prince'. The feminine form means 'girl' or 'daughter'.

Kurt see CONRAD

Kushal *m*
An Indian name meaning 'clever'.

Kyle *f* and *m*
This is a Scottish place and surname meaning 'a strip of land'. It is more usual as a name for boys than girls, for whom **Kyla** is also used.

Kylie *f*
Originally an Australian Aboriginal word for a 'curled stick' or 'boomerang', it was this name's pleasant sound, at a time when similar-sounding names were popular, rather than its meaning, that appealed to parents. It first became familiar to white Australians through the novelist Kathleen Tennant (b. 1912), whose nickname and pen name were both Kylie. Its use spread from Australia throughout the English-speaking world, particularly after being given publicity by the actress and singer Kylie Minogue. **Kylee** and **Kyleigh** are also found.

Kym see KIM

Kyra *f*
While this name can be interpreted as a feminine form of KIERAN or CYRUS, its popularity is more likely to come from the attractive character of **Kira** Neris in the *Star Trek* sequel *Deep Space Nine*. It is also found as **Kera**.

Lacey *f*
Although this is on the surface the surname, which comes from a French place name used as a first name, its recent popularity in the USA probably owes much to its associations with 'lace'.

Lachlan *m*
From Gaelic **Lachlann** or **Lochlann**. Primarily a Highland name, it was introduced as a term for Viking settlers there but was taken by Scots emigrants to Australia and Canada where it flourished. Short forms are **Lachie** and **Lochie**, and there is an occasional feminine form, **Lachina**.

Laeta, Laetitia see LETITIA

Laila see LEILA

Lakeisha *f*
An adaptation of the name KEISHA used by African-American parents. The prefix 'La-', in use since at least the 1920s, became fashionable in the early 1970s in names such as LATASHA and LATOYA, and was popular until the 1990s when it began to be replaced by 'Sha-', although this, too, has largely gone out of fashion. Other names with this prefix include **Laquisha**, **Lashay**, **Lashonda**, **Latisha**, **Latrice** and **Latonya**. The La- prefix can also be found used for men, most often in names such as **Lamar(r)** – probably taken directly from the surname meaning '(from) the pool'.

Lakshmi *f* and *m*
The name of the Hindu goddess of wealth and good fortune. Lakshmi derives from the Sanskrit for 'mark', referring to a lucky birthmark.

Lal *m*, **Lalita** *f*
An Indian name and endearment. As a Hindi term of address the male form, Lal, means 'darling boy', although it derives from a Sanskrit word meaning 'caress'. Lalita, the feminine form, means 'playful' or 'charming'. The name has been in use since the Middle Ages.

Lalage *f*
From the Latin for 'one who prattles'. Short forms are **Lal** and **Lally**.

Lamar(r) see Lakeisha

Lana see Alan

Lancelot *m*
A name of disputed meaning, possibly from the Old French for 'servant'. It can also be spelt **Launcelot** and was used in Britain from the 13th century because of the popularity of Sir Lancelot, the knight without equal, in stories of King Arthur. The short form **Lance** is more common today, although this can also be from a German root meaning 'land'.

Landon *m*
This surname, a form of the place name Langdon, 'long hill', has been used increasingly in North America in recent years. It is occasionally used for girls.

Lanta, Lanty see Atalanta

Laquisha see Lakeisha

Lara *f*
A short form of the Russian name **Larissa** (the meaning of which is uncertain) although it may well be used by some parents as a variation of Laura. Lara came into general use in the 1960s after the success of the 1965 film of Boris Pasternak's novel *Dr Zhivago*, with its tragic heroine with this name.

Laraine see Lorraine

Larissa see LARA

Lark see RAVEN

Larrie, Larry see LAURENCE

Lashay, Lashonda see LAKEISHA

Latasha *f*
There is a strong tradition of name-creating among certain sections of American society, which goes back to at least the 19th century. This name, LAKEISHA and LATOYA are among the commonest of a large group of names that have grown up, particularly in the African-American community, over the last sixty years. They are mostly blends, or combinations of syllables taken from different names, which work because they sound right at the time, echoing the sounds from other popular names. Many of them start with 'La' and particularly 'Lat'. Since names such as **Laverne** (with the option of **Leverne** for boys) were popular with an earlier generation, it may be that the French influence found in place and surnames in the southern USA is the source, although it could just as well come from the many girls' names that begin with these letters. See also Latisha at LETITIA.

Latif *m*, **Latifa** *f*
These are Arabic names from the word for 'gentle, kind'. The American rapper Queen **Latifah** shows another spelling

Latrice, Latonya see LAKEISHA

Latoya *f*
A name introduced to African-Americans by the well-known singer **LaToya** Jackson. Her mother invented the name, making use of the fashionable prefix 'La-'. **LaToy** and **Toya(h)** are also used.

Launcelot see LANCELOT

Laura, Lauren *f*
Laura comes from the Latin for 'laurel', a symbol in the classical world of victory and poetic genius. **Lauretta** is the diminutive form.

Together with **Laurencia** and **Lora**, these names were common from the 12th century. **Lauren** or **Loren** (see also LAURENCE) and **Lori** and **Lauryn** are popular variants, with **Laurine** used in France. Other diminutives that are sometimes used are **Laureen**, **Laurene** and **Laurissa**, and **Loretta** and **Lolly**. **Laurel**, the plant name, sometimes spelt **Lorel**, is also found (see also LARA, LORRAINE). Both Laura and Lauren are popular choices at the moment.

Lauraine see LORRAINE

Laurence, Lawrence *m*
From the Latin, meaning 'of Laurentium', a Roman town that took its name from the laurel plant, symbol of victory. It became common in the 12th century. St Laurence, the 3rd-century archdeacon of Rome, was a favourite medieval saint. The name was popular in Ireland because of St Laurence O'Toole, a 12th-century archbishop of Dublin whose real name was **Lorcan** (Irish for 'fierce'). **Larrie** or **Larry** is the usual abbreviation in England, while **Laurie** or **Lawrie** is typically used in Scotland. **Loren** is a form of the name used for both boys and girls. **Laurent** is the French form of the name, and the Italian/Spanish form **Lorenzo** is well used in the USA.

Laverne see LATASHA

Lavinia *f*
The meaning of this name is unknown, but in classical legend it was the name of Aeneas' wife, for whose hand in marriage he fought and defeated a rival suitor. The town of Lavinium, originally called Latium, was renamed after her. The name was very popular for a while during the Renaissance, but then faded out, returning to fashion only in the 18th century. **Lavina** is probably a variant.

Lawrence, Lawrie see LAURENCE

Layla see LEILA

Lea see LEAH, LEE, LEO

Leah *f*
A Hebrew name, probably meaning 'cow'. In the Bible, Leah was the sister of RACHEL and the first wife of JACOB. **Lea** and **Lia**, the Italian form of the name, are sometimes used, although they can also be a short form of a number of names ending in the sound, while in France **Léa** has topped the charts for girl's names.

Leanne see LIANNE

Leanora, Leanore see LEONORA

Lee, Leigh, Lea *f* and *m*
From the various forms of the surname meaning 'meadow'. Its use may have spread from the southern US, and probably owes its popularity there to the Confederate general, Robert E. Lee (1807–70). It has been a popular choice for many years, and its sound has influenced the development of a number of other names (see also KAYLEIGH). Some parents choosing names such as **Leanne** (see LIANNE) may analyse them as Lee + another name, in this case Lee + ANNE.

Leena *f*
An Indian name that means 'devoted'. In some cases it may be a form of the Arabic name LINA.

Leeta see LITA

Leigh Ann see LIANNE

Leila *f*
A Persian name meaning 'night', probably indicating 'dark-haired'. Byron started the fashion for it in the 19th century by using it in a poem with an oriental setting called *The Giaour*. The name also appears in the Persian romantic legend of *Leila and Mejnoun*, the Persian equivalent of the Greek story of Cupid and Psyche. **Laila** is also used, but the commonest variant is **Layla**, the form used by Eric Clapton in his song that managed the remarkable feat of being a hit in 1972, 1982 and 1992.

Len see LEONARD

Lena see HELEN

Lennie, Lenny, Lennard see LEONARD

Lenore see LEONORA

Leo *m*, **Leonie** *f*
From the Latin for 'lion'. Six emperors of Constantinople and thir-
teen popes were named Leo. **Leon** is the French form, from which
the feminine **Leonie** comes. Other versions used for girls include
Lea, Leola, Leona and **Leontine** or **Leontyne**. In the UK the appearance of Leo among popular names has coincided with the choice of
the name by the Prime Minister's family for their youngest child,
but Leon is still a more popular choice.

Leon see LEO, LIONEL

Leonard *m*
From the Old German, meaning 'brave as a lion'. The 6th-century
St Leonhard was a Frankish nobleman who was converted to
Christianity. He became a hermit and devoted his life to helping
prisoners, of whom he is the patron saint. His popularity made the
name common in medieval England and France, and it was revived in the 19th century. The usual shortened forms are **Len**,
Lennie and **Lenny**. It is sometimes spelt **Lennard**. The Italian and
Spanish form, **Leonardo**, is increasingly used in the United States,
probably influenced by the fame of Leonardo DiCaprio, the film
actor.

Leonie see LEO

Leonora, Lenore, Leonore *f*
These names are European forms of ELEANOR, all of which have
been used from time to time elsewhere, although none of them
appeared widely before the 19th century and their introduction
was probably due to contemporary literary and musical influ-

ences. The spellings **Leanore** and **Leanora** are also found. A short form that all these names share is NORA.

Leontine, Leontyne see LEO

Leopold *m*
From the Old German words meaning 'people' and 'bold'. This name came to Britain in the 19th century through Queen Victoria's uncle, King Leopold of Belgium, after whom she named her fourth son. It was not used much in the 20th century.

Leroy *m*
A surname from the Old French meaning 'the king', which was probably given to royal servants. It has been used as a first name in the USA, particularly among African-Americans.

Leslie, Lesley *m* and *f*
These were respectively the usual masculine and feminine spellings of the name, although they are both now used for girls. It is a Scottish surname, perhaps meaning 'garden of hollies', used originally by the Lords of Leslie in Aberdeenshire. It was taken into general use as a first name in the late 19th century but is now uncommon for boys.

Lester *m*
This is a form of the name of the English city Leicester used as a first name. The city is an ancient one: that it was a Roman town is shown by the -cester ending (a form of the more common 'chester' from Latin *castra*, 'military camp'). The first part of the name refers to the local British Ligore tribe in whose territory it stood.

Letitia *f*
From the Latin meaning 'gladness'. **Lettice** was the usual form of this name from the 12th to the 17th centuries, during which time it was very popular. In the 18th century the Latin **Laetitia** superseded it, now more frequently spelt Letitia. The phonetic form **Leticia** has recently become quite popular in the USA, giving a short form, **Tiesha**, used independently and, most importantly, developing

into **Latisha**, one of the most popular of the La- names (see further LATASHA). **Laeta** is also found. The short forms of Lettice, **Lettie** and **Letty**, are sometimes used independently.

Leverne see LATASHA

Levi *m*
This is a Hebrew name, meaning 'associated', that has recently become more popular in the USA, possibly because of familiarity with the word as a brand name. It is occasionally given to girls, and has been elaborated into **Levon**.

Lewis, Louis *m*
Old German *Chlodowig*, meaning 'famous warrior', was latinised into Ludovicus (source of **Ludovic**). This became **Clovis** in Old French, which was the name of the founder of the French monarchy. His name later became **Louis**, the name of 18 other French kings. The Normans brought the name to England where it became **Lewis**. The reintroduction to the UK of the French form, Louis, is comparatively recent, with Robert Louis Stevenson (1850–1894) an early example, but it is the usual form in the USA. Both Louis and Lewis are currently popular in the UK, and the Spanish form, **Luis**, well used in the USA. Short forms are **Lou** and **Louie, Lew** and **Lewie**.

Lex see ALEXANDER

Lexi(e) see ALEXIS

Lexus see ALEXIS, PORTIA

Lia see LEAH

Liam *m*
This popular boy's name is an Irish short form of the name WILLIAM.

Lianne, Leanne *f*
This started out as pet form of the name JULIANA, via the French **Julianne**. It can also be spelt **Liane** and occurs in such forms as **Leigh Ann**.

Libby see ELIZABETH

Liberty see SAOIRSE

Liese, Liesel see ELIZABETH

Lilian, Lily *f*
Originally these names may have been pet forms of ELIZABETH. **Lillian** is found in Shakespeare's time, but the name was probably associated with the lily flower even then. In the 19th century **Lily** was definitely given as the name of the flower, which is a Christian symbol of purity. **Lil** is the usual abbreviation. Other forms of the name include **Lillah** or **Lila** (recently chosen by the model Kate Moss for her daughter) and, **Lil(l)ian(n)a** and, in Scotland, **Lillias**. However, for one of the most famous bearers of the name, the Edwardian actress **Lillie** Langtry, the name was a pet form of her given name, Emilie.

Lilith *f*
From the Hebrew, meaning either 'serpent' or 'belonging to the night'. In mythology Lilith was an evil spirit who haunted the night and who had been Adam's rejected wife before Eve. It has been used very rarely.

Lily see LILIAN

Lin see LINDA, LYN

Lina *f*
A short form of names ending in '-lina', such as Angelina and Carolina, used as an independent name. It can also be used as a pet form of these names. In the Arab world it derives from a word meaning 'tender'. Some Arabic experts refer the name to a type of palm tree.

Linda *f*
This was a common ending for girls' names in Old German, and comes from the word for a snake, an animal that was held in great reverence by early German tribes. It represented wisdom and suppleness, and the names derived from it were therefore complimen-

tary. In Spanish *linda* means pretty, and this may have had some effect on the use of Linda as an English first name, which dates only from the 19th century. It is also used as a contraction of BELINDA. Linda is also spelt **Lynda**, while **Lindy**, **Lindi(e)**, **Lin** and LYN are pet forms.

Lindsey *f* and *m*
From the Scottish surname meaning 'pool island'. Together with its other forms, **Lindsay**, **Linsey** and **Linsay**, this name is used for both boys and girls. The form Lindsay tends to be the more usual one for boys. At the moment all forms of the name are used much more frequently for girls than for boys and can then take the form **Linzi**.

Linet, Linette see LYNETTE

Linn, Linne see LYN

Linnet see LYNETTE

Linus *m*
Linus comes from the Greek word for 'flax'. The name entered the general fund of Western names because it is mentioned in the Bible, in the second epistle to Timothy. The Linus mentioned there is traditionally identified with the St Linus who became the third Pope. Although not a common choice, the name is well known through several prominent bearers – the scientist Linus Pauling, who won the Nobel Prize twice: once for chemistry and once for peace as a result of his anti-nuclear campaigning; Linus Torvalds, the creator of the Linux open computer operating system, and the actor Linus Roach.

Linzi see LINDSEY

Lionel *m*
This name means 'young lion'. A French diminutive of **Leon**, it thus derives from the same root as LEO. It was the name of one of King Arthur's knights and was given by Edward III of England to his third son, later Duke of CLARENCE. The name was very popular in the Middle Ages and survived into more recent times, particularly

in the north of England. It is not a frequent choice at the moment.

Lisa, Lisette, Liz, Liza, Lizzy see ELIZABETH

Lita *f*
This can come from any first name ending in –lita, such as Lolita (see LOLA), but is most often associated with the name CARMEL. In Spanish the ending –ita can been added to a name to show affection, and Carmelita, 'little Carmel', is common. This then gets shortened to Lita (or sometimes **Leeta**), which in turn can be used independently.

Liv *f*
Although rare, this name has been given prominence by two actresses – the Norwegian Liv Ullmann and the American Liv Tyler. The name is an ancient one, coming from the Old Norse word *hlif*, 'protection', although in modern use it is associated with the Scandinavian *lif*, 'life'. It has also been recorded as a pet form of OLIVIA.

Llewellyn see LYN

Lloyd *m*
A Welsh name meaning 'grey'. **Floyd** is a variant form that has developed from the difficulty of pronouncing the Welsh 'll'.

Lo see DOLORES, LOIS

Lochie, Lochlann see LACHLAN

Logan *f* and *m*
This Scottish place name, meaning 'little hollow', became a surname, which led in turn to its use in Scotland as a first name. It is well used in Scotland today, although not in the rest of the UK, and has been popular since the early 1990s in North America, where it is also used for girls. For girls it has been recorded as **Logann(e)**.

Lois *f*
In the New Testament Lois was the grandmother of TIMOTHY. As the rest of the family had Greek names, Lois is probably Greek also, but

its meaning is not known, although *loion*, meaning 'better, superior', has been suggested. Like many obscure biblical names, it was adopted in the 17th century by Puritans. It fell out of use but was revived at the beginning of the 20th century. Despite the fictional fame of Superman's girlfriend, Lois Lane, however, it does not seem to be widely used. **Lo** has been used as a pet form.

Lola *f*
This was originally a diminutive of the Spanish DOLORES and of Carlotta (see CHARLOTTE). The pet form, **Lolita**, became well known in the 20th century through Vladimir Nabokov's novel of that name.

Lolly, Lora, Lorel, Loren, Loretta see LAURA

Lorcan see LAURENCE

Loren see LAURA, LAURENCE

Lorenzo see LAURENCE

Lori see LAURA, LORRAINE

Lorna *f*
This name was created by R. D. Blackmore for the heroine of his novel *Lorna Doone*, published in 1869. In the book she was the lost daughter of the Marquis of **Lorne**, an ancient Scottish first name sometimes used for boys.

Lorraine *f*
This is the French district the name of which derives from the Old German place name Lotharingen, meaning 'Lothar's place'. **Lothar** was an Old German warrior name meaning 'famous army'. Lorraine is the form used in France. In Britain and North America it sometimes takes forms such as **Loraine**, **Laraine** or **Lauraine**, and it is not always possible to distinguish between variants of this name and forms of LAUREN. **Lori** is a pet form.

Lottie, Lotty see CHARLOTTE

Lou see LEWIS, LOUISA

Louella see LUELLA

Louie see LEWIS, LOUISA

Louis see LEWIS

Louisa, Louise *f*
Louise is the French and **Louisa** the Latin female form of Louis (see LEWIS). Alhough common much earlier in France, Louise did not come to Britain until the 17th century when Louise de Keroual became Charles II's mistress. It was popular for about a century until Louisa replaced it but nowadays Louise is once more the popular form. Pet forms are **Lulu, Lou** and **Louie**. See also LUELLA.

Lourdes *f*
In 1850 St Bernadette of Lourdes, in southwest France, had numerous visions of the Virgin Mary at a grotto near her home town. It has since become one of the major pilgrimage sites in Europe. When the singer Madonna (see DONNA) had a daughter she chose the name Lourdes Marie, a name linked with her own, which has since come into more general use.

Loveday *f* and *m*
This name was common in the Middle Ages but is now mainly restricted to those of Cornish descent. It used to be used for both sexes but is now rarely used for boys. In the past a loveday was a day when members of a community who had had a quarrel were called to meet to see if they could sort things out without going to law. **Lowdy** is an old pet form.

Lowena *f*
Lowena is an old Cornish name meaning 'joy', which can also be spelt **Lowenna**. Its popularity has been growing rapidly in Cornwall, and it is beginning to spread to other areas. The name **Lowenek**, 'joyful', can also be used. Both names are stressed on the second syllable.

Loy see ELOY

Lucas see LUKE

Lucasta, Lucette, Lucia see LUCY

Lucille *f*, **Lucius** *m*
From the Latin word *lux*, meaning 'light' (see LUCY). For girls, **Lucilla** retains the Latin form, and **Lucille** is French. The male form is **Lucius** and its variants, **Lucien** and **Lucian**.

Lucina see LUCY

Lucinda *f*
Originally a poetic form of LUCY, this name is now given independently and has recently become more common. The short forms CINDY, **Cindi** or **Cindie** are sometimes used as names in their own right.

Lucretia *f*
This is a Roman family name of unknown meaning. Its use as a first name in Renaissance Europe was the result of the story of the Roman matron Lucretia who was raped by Tarquin and committed suicide rather than live with the shame. This incident led to the expulsion of the Tarquin dynasty from Rome and the foundation if the Roman republic. Lucretia was regarded as a noble example of how a married woman should behave. Shakespeare's poem *The Rape of Lucrece* spread the use of the name in this form. Lucretia was a common name in Britain between the 16th and 18th centuries and has never entirely died out.

Lucy *f*
Lucy is the usual English form of the Latin **Lucia**, from *lux*, 'light'. In Roman times the name was often used for a child born at dawn; the goddess **Lucina** was the patroness of childbirth, bringing children into the light of day. St Lucy was a Sicilian martyr who was much beloved in the Middle Ages, and the name became well established after the Norman Conquest. Other forms are **Lucette**,

LUCINDA, **Lucasta** and **Lulu**. Lucy has long been a popular name in the UK and Australia but is less well used in North America.

Ludovic, Luis see LEWIS

Luella *f*
This is one of the older American names created by blending two popular names together – in this case LOUISE and ELLA. **Louella** is an alternatve spelling.

Luis see LEWIS

Luke *m*
A Greek name, latinised as **Lucas**, meaning 'a man of Lucania', in southern Italy. St Luke the Evangelist is the patron saint of doctors and also of painters, and the name was often given by a craftsman to his son. The name appeared in the 12th century as Lucas but a century later it was well established in the English form, Luke. Luke is widely popular at the moment, and Lucas increasingly being used.

Lulu see LOUISA, LUCY

Luned see LYNETTE

Lupe, Lupita see DOLORES

Luther *m*
From the Old German, meaning 'people's warrior'. The modern use of Luther as a first name is entirely because of Martin Luther, the German leader of the Reformation, and the American civil rights campaigner Martin Luther King, named after him.

Lydia *f*
From the Greek, meaning 'a Lydian girl'. Lydia was a district of Asia Minor where the people were famous merchants and were said to have invented coinage. In the Acts of the Apostles, Lydia was a widow of Philippi who was converted by St Paul when he stayed at her house. The name was not used in the UK before the

17th century. It is currently quite well used in the UK and rising in popularity in the USA.

Lyn *f* and *m*
A short form of such names as LINDA, LYNETTE and Carolyn (see CAROLINE) when used for girls. It can also take the form **Lin**, **Linne**, **Linn**, **Lynn** and **Lynne**. As a boy's name it can take the form **Lyn** or **Lynn** and is derived either from a surname or from a short form of the Welsh name **Llewellyn**, a name of uncertain meaning.

Lynda see LINDA

Lynette *f*
From the Welsh name **Eluned**, which probably comes from a word for 'idol', via its short form, **Luned**. The form Lynette was introduced by the 19th-century poet Tennyson in the story of 'Gareth and Lynette' in his *Idylls of the King*. It is also spelt **Linet**, **Linnet** (although this can also be from a bird's name), **Linette** and **Lynnette**, and LYN is used as a short form.

Lynn, Lynne see LYN

Lyric see MELODY

Mabel *f*
Mabel is a shortening of Amabel, with **Mabella** as the Latin form. Both were current from the 12th to the 15th centuries but were rare thereafter until Mabel was revived in the 19th century and became very common. It then suffered another fall from favour. The pet form often used is May. **Maybelle** and **Maybelline** are developments of the name.

Macauley *f* and *m*
Made famous by the actor Macauley Culkin, this Scottish surname is now used for children of both sexes, although more frequently for boys. It can be spelt starting with a Mc-, and the final syllable is sometimes -lee or -leigh. The similar-sounding **Mackinley**, originally meaning 'son of Finlay', is also found.

Mackenzie *f* and *m*
As a Scottish surname, this refers to a 'son of Coinneach', a Gaelic name that usually takes the anglicised form Kenneth. It was popularised as a girl's name by the actress Mackenzie Phillips, who appeared in a 1970s' American TV series. In the USA the short form **Kenzie** is also used. The similar **Mckenna**, originally from a Scots surname meaning 'ardent love', is also found but more rarely.

Mackinley see Macauley

Macsen see Maximilian

Macy *f*
This name, famous in the USA from Macy's department stores, has been used increasingly by American parents for some years. The surname was originally French, from a place name meaning 'Marcius' estate'. It is also found as **Macey** and **Maci**.

Maddison see MADISON

Madel(e)ine *f*
Magdalene, the original form of the name, is Hebrew and means 'woman of Magdala', a town on the Sea of Galilee that was the birthplace of St Mary Magdalene. From about the 12th century the name was used in England in the French form **Madeline**, often abbreviated to **Maudlin** and **Madlin**. **Magdalen**, the biblical form, was adopted after the Reformation. It was usually pronounced Maudlin, but because the meaning of this word developed the sense of 'weak and sentimental', this form was replaced by the current pronunciation. It now sometimes takes the form **Madelyn** (**Madlyn**, **Madilyn**) and shares the short form **Madge** with MARGARET. **Maddie** or **Maddy** is also used. A Continental short form is **Magda** (shortened from **Ma(g)dalena**), which has also been given as an independent name.

Madge see MADELINE, MARGARET

Madison *f*
Use of Madison as a first name derives ultimately from the surname, which means 'son of MAUD or MADELEINE'. The name was used by a character in the 1984 film *Splash*, sparking its real-life use as soon as the film was released. It continues to grow in popularity and now takes forms such as **Madisen**, **Madisyn**, **Maddison** (prominent in Australia), **Madyson**. It is very popular in North America, well used in Australia and beginning to enter the charts in the UK.

Madlin, Madlyn see MADELEINE

Madoc, Madog *m*
A Welsh name meaning 'fortunate'. It is rarely used outside Wales. See also MARMADUKE.

Madonna see DONNA

Madyson see MADISON

Mae see MAY

Maegan see MEGAN

Maeleachlainn see MALACHI

Mael Maedoc see MARMADUKE

Maeve *f*
The more usual phonetic form of the Irish name **Meadhbh**, meaning 'she who makes drunk'. It was the name of a famous queen in Irish legend. A diminutive is **Meaveen**, and the name is occasionally spelt **Meave** or **Mave**. It is popular in Ireland but not much used elsewhere, except in France where the form **Maeva** is popular.

Magda, Magdalen(e) see MADELEINE

Maggie see MARGARET

Magnus *m*
This is a Latin adjective meaning 'great'. The spread of this name was because of the Emperor Charlemagne, *Carolus Magnus* in Latin. Some of his admirers took Magnus for a personal name, and among those who christened their sons after him was the 10th-century St Olaf of Norway. The name spread from Scandinavia to Shetland and Ireland. From Shetland the name became well established in Scotland. In Ireland it became **Manus**, hence the common Irish surname McManus.

Mahalia *f*
This is a form of the Hebrew name **Mahala**, meaning 'tenderness'. No longer a very usual name, it is best known from the singer Mahalia Jackson.

Mahomed, Mahommed see MOHAMMED

Mai see MAY

Maia see MAYA

Mair, Maire see MARY, MOIRA

Mairead see MARGARET

Mairi see MARY

Mairin see MAUREEN

Maisie see MARGARET

Makayla see KAYLA, MICHAEL

Malachi, Malachy *m*
Malachi is a Hebrew name meaning 'my messenger' borne by one
of the prophets of the Old Testament. It is sometimes spelt **Malachai**.
The form **Malachy** is well used in Ireland, and has a different history.
Malachy is a form of the Irish name **Maeleachlainn**, which has been
altered to conform to the biblical name. Maeleachlainn was the
name of one of the Irish High Kings who fought effectively against
the Norse invaders, defeating them at the battle of Tara in 980 and
driving them out of Dublin. His name means 'devotee of St
Sechnall'. St Sechnall, whose name is an Irish form of a Latin name,
Secundinus, from a name indicating a second child, was a 5th-cen-
tury companion of St Patrick who became the first bishop of
Dunshaughlin.

Malcolm *m*
From the Gaelic *mael Colum*, 'follower of St Columba'. This was a
very popular Scottish name, borne by four kings of Scotland. It was
used very occasionally in medieval England, but became common
outside Scotland only in the 20th century. Short forms are **Mal** and
Col(u)m. See CALLUM.

Malia see MARY

Malik *m*
From the Arabic for 'king'. The African-American activist and
leader of the Nation of Islam, otherwise known as Malcolm X, took
the name El-Hajj Malik El-Shabazz, which has led to the use of this
name in the USA.

Mallory *f*
This name has a pleasant sound but a less pleasant meaning: as a

surname it derives from the French and means 'ill-omened' or 'unfortunate'. It was nevertheless well used by American parents in the 1990s, having been given prominence by a character in the TV series *Family Ties*. The English-born author **Malorie** Blackman shows another spelling of the name

Malvina *f*
A name invented by the Scottish poet James Macpherson (1736–1796). He may have taken it from the Gaelic, meaning 'smooth brow'. The form **Melvina** is also found.

Manish *m*, **Manisha** *f*
An Indian name that refers to the Sanskrit for 'intellect' or 'intelligence'.

Manju *f*
An Indian name derived from the Sanskrit for 'beautiful'. Similar names are **Manjubala** and **Manjulika**, both meaning 'beautiful girl'.

Mamie see MARY

Mandy see AMANDA

Manny see EMANUEL

Manon see MARY

Manuel see EMANUEL

Manus see MAGNUS

Maol Mhuire see MILES

Marc, Marcel see MARCUS

Marcia *f*
The feminine form of the Latin Marcius, a Roman clan name that probably was derived from Mars, the god of war. St Marcia was an early Christian martyr. The name can be pronounced with either three syllables or with two, reflected in the alternative spelling **Marsha**. **Marcy** is used as a short form. **Marcella**, **Marcelle**, **Marcelline** and **Marcine** are all developments of the name.

Marcus see MARK

Marcy see MARCIA

Maredudd see MEREDITH

Margaret *f*
From the Latin *margarita*, derived from the Greek word meaning 'a pearl'. The ultimate origin, however, is said to be Persian for 'child of light', the ancients believing that pearls were formed when oysters rose from their beds at night to look at the moon, and trapped a drop of dew in their shells that was then transformed into a pearl by the moonbeams. The name first appears in Scotland in the 11th century, thanks to St Margaret, wife of Malcolm III. She was born in Hungary where the name had spread through respect for St Margaret of Antioch, a 3rd-century martyr. The name became very common in medieval England and, after a decline, regained popularity in the 19th century. The most common pet forms are **Maggie**, **Madge**, **Meg** and **Peg(gy)**. **Maisie**, increasingly popular in the UK, was a particularly Scottish variant, and **Marget** or MEGAN, Welsh. The Irish form is **Mairead** ('mar-ed'). Other diminutives sometimes used are the Swedish GRETA, French **Margot** (now also spelt **Margaux**) and **Marguerite**, and RITA, from **Margarita**, which is also the source of the Scandinavian pet form **Meta**. Other forms include **Marghanita**, **Margaretta** and **Margoletta**. See also DAISY, MARGERY, MAY, PEARL.

Margery, Marjorie *f*
Margerie was originally a pet form of the French **Marguerite** (see MARGARET), but it became established in England as early as the 12th century. **Marjorie** is the spelling in Scotland, where the name was popular from the late 13th century after Robert the Bruce gave it to his daughter, who was founder of the Stewart or Stuart dynasty through her marriage to Walter the Steward. **Marge** and **Margie** are pet forms.

Marget see MARGARET

Marghanita, Margot, Margoletta, Marguerite see MARGARET

Mari, Maria(h) see MARY

Mariam, Mariamne see MIRIAM

Marian *f*
Marian or **Marion** was originally a pet form of the French Marie (see MARY), which was early established as an independent name and was common on both sides of the Channel in medieval times. Marian was later extended to **Marianne**, giving rise to the double name **Mary Anne** in the 18th century. **Marianna** is the Spanish equivalent, which is sometimes given in England. In the USA Marion is occasionally found as a boy's name, as in the case of Marion Morrison, the real name of actor John Wayne (1907–1979). In such cases it uses the surname Marion as a first name, possibly influenced by Francis Marion, who played an important part in the American War of Independence.

Marie, Mariel(la), Marielle, Marietta, Mariette see MARY

Marigold *f*
This name, borrowed from the flower, was adopted with other flower names in the late 19th century but has never been common.

Marilyn *f*
This diminutive of MARY is now used independently. Its popularity was heightened by the film actress Marilyn Monroe (1926–1962).

Marina *f*
From the Latin *marinus*, meaning 'of the sea'. The name has been used occasionally from at least the 14th century, probably on account of St Marina of Alexandria, a martyr of the Greek church. The name became more popular in Britain in 1934, when Prince George married Princess Marina of Greece, who later became Duchess of Kent. In France, the equivalent name **Marine** is very popular, with **Océane**, with a similar meaning, even more so. MORGAN and MURIEL are British names with a similar meaning.

Marion see MARIAN

Marisa, Marise, Marisol, Marissa see MARY

Marius *m*
From a Roman family name that was adopted as a first name during the Renaissance. It has never been common, although the Spanish and Italian form **Mario** is well used on the Continent and in the USA. The name is probably derived from Mars, the Roman god of war, and so related to MARK.

Marjorie see MARGERY

Mark, Marcus *m*
These names are probably derived from Mars, the Roman god of war, and were used as Roman family and personal names. Although it occurs from the Middle Ages in Britain, **Mark**, the modern form of the name, has become common only since the 1950s. The French forms, **Marc** and **Marcel**, the latter derived from the Latin diminutive of the name Marcellus, are also used in Britain today. **Marcelle** can be used for girls.

Marlene *f*
This is a German shortening of Mary Magdalene (see MADELEINE). It was introduced to English speakers by the song *Lili Marlene*, a favourite on both sides of the conflict in the Second World War, and by the actress Marlene Dietrich (1901–1992). **Marlena** is a form that reflects the German pronunciation of the name, but a two syllable pronunciation, the second half of the name sounded as in the word 'lean' as opposed to the German 'lane', is common with English speakers (see also ARLENE). A shortening, **Marlee (Marley)** is also used.

Marlon *f* and *m*
A name of unknown origin, brought into use through the fame of the actor Marlon Brando (b. 1924). **Marlin** and **Marlo** have also been used for both sexes in the United States, while **Marlen** for girls seems to be half way between this and MARLENE.

Marmaduke *m*
From the Irish **Mael Maedoc**, meaning 'servant of MADOC'. The name
is mainly confined to Yorkshire, where Celtic civilisation lingered
after the Norse invasions of northern England. **Duke** is sometimes
used as an abbreviation, but in America its use usually derives
from the title.

Marsha see MARCIA

Martha *f*
From the Aramaic, meaning 'lady'. In the New Testament Martha
was the sister of Mary and Lazarus. The name was common in
France in the Middle Ages where there was a legend that Martha
had come to France after the Crucifixion. It was not adopted in
Britain until after the Reformation. Variants include **Marta** and
Martella. **Martie** is the commonest pet form.

Martin *m*, **Martina** *f*
From the Latin *Martinus*, a diminutive of *Martius*, meaning 'of
Mars', the Roman god of war. According to popular legend, St
Martin was a 4th-century soldier who cut his cloak in half to share
it with a beggar one winter's night; he later became bishop of Tours
in France. Martin has been used more or less without a break since
the 12th century. **Martyn** is the Welsh spelling and **Marty** a short
form. **Martina** and **Martita** are the female forms of the name.
Martinella and the French feminine **Martine** are also found for girls.

Marvin see MERVYN

Mary *f*
A biblical name, traditionally meaning 'dew of the sea', but possibly going back to an ancient Egyptian name. The earliest form of
the name was MIRIAM, which later translations of the Bible changed
to **Mariam** and **Maria** (now also spelt **Mariah** and pronounced with
a long 'i' sound), and finally Mary. Out of respect for the Virgin
Mary, the name was held to be too sacred for general use until about
the 12th century when the French form, **Marie**, and the diminutive

Marian were common. The Scots kept the French Marie and used the Gaelic **Mairi** and **Mhairi** or **Mhari**. **Maire** is the Irish form, and **Mair** or **Mari** the Welsh. The latinised Maria was adopted in the 18th century, giving a pet form of **Ria**. **Marise** and **Maris(s)a** are Continental forms of the name. Other elaborations are **Mariel(le)**, **Marietta**, **Mariette** and **Mariella**. Pet forms of Mary are **Molly** or **Mollie**, currently a popular choice in the UK, **Polly**, **Mimi**, **Mamie** and MAY, with **Manon** a French pet form that is currently one of the most popular names in France (see also MARIAN, MARILYN, MAUREEN, MAYA, MIA, MIRIAM, MOIRA).

A recent trend has been to adopt the Continental habit of linking Marie with another name to produce names such as **Marie-Rose** and **Marie-Louise**. One such combination, **Marisol**, combining Mary with the Spanish name **Sol**, 'sun', is particularly popular with Spanish speakers. Perhaps the most exotic form of Mary is the Hawaiian **Malia** (**Mahlia**), increasingly being used in the United States, which developed because the Hawaiian language does not support the 'r' sound of Western forms.

Maryann, Maryanne, Mary Anne see MARIAN

Mason *m*
The surname, which comes from the occupation, used as a first name. Well used in the USA for some years, it is now entering the UK charts.

Matilda *f*
From the Old German, meaning 'mighty in battle'. This name was particularly popular in medieval court circles, introduced by William the Conqueror's wife who bore the name. Later, their granddaughter, sometimes known as MAUD, fought her cousin Stephen for the throne. The name fell into disuse but returned to favour in the 18th century. **Matty**, **Tilda** and **Tilly** are pet forms. Although by no means common, there has been a recent increase in the use of this name, and the French form **Mathilde** is among the top dozen names for girls in France.

Matthew *m*

From the Hebrew, meaning 'gift of God', and the name of one of the Evangelists. The name was particularly popular from the 12th to the 14th centuries. After the Reformation the Greek form, **Matthias**, was adopted. In the Bible it is used for the name of the apostle chosen to succeed Judas Iscariot. Today Matthew is one of the most popular choices for English speakers. The usual short form is **Matt**.

Matty see MATILDA

Maud *f*

The Old French form of the name MATILDA. This name was popular in Britain after the Norman Conquest but fell out of use about the 15th century. It was revived in the 19th century by Tennyson's well-known poem *Maud* (1855). It is also spelt **Maude**, and **Maudie** is sometimes used as a pet form.

Maudlin see MADELEINE

Maura see MOIRA

Maureen *f*

A phonetic form of the Irish **Mairin**, meaning 'little Mary'. The variant forms in Britain are **Moreen** and MOIRA. The Irish also have a name **Mor**, meaning 'tall', with a pet form **Moirin**, which can be anglicised as **Moreen**.

Maurice, Morris *m*

From the Latin *Mauritius*, meaning 'a Moor'. The spread of the name was because of St Maurice, a 3rd-century martyr in Switzerland after whom the town of St Moritz was named. The Normans brought the name to England as **Meurisse**, which was soon anglicised to **Morris**. The more modern French form, **Maurice**, has now largely replaced the English form, although it is usually pronounced the same way in the UK: in the USA it is often pronounced in the French manner, with the stress on the second syllable. There is a Welsh equivalent, **Meurig**, which occurs from the 5th century. Short forms are **Morrie** and **Maurie**.

Mave see MAEVE

Mavis *f*
From the old word for song thrush. It was first used by Marie Corelli in her novel *The Sorrows of Satan* (1895).

Maximilian *m*
Maximus in Latin means 'greatest'. Two 3rd-century saints bore its derivative, **Maximilian**, yet it is popularly thought to have been invented by the German Emperor Frederick III, combining the last names of Quintus Fabius Maximus and Scipio Aemilianus, two renowned Roman generals. His son, later Emperor Maximilian I, was a famous huntsman and fighter, and the name became very popular in German-speaking countries. The name has recently become more popular in the UK, particularly in its short form, **Max**. **Macsen** is the Welsh form of Maximus. **Maxime** is used in France for both sexes and is currently popular there for boys, with **Maxence** also well used, but in Britain this, or **Maxine**, tends to be used for girls, keeping **Maxim**, also a Russian form of the name, for boys. Max can also be a short form of **Maxwell**, from a Scottish surname and place name meaning 'Mac's well'.

May *f*
This was originally a pet form of MABEL, MARGARET or MARY, but it has more recently been associated with the month, and it is now a separate name. Variants are **Mae**, as in the actress Mae West (1892–1980), and **Mai** (see also AVRIL / JUNE). Forms such as **Mayra** fall somewhere between May and Maria (see MARY).

Maya *f*
In India this name derives from a Sanskrit word meaning 'illusion', an important word in Hindu philosophy. In America the author Maya Angelou has made the name famous. In her case it is a nickname, derived from her brother's way of pronouncing 'my sister'. The name can also be interpreted as a pet form of Maria (see MARY). It is also found as **Maia**.

Maybelle, Maybelline see MABEL

Maygen see MEGAN

Mcauley see MACAULEY

Mckenzie, Mckenna see MACKENZIE

Mckinley see MACAULEY

Meadhbh, Meave, Meaveen see MAEVE

Meena *f*
From the Sanskrit for 'fish, Pisces', this is the name of a Hindu goddess.

Meera *f*
A Hindi name that means 'saintly woman'.

Meg see MARGARET

Megan *f*
Megan started life as a Welsh pet form of **Meg**, itself a pet form of MARGARET. It is currently very popular throughout the English-speaking world. In Australia, Canada and the USA it is quite often spelt as **Meghan**, as if it were an Irish name, and Americans also use forms such as **Maegan** and **Maygen**.

Mehul *f*
This Hindi name refers to 'rain clouds'. It is also found as **Mehal**.

Mel see MELANIE, MELVIN

Melanie *f*
From the Greek for 'black' or 'dark-skinned'. Melania was an ancient name used by both the Greeks and the Romans. It came to England from France in the mid-17th century in its French form, Melanie, which also became **Melony** or **Mel(l)oney** and **Melany** in Britain. It is shortened to **Mel**.

Melicent, Melisenda, Melisande, Melisent see MILLICENT

Melissa *f*
From the Greek meaning 'a bee' and the name of a nymph in Greek
mythology. It was used occasionally in the 18th century and has
been popular in recent years. Other names with the sense of 'bee'
or 'honey' that are used are **Melinda**, sometimes shortened to **Mindy**,
and **Melita**.

Melloney, Meloney, Melony see MELANIE

Melody *f*
This vocabulary word has come into first-name use in recent years,
particularly in the USA. Other names with musical associations
that are sometimes used are **Harmony** and **Lyric**.

Melvin, Melvyn *m*
Various theories have been put forward as to the source of this
name. It seems likely that it comes from a surname, which can come
from a variety of sources, several of them Scottish. **Mel** is the short
form.

Melvina see MALVINA

Mercedes see DOLORES

Mercy *f*
This is the virtue used as a first name, in the same way as HOPE. The
pet form is **Merry**, which is also used as an independent name.

Meredith *f* and *m*
From the surname from the ancient Welsh **Maredudd** or **Meredydd**,
'great chief'. It can be spelt **Meridith** and shares **Merry** as a short
form with MERCY. Use of the name for girls was a 20th-century in-
novation.

Meriel see MURIEL

Merle *f* and *m*
This is the French for 'blackbird', originally derived from Latin. It
was adopted as a first name in the 19th century. It became well

known as the name of the film actress Merle Oberon (1911–1979). As a boy's name its use is mainly restricted to the USA, and in this case is probably from a form of the surname **Merrill** (occasionally used for both boys and girls), which in turn comes from the name MURIEL.

Merlene, Merlin, Merlyn see MERVYN

Merrill see MERLE, MURIEL

Merry see MERCY, MEREDITH

Mervyn *m*
From the Welsh name **Myrddin** ('sea fort'), which is the true form of **Merlin**, the name of King Arthur's legendary magician. It is also spelt **Mervin**. Merlin has recently come to be used for girls, sometimes in the forms **Merlene** or **Merlyn**. **Marvin**, also a common surname, is probably a form of Mervyn, although some would dispute this.

Meryl see MURIEL

Meta see MARGARET

Meurig see MAURICE

Mhairi, Mhari see MARY

Mia *f*
A Scandinavian pet form of MARY, although some associate it with the Italian and Spanish word for 'my'. The actress Mia Farrow brought the name into more general use. **Mya(h)** is also found.

Michael *m*, **Michelle** *f*
From the Hebrew, meaning 'who is like the Lord?' In the Bible Michael was one of the seven archangels and their leader in battle, and he therefore became the patron saint of soldiers. The variant form **Micah**, the name of a minor prophet in the Old Testament, was used in the 17th century among Puritans and can now be found

used for both sexes, sometimes as **Mica** or **Myka**. Michael has pet forms **Mike**, **Mick** or **Micky**. The surname **Mitchell**, derived from Michael, is also popular as a boy's name, with the short form **Mitch**. **Michelle** is the French female form of the name, also found as **Michele**, which can be shortened to **Shelley**. **Michaela** is another feminine form of the name currently popular in the USA, where it can take numerous exotic forms such as **Makayla** or **Mykala** (see also KAYLA). **Misha** or **Mischa** is in Russia a pet form of Michael, but because of the 'a' ending is sometimes thought of as a girl's name. Spanish forms are **Miguel** (*m*) and **Miguela** (*f*).

Milan *m*
In Europe this name usually derives from the Czech for 'grace'. As an Indian name the derivation is from a word meaning 'union'.

Mildred *f*
The 7th-century King Merowald of the Old English kingdom of Mercia had three daughters: Milburga ('gentle defence'), Mildgyth ('gentle gift') and Mildthryth ('gentle strength'). It was from the last of these that Mildred developed and the popularity of the three sisters, all of whom became saints, led to the name becoming common in the Middle Ages. It was revived in the 19th century.

Miles *m*
An old name of unknown meaning. The Normans brought to Britain the forms Miles and **Milo**. It has also been used to transliterate the Irish **Maol Mhuire** ('devotee of Mary') and its Gaelic form **Mael Moire**. A variant spelling is **Myles**.

Millicent *f*
From the Old German, meaning 'strong worker'. This name was common in France about a thousand years ago, when it had the form **Melisenda**, now also **Melisande**. The French brought it to England in the late 12th century in the form **Melisent**, and it survived, with minor changes of spelling such as **Melicent**, well into the 17th century. In the 19th it was revived. **Millie** or **Milly** is a common abbreviation.

Millie, Milly see AMELIA, CAMILLA, EMILY, MILLICENT

Milo see MILES

Milton *m*
From the Old English surname derived from a place name meaning 'mill-enclosure'. Initial use as a first name may have been because of the poet John Milton (1608–1674). It has been particularly popular in the US.

Mima see JEMIMA

Mimi see MARY

Mindy see MELISSA

Minerva see ATHENE

Minna, Minnie see WILLIAM

Minta, Minty see ARAMINTA

Mira see MYRA

Miranda *f*
From the Latin, meaning 'deserving admiration'. This name was coined by Shakespeare for the heroine of *The Tempest* (1612), a young woman blessed with many admirable qualities. Like other Shakespearean names it came into use in the 20th century. **Mirabel** (**Mirabelle**, **Mirabella**) from the Latin 'admirable, wonderful' is related.

Miriam *f*
This is the old form of MARY, and in the book of Exodus in the Old Testament it was the name of the sister of MOSES and AARON. It is traditionally interpreted as meaning 'dew of the sea', but possibly, like Miriam's brothers' names, goes back to ancient Egyptian sources. It first became common in Britain in the 17th century. **Mariam** and **Mariamne** are variant forms that have recently gained popularity. **Mitzi** can be a short form of Miriam or Maria.

Mischa, Misha, Mitch, Mitchell see MICHAEL

Mitzi see MIRIAM

Mohammed *m*
The name of the Prophet of Islam, which comes from the word 'praise'. It is probably the most popular Islamic name, the only one to enter the top 50 boy's names in the UK, and is spelt in various ways, **Muham(m)ad, Mahom(m)ed** and **Moham(m)ad** being the common variants.

Mohan *m*, **Mohana** *f*
In early times a name of KRISHNA's, from the Sanskrit for 'attractive, bewitching'.

Moira, Moyra *f*
Moira or **Maura** is an English phonetic spelling of **Maire**, the Irish form of MARY. MAUREEN has the same origin, but has developed as a separate name, although Moira is occasionally used as its short form.

Moirin see MAUREEN

Molly see MARY

Mona *f*
This name is derived from a diminutive of the Irish **Muadhnait** ('mooa-nid'), meaning 'noble, good'. It came into use in the late 19th century along with other Irish names that spread throughout Britain at that time, during a general revival of interest in Celtic culture. It can also be a short form of MONICA.

Monica *f*
The etymology of this name is uncertain, but it could be connected with the Greek word *monos*, meaning 'alone', or Latin *monere*, meaning 'to advise'. St Monica was the mother of St Augustine and was a paragon of motherly virtues. MONA is sometimes used as a short form, and there are French and Scandinavian forms, **Monique** and **Monika**.

Montagu(e), Montgomery *m*

Founder of the ancient noble family of Montague was Drogo de Montacute, William the Conqueror's companion who received estates in Somerset. He took his name from Mont Aigu, a 'pointed hill' in Normandy. **Montagu(e)**'s first-name use dates from the 19th century, when many aristocratic surnames, e.g. CECIL, HOWARD, DUDLEY, MORTIMER, PERCY, were adopted by the public. It shares **Monty** as a short form with **Montgomery**, from the Old French meaning 'mountain of the powerful one'.

Montserrat see DOLORES

Montana *f*

The name of the mountainous American state is starting to appear as a first name, sometimes spelt **Montanna**.

Moosa see MOSES

Morag *f*

A Scottish name from the Gaelic and Irish name **Mor**, meaning 'great' or 'tall'. See also MAUREEN.

Moray see MURRAY

Moreen see MAUREEN

Morgan *f* and *m*

In its earliest form, Morcant, this name meant 'sea-bright' (see MURIEL), but it later absorbed another name, Morien, meaning 'sea-born'. Its earliest celebrated male bearer was the first recorded British heretic, who was known as Pelagius (*c*.353–*c*.425), a Greek translation of the name. It was almost always a male name until the 20th century but now is common for girls. The most famous female precedent for the name was **Morgan(a)** le Fay, King Arthur's wicked half-sister. The feminine form **Morgane** is currently popular in France.

Morna, Myrna *f*

Both these names come from the Gaelic name **Muirne**, which means either 'gentle', the traditional interpretation, or possibly 'high-spirited'.

Morrie, Morris see MAURICE

Mortimer *m*
An aristocratic surname adopted as a first name in the 19th century. The surname was derived from a French place name meaning 'dead sea'. The Mortimer family connect it with the Dead Sea in Palestine, where their ancestors fought in crusading times. The pet form **Morty** was also used independently in Ireland as a form of the Irish name **Murtaugh** or **Murty** ('skilled sailor'). The short form **Mort** is also used.

Morven *f*
A Scottish name, from an old name for the northwest of the country. In legend it is the name of the kingdom of FINGAL and means 'high mountains'. It became a first name as a result of its inclusion in James Macpherson's poems, in much the same way as SELMA did.

Morwenna *f*
Morwenna comes from Welsh and probably means 'maiden'. There was a 5th-century saint of this name about whom little is known, and the name used to be confined to Wales and Cornwall but now seems to be spreading. It is also found as **Morwen**.

Moses *m*
The meaning of this name is uncertain and it is possibly Egyptian rather than Hebrew. It became common among Jews after their return from captivity in Babylon. In Britain it first appears in the Domesday Book as **Moyses**, which became **Moyse** or **Moss** in general use. The present form, Moses, which was not used until the Reformation, is the form used in the Authorised Version of the Bible. **Moosa** or **Musa** is the Arabic form of the name.

Moyra see MOIRA

Muadhnait see MONA

Muhammed see MOHAMMED

Muhsin *m*, **Muhsina** *f*
A popular name in the Arab world, derived from an Arabic word meaning 'charitable' or 'benevolent'.

Muirne see MORNA

Muneer see MUNIR

Mungo *m*
This name was originally a term of affection given to St Kentigern by his followers and in Gaelic means 'beloved'. Kentigern was a 6th-century bishop of Glasgow and is generally known as St Mungo. The name is pretty well confined to Scotland, and the most famous bearer was Mungo Park, the 18th-century explorer of the River Niger.

Munir *m*, **Munira** *f*
From the Arabic for 'brilliant' or 'illuminating'. The name has the alternative male form **Muneer**.

Murali *f*
From the Sanskrit word for 'flute'. The reference is to the young KRISHNA, who played the flute to attract female cowherds to his side.

Murdo, Murdoch *m*
This Scottish name is derived from the Gaelic, meaning 'seaman', and is equivalent to the Irish Murtaugh (see MORTIMER).

Muriel, Meriel *f*
A Celtic name meaning 'sea-bright'. It came to England at the time of the Norman Conquest, via the many Celts who had settled in Brittany and Normandy in earlier centuries. Both forms were in common use until the mid-14th century. **Muriel** was revived in the 19th century and **Meriel** came back into use at the beginning of the 20th century. Other forms such as **Meryl** and **Merrill** have appeared more recently.

Murray *m*
From the Gaelic meaning 'sea'. The Scottish clan of Murray, or **Moray**, probably took its name from the Moray Firth in the northeast of Scotland. James Stewart, Earl of Moray, was half-brother of Mary, Queen of Scots, and he acted as Regent when she was imprisoned in Lochleven Castle. His fame gave rise to the use of Moray as a first name in Scotland, but today the form Murray is more common, with **Murry** a variant.

Murtaugh, Murty see MORTIMER

Musa see MOSES

Mustafa *m*
From the Arabic, meaning 'chosen'. It is one of the names used to describe the Prophet Mohammed.

Mya(h) see Mia

Myka, Mykala see MICHAEL

Myfanwy *f*
A well-known Welsh name meaning 'my fine one'. The commonest short forms in Wales are **Fanny** and **Myfi**.

Mylene *f*
This name, a running together of the parts of the French name Marie-Helène, has become widely known through the success of the Canadian-born French singer Mylène Farmer and use is rapidly spreading. **Mye** is used as a short form.

Myles see MILES

Myra *f*
This name appears to have been invented in the 16th century by Fulke Greville, Lord Brooke, for the heroine of his love poems, and until the 19th century it was used exclusively by poets and novelists. He may have wanted to echo the sound of 'admired'. The variant form **Mira** is found, but this can also be a short form of **Mirabel**, 'admirable', or MIRANDA.

Myrddin see MERVYN

Myrna see MORNA

Myron *m*
The Greek word for 'fragrant'. It was the name of a famous sculptor in the 5th century bc.

Myrtle *f*
One of the flower names, it has been used as a name since the 19th century. The name is Greek, and in Ancient Greece the myrtle was a symbol of victory, while in the 19th century, myrtle was a traditional element in a bride's bouquet. The variant form **Myrtill(a)** is also found occasionally.

Nadim *m*
This Arabic name refers to a 'drinking companion' or 'friend'. It is also spelt **Nadeem**.

Nadine *f*
A French name, derived from the Russian for 'hope'. Variants are **Nada** and **Nadia**.

Naeem, Naeema see NAIM

Nafisa(h) *f*, **Nafis** *m*
From the Arabic for 'precious, delicate'. It is more commonly used for girls and has other spellings, such as **Nafeesa**.

Naim *m*, **Naima** *f*
From the Arabic word meaning 'comfortable', 'contented' or 'tranquil'. Some families prefer to spell the names **Naeem** and **Naeema**.

Nan see ANNE

Nanak *m*
This is a Hindi name, the meaning of which has been lost. As one of the names of the Guru Nanak Dev Ji, founder of the Sikh religion, it is particularly attractive to his followers.

Nancy *f*
This was originally a pet form of ANNE but has long been established as a name in its own right. **Nancie** is occasionally found, and **Nanette** and **Nana** are French forms.

Nandy see FERDINAND

Nanette, Nanny see ANNE, NANCY

Naomi *f*
From the Hebrew, meaning 'pleasant'. In the Old Testament Naomi was the mother-in-law of RUTH and loved her daughter-in-law so much that when their menfolk died she left her home to travel back to Israel with Ruth. The name was adopted by the Puritans in the 17th century and has recently increased in popularity. **Noémie** is a French form.

Nastasia see ANASTASIA

Nat see NATHAN, NATHANIEL

Natalie, Natasha *f*
These names come from the Latin *natale domini*, meaning 'the birthday of the Lord', and were originally restricted to children born around Christmas. **Natalie** comes from Russia, where it is spelt **Natalya**, and has the pet form **Natasha**, both popular choices in recent years. **Natasha** is sometimes spelt **Natacha** or **Natasja** and can have the short form **Tasha**. **Natalia** or Natalie can be shortened to **Talia, Talya** or **Tally**.

Nathan, Nathaniel *m*
Nathan comes from the Hebrew, meaning 'gift'. It was the name of the prophet in the Old Testament who condemned King David for killing Uriah by putting him in the front line of battle so that David could marry his widow, BATHSHEBA. The name shares the short form **Nat** with **Nathaniel**, meaning 'gift of God'. It was the name of the apostle who was better known by his second name, BARTHOLOMEW. Both names are increasingly popular.

Nayan *m*, **Nayana** *f*
An Indian name derived from the Sanskrit for 'eye'. The feminine form refers to a girl with lovely eyes.

Neal see NIGEL

Neelofar see NILOUFER

Ned, Neddy see EDWARD

Neha *f*
This Indian name comes from the Sanskrit for 'rain'.

Neil see NIGEL

Neirin see ANEURIN

Nell, Nelly *f*
These are pet forms of HELEN and ELEANOR. They were already in use in Britain in the Middle Ages. A famous holder of the name was Nell (Eleanor) Gwyn, the mistress of Charles II.

Nelson see NIGEL

Neris see NERYS

Nerissa *f*
This is one of the less common names taken from Shakespeare, in this case Portia's witty maid in *The Merchant of Venice*. It is not clear what Shakespeare meant by the name, but he may have taken it from *nereis*, the Greek word for a sea nymph.

Nerys *f*
An unusual Welsh name, meaning 'lady', that has become widely known through the actress Nerys Hughes. It is sometimes found in the form **Neris**.

Ness, Nessa see AGNES, VANESSA

Nessie, Nest, Nesta see AGNES

Net, Netta, Nettie see ANTHONY, JANET

Neville *m*
From the French surname Neuville, meaning 'new town'. It was introduced into England at the time of the Norman Conquest, when the Neville family, which came over with William the Conqueror, was very powerful. Their influence continued, but the name was not adopted as a first name until the 17th century. **Nevil** is a variant spelling.

Nia see NIAMH

Niall see NIGEL

Niamh *f*
This name, pronounced 'nee-av' or 'neev', is currently very popular in Ireland and the UK. It means 'radiance, brightness' and was originally the name of a pagan goddess. In Irish legend Niamh was a fairy woman who fell in love with OSSIAN and carried him off to the magical Land of Promise. **Nia** is a pet form but when used by African-Americans can also represent a Swahili word meaning 'intention, purpose'.

Nic see DOMINIC

Nic(c)i see NICOLA

Nicholas *m*
From the Greek, meaning 'victory of the people'. The name was common in the Middle Ages as a result of the popularity of St Nicholas, the patron saint of children and of sailors. The usual form at that time was **Nicol**. In Latin the name is **Nicholaus**, and the use of **Claus** in 'Santa Claus' is taken from **Klaus**, the modern German development of the Latin. **Nick(o)** and **Nicky** are the pet forms. See also COLIN, NICOLA. Nicholas is widely popular at the moment.

Nicola, Nicole *f*
Nicola is one of the Italian forms of NICHOLAS, others being **Nicolo** and **Niccolo**. The feminine Italian form is **Nicoletta**, but **Nicola** has wrongly been assumed by English speakers to be feminine because of the '-a' ending. **Nicole** is the French feminine form of Nicholas. Both are popular at the moment. The names are also spelt **Nichola** and **Nichole**, and **Nicolette** is also used. **Nickie**, **Nikki** and **Nici** or **Nicci** are short forms shared with Nicholas (see also DOMINIC), and **Cole** (see also COLETTE) is also found.

Nigel, Niall, Neal, Neil *m*
The origin of these names goes back to an Irish name, the meaning

of which could be 'champion' or 'cloud' or 'passionate'. **Niall** is the Irish spelling of the name, but it early on developed different spellings. When medieval scribes wanted to write the name in Latin documents they gave it the form *Nigellus*, as if it were a name that came from the Latin *niger*, meaning 'black'; and when interest was strong in all things medieval in the 19th century, this Latin form was adopted as **Nigel**. Nigel has rare girls' forms, **Nigella** (as used by the TV chef, Nigella Lawson) and **Nigelia**. **Nelson** is an old surname meaning 'Neal's son'.

Nikhil *m*
An Indian name derived from the Sanskrit for 'entire', 'complete'.

Nikita *f* and *m*
Nikita was originally a Russian, masculine name from the Greek, meaning 'unconquered', and adopted by Russians in honour of a 2nd-century pope. However, in many languages it looks like a feminine name, and after its use for a woman in the successful 1990 French film *La Femme Nikita* and the subsequent American television series based on it, it has come to be used as a girl's name. Nikita or **Nikhita** is also an Indian name used for both sexes, from the Sanskrit for 'the earth'.

Nikki see NICOLA

Niloufer *f*
An Indian name that means 'celestial being'. It occurs in various spellings, such as **Neelofar**.

Nina *f*
A pet form of various Russian names ending '-nina', which is now established in this country as a name in its own right.

Ninian *m*
The name of a 5th-century saint who converted the Picts in the south of Scotland to Christianity. It is mainly found in Scotland.

Nique see DOMINIC

Nisha *f*
A Sanskrit name meaning 'night'. **Nishant** means 'dawn', the end of the night.

Nita see JOAN

Noah *m*
Despite the wide fame of Noah and his Ark, this Hebrew name, meaning 'rest', has been rare in the past. In recent years, however, the name has been well up in the top 50 names for boys in the United States.

Noam *m*
This is a modern Jewish name, from the Hebrew word for 'pleasant'. As it has the same root as NAOMI, it was probably coined as the male equivalent. It has gained world-wide recognition from the work of the American peace-campaigner and academic Noam Chomsky.

Noel *f* and *m*
This is an old French name derived from the Latin *dies natalis*, meaning 'birthday'. The name refers to Christmas Day and was often given to children born then. **Nowell** is an English spelling that is also used, and **Noelle** is an alternative girl's form. **Christmas** is also found occasionally as a first name. See also NATALIE.

Noémie see NAOMI

Nola see FENELLA

Nona see ANNE

Nora(h) *f*
An Irish abbreviation of HONORIA, now used as a separate name. It is also found as a short form for ELEANOR and LEONORA. In Ireland the pet forms **Noreen** and **Nonie** are used.

Norma *f*
Possibly from the Latin, meaning 'rule' or 'precept'. The great suc-

cess of Bellini's opera *Norma* (1831) brought the name into popular favour. It has been used as a feminine counterpart of Norman.

Norman *m*
From the Old English for 'Northman', used first of all for the Vikings and then for the descendants of the Viking settlers in France who were known as 'Normans'. It was popular in Scotland, and for a while was considered a purely Scottish name, being used as a substitute for the Gaelic **Tormod** ('protected by Thor'), itself originally a Viking name. **Norm** and **Norrie** are short forms.

Nuala see Fenella

Nye see Aneurin

Oberon see AUBREY

Océane see MARINA

Octavia *f*, **Octavius** *m*
A Roman family name derived from the Latin, meaning 'eighth'. It was also used as a given name for an eighth child in the 19th century, but now that such large families are rare it is used without regard to its original sense. **Octavian** is an alternative masculine form. The short forms **Tavia, Tavian** and **Tavius** are sometimes used independently.

Odette, Odile see OTTILIE

Odysseus see ULYSSES

Oengus see ANGUS .

Oisin see OSSIAN

Olaf see OLIVER

Olga *f*
From the Norse word *helga*, meaning 'holy'. The founder of the Russian monarchy is supposed to have been a Scandinavian traveller, and it was in Russia that Olga evolved from the Scandinavian form, HELGA. St Olga was the wife of the Duke of Kiev in the 10th century, and she helped spread Christianity in Russia.

Oliver *m*
In Old French legend Oliver was one of Charlemagne's greatest knights. Since these knights were of Frankish origin – that is to say of Germanic ancestry – their names are likely to be from Old Ger-

man. Thus it is thought that this name goes back to the same source as the Scandinavian **Olaf** ('heir of his ancestors', often written as Olvir in the Middle Ages). However, users probably associate it with the more obvious source of the olive tree, symbol of peace. Oliver was popular until the parliamentary revolt led by Oliver Cromwell in the 17th century, after which the name fell out of favour. It was revived in the 19th century and is now very popular in the UK. **Ol** and **Ollie** are short forms.

Olivia *f*

The female form of OLIVER but even more strongly associated with the Latin *oliva*, meaning 'olive'. St **Oliva** was venerated as the protectress of the olive crops in Italy. Olivia was first found in England in the early 13th century, was used by Shakespeare in *Twelfth Night* and is currently very popular with English speakers. LIV has been recorded as a short form. **Olive** is a rarer form, although well known as the name of the cartoon character Olive Oyl, Popeye's girlfriend.

Olwen, Olwyn *f*

From the Welsh, meaning 'white footprint'. The name first occurs in an old Welsh legend in which Olwen, a giant's daughter, is wooed by a prince, who has to get help from King Arthur to do the tasks that are set him. She was named Olwen because white clover sprang up wherever she trod. The name became very popular in Wales and spread to England in 1849 when a new translation of the story was published.

Omar *m*

A popular Muslim name from the Arabic for 'flourishing, long life'. It was the name of the Prophet Mohammed's lifetime companion and supporter. Another form of the name is **Umar**. **Omari**, the Kiswahili form, is sometimes used by African-American parents.

Oona, Oonagh see UNA

Ophelia *f*

From the Greek, meaning 'help'. Its use is because of Shakespeare's

Hamlet (1601). In the play, Ophelia is Hamlet's lover, but she goes mad after he murders her father and abandons her, and is finally drowned.

Oprah *f*
This name is well known through the American talk show host Oprah Winfrey, but perhaps because of this close association with one person, it has not yet come into general use in either the USA or Britain. Oprah Winfrey has explained that her parents intended to call her Orpah, a biblical place name that possibly means 'gazelle'. The registrar misspelt the name as Oprah, which her parents then preferred.

Oriel, Oriole see AURELIA

Oran *m*, **Orna** *f*
Oran, in Irish **Odhrán**, means 'grey-brown, dark' and was the name of a number of early saints. It is found in Ireland but rare elsewhere, except in the USA where names such as **Orin**, **Or(r)en** and **Orran** probably come from this, although they can also derive from a Hebrew name meaning 'palm tree'. **Orna** is the feminine form.

Orla *f*
An Irish name meaning 'golden princess'. It also occurs as **Orlagh** and in the Old Irish spelling **Orlaith**, and is currently popular in Ireland.

Orlando *m*
This is the Italian form of ROLAND. Italian names were fashionable in the 16th century and Shakespeare used this one in his play *As You Like It* (1600). It has become rather more common recently. There is a rare feminine, **Orlanda**.

Orna, Orran, Orren see ORAN

Orville *m*
A name invented by the 18th-century novelist Fanny Burney for the hero of her novel *Evelina*. It is fairly rare in Britain. A famous

American example was Orville Wright, aviation pioneer and brother of WILBUR.

Osbert *m*
From the Old English, meaning 'bright god'. It shares **Oz** and **Ozzy** as pet forms with OSWALD.

Oscar *m*
In the 1760s James Macpherson gave this name to OSSIAN's warrior son in his poems on the legendary past of Scotland, and Napoleon's enthusiasm for the Ossianic legend caused him to give the name Oscar to his godson, later King of Sweden. As a result, it became widespread on the Continent and was regularly used in England and Ireland. The trial of Oscar Wilde in 1895 for homosexuality caused an abrupt fall in the name's popularity in Britain for many years (although it is now increasing in popularity), but it remained in use in the US, where it is also found as **Oskar**, the Scandinavian spelling. It probably means 'deer-lover'.

Osman see UTHMAN

Ossian *m*
In legend Ossian ('little deer') is the son of FINN and father of OSCAR. It is spelt **Oisin** in Irish, a form currently popular in Ireland, while **Osheen** reflects the Irish pronunciation, although it is usually pronounced as it is spelt in England. A female form, **Ossia**, also exists.

Oswald *m*
From the Old English, meaning 'god power'. Oswald, King of Northumbria in the 7th century, was killed fighting the Welsh at Oswestry. He was later canonised, and the place is said to take its name from him. A second St Oswald helped St DUNSTAN with his church reforms in the 10th century. Because of these two saints, the name was popular in the Middle Ages and has never entirely died out. **Oz** and **Ozzy** (**Ozzie**) are pet forms shared with OSBERT.

Ottilie *f*
This is a modern form of **Ottilia**, which comes from the Old German

meaning 'prosperity'. St Ottilie is the patron saint of Alsace. **Ottoline** is another form of the name, and the French forms **Odette** and **Odile** have also been used in Britain. The Continental male form, **Otto**, is less common..

Owen, Owain *m*

This is one of the most popular of all Welsh names, but its origin is uncertain. It may well have come from the Greek name EUGENE, meaning 'well-born', or from Welsh *oen*, meaning 'lamb'. There are many bearers of the name in Welsh history and legend, but the best known is Owen Glendower, who fought for Welsh independence in the 15th century. The name has spread to the rest of Britain and to North America.

Oz, Ozzie, Ozzy see OSBERT, OSWALD

P

Paayal see PAYAL

Paddy see PATRICK

Padma *f* and *m*
This Indian name, usually identified with the goddess SRI or LAKSHMI, derives from a Sanskrit word meaning 'lotus'. Other forms are **Padmal, Padmini** and **Padmavati**. In some parts of India Padma and **Padman** are used as boys' names.

Padraig see PATRICK

Paige *f*
The surname, originally given to someone who acted as a page, used as a first name. It has been popular for some time in the USA and has recently become well used in the UK, probably because of the name's prominent use in several imported television series.

Paloma *f*
This means 'dove', the symbol of peace. Its use by the artist Pablo Picasso for his daughter made the name more widely known.

Pamela *f*
From the Greek meaning 'all honey'. This name dates from the late 16th century when it was coined by Sir Philip Sydney for his romance *Arcadia*. It did not come into general use until the publication of Samuel Richardson's novel *Pamela* (1740). It has been most used in the 20th century, and **Pam(mie)** is the usual pet form.

Pandora *f*
In Greek legend Pandora ('all-giving') is a beautiful but foolish woman created by the gods to plague mankind. She opened the box that contained all the ills that afflict us. After their escape, only

hope, which had been sealed up with them, was left to help mankind.

Pansy *f*
One of the more old-fashioned flower names, now generally out of favour. Use in the UK may have been affected by the cartoon character of Pansy Potter the Strong Man's Daughter which ran in the *Beano* from 1938. The flower gets its name from the French *pensée*, 'thought', because of the way the flower appears to bear a face, often turned down or aside as if in thought.

Paris *f* and *m*
This has been an increasingly popular choice in the USA for some years and is beginning to make headway in the UK. It is difficult to tell if parents select it for the glamorous associations of the French capital or for the Trojan prince who had to choose between three goddesses and was given the beautiful Helen of Troy as his reward, although the former seems the more likely.

Parminder *f*
This name, which means 'highest God', has recently received much publicity through the British actress Parminder Nagra, who starred in the film *Bend it Like Beckham*. It is one of the Punjabi names popular with Sikhs.

Parvais *m*
An Urdu name, from the Persian meaning 'commendable'. It is sometimes found as **Pervez**. Parvais was the name of the son of the great Mogul Emperor **Jahangir**, whose name means 'holder of the world' in Persian.

Parvati *f*
An Indian name, from the Sanskrit meaning 'of the mountain', a reference to the wife of SHIVA. See also BHAVINI.

Pascal *m*, Pascale *f*
A French name meaning 'Easter', which has come into general use since the 1960s.

Patience *f*

This name was fashionable in the 17th century when girls were named after abstract virtues and Sir Thomas Carew could call his four daughters Patience, **Temperance**, **Silence** and PRUDENCE.

Patricia *f*

The feminine of Latin *patricius*, meaning 'nobleman'. It was originally only used in Latin records to distinguish a female bearer of the name PATRICK, then used for both sexes, but it was used independently from the 18th century. It has become common only in the last hundred years, possibly encouraged by the popularity of Queen Victoria's granddaughter Princess Patricia of Connaught. Current abbreviations are **Pat**, **Patsy**, **Patti(e)**, **Patty** and **Tricia**.

Patrick *m*

From the Latin *patricius*, meaning 'nobleman'. St Patrick adopted this name at his ordination. He was born in Britain in the late 4th century, captured by pirates when still a boy and sold as a slave in Ireland. Although he escaped, he wished to convert the Irish to Christianity, so after training as a missionary in France, he returned to devote his life to this cause. **Pat** and **Paddy** are short forms, and **Padraig** the Irish form. **Patsy**, used for girls, was once a common short form for Patrick and is still occasionally found.

Paul *m*

From the Latin *paulus*, meaning 'small'. The New Testament tells how SAUL of Tarsus adopted this name after his conversion to Christianity. The name was not common until the 17th century. It was often coupled with the name PETER, as the saints Peter and Paul share the same feast day.

Paula, Paulina, Pauline *f*

The female forms of PAUL. The 4th-century St **Paula** founded several convents in Bethlehem, and thus established the name in the Middle Ages. **Paulina** and **Pauline** or **Paulette** are respectively the Latin and French forms. **Polly** is sometimes used as a pet form that is shared with MARY.

Payal *f*
An Indian name meaning 'anklet'. It is also spelt **Paayal**.

Pearl *f*
This name first became common in the 19th century, with other gem names such as BERYL and RUBY. It has also been used as a pet name for MARGARET, which is derived from the Greek word for 'pearl'.

Peg, Peggy see MARGARET

Penelope *f*
In Greek legend Penelope was the name of Odysseus's faithful and astute wife, who waited 20 years for her husband to return from the Trojan Wars. The name has been used regularly since the 16th century. It is often abbreviated to **Pen** or **Penny**.

Percy, Percival *m*
Percy is an English aristocratic family name, ultimately from a village in Normandy, that became popular in the 19th century, partly because of the fame of the Romantic poet Percy Bysshe Shelley (1792–1822). It is also a short form of **Percival** (**Perceval**), the name, in the medieval story, of one of King Arthur's knights, although as a surname it also comes from a village in Normandy. Both can be shortened to **Perce**; and Percival can become **Val**.

Perdita *f*
This is from the Latin, meaning 'lost'. It was coined by Shakespeare for the heroine of *A Winter's Tale*, where the finding of a baby who was abandoned at birth is an important part of the plot.

Peregrine *m*
From the Latin *peregrinus*, meaning 'stranger' or 'traveller' and hence 'pilgrim'. There was a 7th-century saint of this name who was a hermit near Modena in Italy. The name has been used in the UK since about the 13th century, but it has always been rather uncommon. PERRY is used as a short form, or, in the case of the character in J. R. R. Tolkien's *Lord of the Rings*, **Pippin**.

Pernilla, Pernille, Peronel see PETRONELLA

Perry *m*
This name sometimes occurs as an abbreviation of PEREGRINE, but it is also a surname used as a first name. It was the surname of two 19th-century American admirals, one of whom inflicted a defeat on the British while the other led the expedition that opened up Japan to the west. Their exploits probably encouraged the use of the name in the US. The singer Perry Como, who helped spread the popularity of the name, was born **Pierino**, a pet form of PETER.

Persephone see CORINNA

Pet see PETULA

Peter *m*
From the Greek *petras*, meaning 'rock'. *Cephas* is the Aramaic equivalent, which Jesus gave as a nickname to Simon bar Jonah, better known as Peter, to symbolise steadfastness in faith. Peter was chief of the Apostles and became the first bishop of Rome. He was a favourite saint of the medieval church, and his name was very popular throughout Christendom. In England the name is first recorded in the Domesday Book in the Latin form, *Petrus*. The Normans brought over the French form, **Piers** (or **Pierce**), which was usual until the 14th century when Peter became predominant, although Piers is now quite fashionable once again. The name was unpopular after the Reformation because of its association with the Papacy and did not return to fashion until 1904, when James Barrie's *Peter Pan* was published. A short form is **Pete**. **Peta**, **Petra** and **Petrina** are modern female forms of the name.

Petronella, Petronilla *f*
These are derived from Petronius, a Roman family name. **Petronilla**, a 1st-century martyr, came to be connected with St PETER and was even thought by some to be his daughter. Because of this, the name was popular in the Middle Ages and used as Peter's female equivalent. **Petsy** has been used as a short form. The name became **Pernilla**

in Swedish and **Pernille** in Danish, and these, together with the medieval English form **Peronel** are sometimes found.

Petula *f*
This name is a 20th-century coinage, although its origin has been linked to the Latin, meaning 'seeker'. It is shortened to **Pet**. It is a very rare name, although the singer Petula Clark has made it well known.

Phebe see PHOEBE

Phelim see FELIX

Philip *m*
From the Greek, meaning 'lover of horses'. It was common in the Middle Ages on account of Philip the Apostle. In Elizabeth I's reign, however, Philip of Spain was the arch enemy of England, and the name suffered accordingly. It was revived in the 19th century. **Phil** is now the most usual short form, although **Pip** and **Flip** are sometimes used. **Phillip** is a variant spelling reflecting the form usually found in surnames.

Philippa *f*
This is the female form of PHILIP but originally was used only to distinguish women (who shared the name Philip with males in the Middle Ages) in Latin records. Its use as a separate name dates from about the 19th century. Often abbreviated to **Pippa**, an Italian form, it can be found as **Phillippa** and **Philipa**. **Philippine** is a much rarer female form of Philip.

Phillip see PHILIP

Phillis see PHYLLIS

Philomena *f*
This name comes from the Greek for 'beloved'. It used to be a popular name in Ireland but is now rather out of fashion. It was thought that there were two saints of this name, but when it was realised that the word Philomena on the inscription on their graves was an

address to the reader and not their names the cult was suppressed; hence the name's fall from favour.

Phoebe *f*
From the Greek, meaning 'the shining one'. It is one of the titles given to the Roman moon goddess, DIANA. It occurs as a personal name in St Paul's Epistle to the Romans and, perhaps for this reason, was adopted after the Reformation, reaching its peak of popularity in the 17th century. It is currently enjoying another rise in popularity in the UK and is sometimes spelt phonetically **Phebe**. It can be used as a pet form of EUPHEMIA.

Phyllis, Phillis *f*
From the Greek, meaning 'leafy'. In legend it was the name of a girl who died for love and was transformed into an almond tree. **Phyllida** is an alternative form that is sometimes found.

Pia *f*
From the Latin, meaning 'pious'. It was not used by English speakers until well into the 20th century.

Pierce, Piers see PETER

Pip see PHILIP

Pippa see PHILIPPA

Pippin see PEREGRINE

Polly see MARY, PAULA

Pooja *f*, **Poojan** *m* and *f*
This Hindi name, which can also be spelt **Puja** and **Pujan**, means 'worship'. **Poojit** (*m*) and **Poojita** (*f*), also found as Pujit and Pujita, mean 'worshipped'.

Poonam *f*
A Hindi name that refers to the 'full moon'. The spelling **Punam** is also used.

Poppy *f*
The flower used as a name. It was particularly popular in the UK at the end of the 19th century and the beginning of the 20th and is rapidly increasing in popularity again.

Portia *f*
Portia is an old Roman family name with the unfortunate meaning of 'pig'. However, Portia, wife of Brutus, became famous for her stoicism and bravery, which probably inspired Shakespeare to choose this name for the heroine of *The Merchant of Venice*. This Portia is beautiful, rich, wise, witty and charming, and it is thanks to her that the name has come into use as a modern girl's name. Although the name **Porsche** looks like a respelling of the name, and the similarity of sound may have helped, it is in fact the most prominent name from a 1990s' fashion, particularly among African-Americans, of naming girls after luxury goods. Other car names include **Delorean**, **Camry**, **Lexus** and **Chevelle**. See also SIERRA and CHANEL.

Pratik *m*
A Hindi name that means 'a symbol'.

Pratima *f*
This name comes from the Sanskrit for 'image, icon'.

Priscilla *f*
The Latin diminutive of *prisca*, meaning 'ancient'. It was the name of a woman mentioned in the Acts of the Apostles and, as with other New Testament names, it was a favourite with 17th-century Puritans. It also appears as **Prisca** but this is very rare. **Pris** and **Prissy** are sometimes found as short forms, but **Cilla** is the most used form.

Priya *m*, **Priyal** *f*
An Indian name from the Sanskrit for 'beloved'. The girls' versions also include **Priyam**, **Priyanka** and **Priyasha**.

Prudence *f*
Prudence first appears as a name in Chaucer's books, and it was

one of the first abstract virtues to be adopted by the Puritans. It is usually abbreviated to **Prue** or **Pru**. See also PATIENCE.

Prunella *f*
Probably from the Latin *prunus*, meaning 'little plum'. It is also the name of a kind of silk and the Latin name for a wild flower, the self-heal, and a bird, the hedge sparrow or dunnock. The actress Prunella Scales has made the name more widely known. It shares short forms with PRUDENCE.

Puja, Pujan, Pujit, Pujita see POOJA

Punam see POONAM

Punit *m*, Punita *f*
A Hindi name that means 'pure'.

Q

Qasim *m*
The name of a son of the Prophet Mohammed, this comes from the Arabic and refers to a 'distributor', one who distributes food and money among the people.

Quanisha see KANISHA

Queenie *f*
This name is sometimes given independently, but it is really a pet name for **Regina**, which is Latin for 'queen'. This name also appears as **Reina** in Spanish, **Regine** or **Reine** in French and **Raina** (**Raena**, **Rayna**) in Polish, all forms that are showing signs of increasing popularity in the USA. Regina was used from the Middle Ages, possibly with reference to the Virgin Mary, Queen of Heaven. Queenie was also used as a nickname for girls christened VICTORIA during Queen Victoria's long reign.

Quentin, Quintin *m*
From the Latin for 'fifth', originally a name for a fifth son. **Quentin** was the French form, which the Normans introduced into England. It became obsolete after the Middle Ages except in Scotland, although it revived in the 19th century, possibly because of Walter Scott's historical romance *Quentin Durward* (1823). **Quinton** and **Quinten** are other forms of the name.

Quiana see KIARA

Quincy *m*
A surname taken from a French place name. Its use in the US may have been because of the prominent New England family of that

name in colonial times. John Quincy Adams (1767–1848), the 6th President, may have received his middle name in honour of this family or it may have been taken from Quincy, Massachusetts, where he was born. It can also be found as **Quincey**.

Quinn *m* and *f*
Quinn is an old Irish family name, literally meaning 'descendant of Conn' (see CONOR) but used to indicate 'chief, leader'. It has recently come into use for both sexes in the USA.

R

Rab, Rabbie see ROBERT

Rabiah *f*
An Arabic name that means 'garden'.

Rachel *f*
From the Hebrew for 'ewe', a symbol of gentleness and innocence. In the Book of Genesis, Rachel was 'beautiful and well-favoured', and JACOB laboured seven years to win her (Gen. 29:20). In Britain the name was adopted after the Reformation and was very popular in the 17th and 19th centuries and is popular today. The usual pet forms today are **Rach**, **Rachie**, **Rae**, **Rai** and **Ray**, and it can be spelt **Rachael** or **Raechel(l)**. The actress **Raquel** Welch shows the Spanish form of the name. From Rachel have developed the forms **Rachelle** (sometimes pronounced with a 'sh' sound) and **Rochelle**, the French for 'little rock', a place name taken from Brittany to the US where the name has been popular. SHELLEY is a short form.

Radha *f*, **Radhakrishna** *m*
Radha is the name of the cowherd loved by Krishna. It derives from the Sanskrit for 'success'. Another form of this Indian name is **Radhika**. **Radhakrishna** is a blend of this and KRISHNA and is meant to symbolise the male and female nature of the supreme god. In southern India it appears as **Radhakrishnan**.

Rae, Raechel(l), Rai see RACHEL, RAYMOND

Raelene see DARLENE

Rafael, Rafaella, Rafaelle see RAPHAEL

Rafe see RALPH

Rahil *f*
An Arabic form of RACHEL. It is also found as **Raheel** and **Raheela**.

Rahim *m*, **Rahima(h)** *f*
From the Arabic, meaning 'merciful' and 'compassionate'. The fuller form of the male name is **AbdurRahim**, 'servant of the Merciful', a reference to one of the attributes of Allah. The spellings **Raheem**, **Raheema** and **Raheemah** are also found, particularly in the USA.

Raina see QUEENIE

Raja *m*
An Arabic name that means 'hope'.

Rajan *m*
An Indian name derived from the Sanskrit word for 'king'. Similar names include **Rajesh** and **Rajendra**.

Rajani *f*
From the Sanskrit, meaning 'the dark one' or 'night'. This is one of the names of the Hindu goddess DURGA.

Rajiv *m*
This Indian name comes from the Sanskrit, meaning 'striped', which is also the name given to the blue lotus. It is sometimes **Rajeev**.

Rajni *f*
An Indian name from the Sanskrit for 'queen', this name can also be a contracted form of RAJANI.

Rajnish *m*
This Indian name derives from the Sanskrit words meaning 'ruler of the night', the reference being to the moon. **Rajneesh** is a variant spelling of the name.

Ralph *m*
From the Old Norse words meaning 'counsel' and 'wolf'. In its earlier form, Radulf, this name was fairly common in England

before the Norman Conquest, and it was reinforced by French use. The medieval spellings were **Ralf** and **Rauf** which were pronounced with the same vowel sound as the word 'ray'. **Rafe** was the common form in the 17th century, and Ralph appears in the 18th century. The current usual pronunciation with a short 'a' and pronouncing the 'l' is 20th-century practice. **Raoul** is the French form of the name, and **Raul** the Spanish.

Rama *m*
From the Sanskrit for 'pleasing'. As the seventh incarnation of Vishnu, Rama is widely worshipped in India. Rama's full name is **Ramachandra**, or **Ramachander** in southern India.

Ramona see RAYMOND

Ranait see RONIT

Ranald see RONALD

Randolph *m*
From the Old English Randwulf, meaning 'shield wolf', which in the Middle Ages became **Ranulf** and **Randal(l)**. The short form, **Randy** (**Randi**), has been used as a name in its own right, particularly in the USA, where it can also be a short form of the girl's name MIRANDA.

Raoul see RALPH

Raphael *m*
This is the name of an archangel, meaning 'God heals' in Hebrew. It is often found in the Spanish spelling **Rafael** in the USA. Use is currently increasing. Feminine forms are the Italian **Raphaella** (**Rafaella**), and **Raphaelle** (**Rafaelle**).

Raqib *m*
A Muslim name from an Arabic word meaning 'guardian' or 'supervisor', especially in religious matters.

Raquel see RACHEL

Rashad *m*
This Arabic name means 'good judgement'. **Rashid** has a similar meaning, 'rightly guided', and has a feminine, **Rashida**.

Rathnait see RONIT

Rauf, Raul see RALPH

Raven *f* and *m*
The name of this large, sleek, black bird has been intensely used by African-American parents since 1989, when an actress of that name appeared in TV's *The Cosby Show*. Other bird names such as **Finch**, **Lark** and **Swan** have occasionally been used in the past. MAVIS, a poetical name for the song thrush, enjoyed a spell of popularity, and ROBIN has long been in use. JAY can also be interpreted as a bird name.

Ravi *m*
The Indian name of the sun god, from the Sanskrit for 'sun'. **Ravindra** is another boy's name based on the same word.

Ray see RACHEL, RAYMOND

Raymond *m*
From the Old German, meaning 'counsel protection'. The Normans brought the name to Britain, and it was particularly popular in crusading times. Two 13th-century saints bore the name. St **Raymund** of Pennafort spent much of his life rescuing Spaniards captured by the Moors. **Redmond** or **Redmund** is a form of the name that developed in Ireland. The short form, **Ray**, is sometimes given independently. There is a feminine form, **Raymonde**, which also has the short forms **Ray**, **Rai** and **Rae**. The Spanish female form is **Ramona**.

Rayna see QUEENIE

Razina *f*
A Muslim name from the Arabic for 'contented'.

Reagan see RYAN

Reanna, Reanne see RHIANNON

Rebecca *f*
In the Old Testament **Rebekah** (the name's Hebrew form, used increasingly today) was the wife of ISAAC and was famous for her beauty. It was a favourite name among Puritans, who took it to North America. It is occasionally spelt **Rebekka** and is currently very popular. **Becky** is the short form.

Redmond, Redmund see RAYMOND

Reece, Reese see RHYS

Regina, Regine see GINA, QUEENIE

Reginald *m*
From the Old English Regenweald, meaning 'power force'. It was not a common Anglo-Saxon name but was reinforced at the time of the Norman Conquest by the French equivalent, Reinald or Reynaud, and developed into **Reynold** or **Reynard**. It can be abbreviated to **Reg**, **Reggie** or REX. See also RONALD.

Reilley see RILEY

Reina, Reine see QUEENIE

René, Renée *m* and *f*
These are the French boys' and girls' names derived from the Latin *renatus*, meaning 'reborn'. The Latin form was sometimes used by Puritans in the 17th century, and the French forms have been used in Britain since the 20th century. The Latin feminine form, **Renata**, is also used occasionally.

Renie see IRENE

Renny see RONIT

Reshma *f*
An Indian name that means 'silken'.

Reuben *m*
From the Hebrew, meaning 'behold a son', it appears in the Bible as the name of a son of JACOB, the founder of one of the tribes of Israel. The form **Ruben** is also found.

Rex *m*
This is the Latin for 'king', which has been used as a first name only in recent times. It is also found as an abbreviation of REGINALD.

Reynard, Renaud, Reynold see REGINALD

Rhiannon *f*
The name of an important figure in medieval Welsh literature. There is evidence that she was originally a Celtic goddess connected with horses. The name means 'great queen, goddess' and has spread outside Wales. The old form was **Riannon**, and a new form, **Rhianna** (also **Reanna**), is also found. **Reanne, Rhian(n)e** and **Rian(n)** are also used, although some forms shade into feminines of RYAN, or in the case of Rhian, analysed as from Welsh *rhiain*, 'maiden'.

Rhoda *f*
Derived from the Greek for 'rose', this is a New Testament name (see Acts 10:11–13) that was taken into use in the 17th century. It was popular in the early years of the 20th century.

Rhodri see RODERICK

Rhona see ROWENA

Rhonda *f*
This is a simplified spelling of the Welsh place name **Rhondda**, which has been used as a first name since the early part of the 20th century.

Rhonwen see ROWENA

Rhydderch see RODERICK

Rhys *m* and *f*
An old Welsh name meaning 'rashness, ardour'. It has had many famous bearers, including a Prince Rhys who checked the Norman advance into Wales. The name's popularity increased rapidly in the mid 1990s, with the alternative spelling **Reece** overtaking Rhys itself in the UK. Rhys is more normal in Australia but hardly used in the USA. Currently, use for girls is mainly restricted to the USA, usually in the form **Reese**.

Ria see MARY

Rian see RYAN

Riann, Riannon see RHIANNON

Richard *m*
This name first appears in Anglo-Saxon as Ricehard, meaning 'strong ruler', which was later developed into Ricard. It was the Normans who spread the present form of the name, the softer, French Richard. The short form **Dick** appears as early as the 13th century, and this is still very common, though **Rich(ie)**, **Dickie**, **Rick(ie)**, **Ricky** and **Dickon** have been used at various times. Female forms of the name include **Richelle**, **Richenda** and **Ricarda**.
Rick, Rickie, Ricky see DEREK, ERIC, RICHARD

Riley *m* and *f*
Riley (**Rilley**, **Reilly**) is an Irish surname of unknown meaning, currently a popular choice for boys in North America and Australia. For girls it is also found as **Rylee** or even **Ryleigh**.

Rio *f* and *m*
This is a recent addition to the store of names, its spread probably helped by a 1982 Duran Duran hit song. It comes from the Spanish word for 'river' and is also the short form of the glamorous Brazilian city of Rio de Janeiro. Use in the UK is no doubt influenced by the popularity of the footballer Rio Ferdinand. In the USA **River**, as in the late River Phoenix (1970–1993), is more usual.

Ríoghnach, Riona see CATRIONA

Rishi *m*
An Indian name that means 'sage' or 'wise man'.

Rita *f*
This is an abbreviation of **Margarita** (see MARGARET). However, it is used much more often as a separate name, and some of its popularity in the 20th century may have been because of its use by the film star, Rita Hayworth (1918–1987).

River see RIO

Robert *m*
This name is derived from the Old German, meaning 'famous and bright'. Although there was an equivalent Anglo-Saxon name, it was the French form that took hold in Britain after the Norman Conquest. King Robert the Bruce popularised the name in Scotland where it has the local short forms **Rab** and **Rabbie**. **Rob**, **Robbie**, **Bob**, **Bobbie** or **Bobby** and **Bert** are also used. **Robin** or **Robyn**, a French pet form of Robert, is now popular in its own right (see also RUPERT). **Roberta** and **Robina** are female forms, particularly used in Scotland. **Bobbie** and **Robin** or **Robyn** are also used for girls.

Rocco *m*
This is a name that came to public attention when it was chosen by the singer Madonna for her son. It is the Italian form of the name of the 14th-century saint, patron of the sick from his work with plague victims, called St **Roch**. It has also been anglicised to **Rock**, a source of the name **Rocky**. It means 'rest'.

Rochelle see RACHEL

Rock, Rocky see ROCCO

Roderick *m*
From the Old German, meaning 'famous rule'. The Goths took the name to Spain where it became **Rodrigo**, and it was established there at least as early as the 8th century. In Britain the name is commonest in Scotland where it was first used to transliterate the

Gaelic name **Ruairi**. In Wales it is used as an English form of **Rhodri**, meaning 'crowned ruler', or **Rhydderch** ('reddish-brown'). Short forms are **Rod**, **Roddy** and RORY.

Roden *m*
This Irish surname from the word *rod*, meaning 'strong', is occasionally used as a first name, especially in the USA.

Ro(d)ge see ROGER

Rodney *m*
This means 'reed island' and was originally a surname. It was not used as a first name until Admiral George Rodney gave it heroic associations in the 18th century. Short forms are **Rod** and **Roddy**.

Roger *m*
Hrothgar, meaning 'famous spear', was an Anglo-Saxon form of this name. It became famous as the name of a legendary king, but it was the Normans who gave us the present form, which was derived from Old German. Roger was a favourite name in the Middle Ages, but from the 16th to the 19th centuries it was thought of as a peasant name and consequently fell from esteem. The ancient short form **Hodge**, once a type-name for a farm labourer, has been replaced by **Ro(d)ge**.

Rohan *f* and *m*
This name comes from a Sanskrit word that can mean either 'ascending' or 'medicine', although some like to interpret the meaning as 'sandalwood'. In Sri Lanka it is the name of a sacred mountain, also known as Adam's Peak, which has on its summit a mark like a footprint that features, with different interpretations, in the legends of all three of the island's great religions – Muslim, Hindu and Buddhist.

Roisin see ROSE

Roland *m*
From the Old German *Hrodland*, meaning 'famous land'. Roland was the most famous of Charlemagne's warriors, and the Normans

brought the name to England. **Rowland** is both the medieval spelling and the form of the surname that comes from this name. They are shortened to **Roly** or **Rowley**. ORLANDO is the Italian form.

Rolf *m*

From the Old German, meaning 'famous wolf'. **Rollo** is a Latin form and Rollo the Ganger ('Walker') was a 9th-century Norwegian exile who, with his followers, founded the Norman race. Rolf developed in Normandy and came to Britain at the time of the Norman Conquest. It was soon absorbed into RALPH but revived in the late 19th century.

Romeo *m*

Romeo, the name of Juliet's lover in Shakespeare's play, has been used occasionally by parents in the USA and was recently brought to public attention in the UK when the Beckhams chose it for their second son. Some 21 parents chose to follow their lead in 2003. It comes from a name meaning 'pilgrim to Rome'. Rome got its name from its legendary founder **Romulus** (which, rather self-defeatingly, means 'Roman'). Other names from the same source are **Roman** and, for girls, **Roma(i)ne** – both well used in France – **Roma** and **Romola**, a name brought to public attention when George Eliot published a novel of that name in 1863. **Romilly**, a French place name that comes ultimately from someone called Romulus, has also been used for both sexes.

Romey, Romy see ROSEMARY

Romilly see ROMEO

Rona see ROWENA

Ronak *m*

This Indian name is from a Sanskrit word meaning 'radiance, embellishment'.

Ronald *m*

Ronald and **Ranald** are Scottish equivalents of **Reynald** and REGINALD, but they are from the Norse (Viking) not the Old English forms. Ranald is still almost exclusively Scottish but Ronald is now widespread. Short forms commonly used are **Ron** and **Ronnie**.

Ronan *m*
An Irish and Scottish name meaning 'little seal', borne by a number of early saints. **Ronat** is the feminine form, although **R(h)ona** (see ROWENA) is also used.

Ronee, Roni see VERONICA

Ronit *f*
This is an anglicised version of the Irish name **Rathnait**, from *rath*, meaning 'prosperity, grace'. It was the name of the patron saint of Kilraghts, County Antrim. It can also be spelt **Ranait** in Irish and has been anglicised as **Renny**. The similar **Ronat**, also found as **Rónnad** and **Rónait** in Irish, is unrelated, being a feminine form of RONAN.

Rory, Rorie *m*
From the Irish and Gaelic **Ruairi**, meaning 'red-haired'. The name became popular in Ireland because of the fame of the 12th-century King Rory O'Connor. It is also widely used in the Scottish Highlands and is sometimes found in England as an abbreviation of RODERICK. It can also be spelt **Ruari** and **Ruaridh**.

Rosa, Rosabel, Rosabella, Rosalba see ROSE

Rosalie *f*
From Latin *rosalia*, the name of a Roman festival when garlands of roses were draped on tombs. Its use as a first name is due to St **Rosalia**, a 12th-century hermit, the patron saint of Palermo in Sicily. Rosalie is the French form.

Rosalind *f*
The origin of this name is the Old German *Roslindis*, either made from elements meaning 'horse' and 'serpent' or 'fame' and 'shield' – the experts disagree. When the Goths took it to Spain it was interpreted as Spanish *rosa* and *linda*, 'pretty rose', and it was with this meaning that it came to England in Elizabeth I's reign. It was used

by Shakespeare for the heroine of *As You Like It* and in another form, **Rosaline**, in two other plays. Largely because of this literary association it has been in use ever since. It developed a number of different forms such as **Rosalyn**, **Rosalin**, **Rosalinda**, **Roslyn** and **Rosaleen**, which is used in Ireland as an alternative form of **Roisin** (see ROSE). **Roz** is a short form.

Rosamund, Rosamond *f*

This comes from the Old German words meaning 'horse' and 'protection', but it has generally been associated with the Latin *rosa munda*, meaning 'pure rose', or *rosa mundi*, 'rose of the world'. The Normans brought the name to England. **Roz** is a short form shared with ROSALIND.

Rose *f*

This flower, the symbol of the Virgin Mary, has been the most popular of all the flower names that are used as personal names. The Normans brought the name to England and it has been consistently popular, giving rise to many derivatives, like **Rosalba** ('white rose'), **Rosetta** ('little rose') and **Rosabel(la)** ('beautiful rose'), as well as **Rosina**, **Rosita** and the pet form **Rosy** or **Rosie** – currently popular in the UK. **Rosa** is a Latin form that has been used occasionally since the 19th century. In Ireland **Roisin**, sometimes spelt **Rosheen** to reflect its pronunciation, is popular. It means 'little rose'. Rose is used as a short form of all the girls' names that begin with its sound.

Roseanne *f*

This is one of the many developments of ROSE, here combined with ANNE. Variants include **Roseanna**, **Rosanna**, **Rosanne** and **Rosannah**, as in Rose + HANNAH.

Rosemary *f*

This is generally considered to be a plant name, although it is sometimes analysed as a combination of ROSE and MARY. The plant name is derived from the Latin *ros marinus*, meaning 'dew of the sea', which describes the misty blue-green of its leaves. It can be spelt **Rosemarie**, and **Romy** or **Romey** and **Rosie** are short forms.

Rosetta see ROSE

Roshan *m* and *f*, **Roshni** *f*
A name from the Persian for 'shining' or 'famous', used by both
Muslims and Hindus in India. **Roxana** or **Roxan(n)e** is the Western
form of the name, usually interpreted by users as meaning 'dawn
light'. It was the name of one of Alexander the Great's wives.

Rosheen, Rosina, Rosita see ROSE

Rosie see ROSE, ROSEMARY

Rosina, Rosita see ROSE

Roslyn see ROSALIND

Ross *m*
From the Gaelic for 'of the peninsula' and the name of a Scottish
clan. Its use as a first name has spread throughout the English-
speaking world, although it is still most used in Scotland.

Rosy see ROSE

Rowan *f* and *m*
From the Irish **Ruadhan**, meaning 'little red-(haired) one'. It was the
name of an Irish saint. Once used exclusively for boys, it is now also
found as a girl's name, in which case it can take the form **Rowanne**
and may be interpreted as a plant name.

Rowena *f*
Probably best thought of as a form of the Welsh **Rhonwen**, meaning
'fair (woman) slender as a lance'. Rowena was the daughter of the
Saxon chief Hengist and her beauty bewitched the British king
Vortigern, bringing about his downfall; she may have had a truly
Saxon name, but her story is transmitted through Welsh-speaking
British writers and seems to have taken on a Welsh form. Its mod-
ern use is because of Sir Walter Scott, who gave this name to the
heroine of his novel *Ivanhoe* (1819). **Rowina** is another spelling.
Rhona or **Rona** has been claimed as a short form of Rhonwen, al-
though it is also the name of a Scottish island.

Rowland, Rowley see ROLAND

Roxana, Roxan(n)e see ROSHAN

Roy *m*
From the Gaelic *ruadh*, meaning 'red'. A well-known example of the name is the famous Highlander Robert Macgregor, commonly known as Rob Roy because of his red hair, who was involved in the Jacobite Rising of 1715. Walter Scott's novel about him may have contributed to the name's popularity.

Roz see ROSALIND, ROSAMUND

Ruadhan see ROWAN

Ruairi, Ruari, Ruaridh see RODERICK, RORY

Ruben see REUBEN

Ruby *f*
This is one of many jewel names introduced during the 19th century. Felt to be rather old-fashioned in the second half of the 20th century, it is now coming back into fashion, particularly in the UK. Other precious substances used as first names include DIAMOND, AMBER, BERYL and PEARL and **Sapphire**, while on the same theme **Tiara** has been quite well used in the USA.

Rudolf, Rudolph *m*
From the Old German *Hrodulf*, meaning 'famous wolf', the same name that gives us ROLF. **Rudolf** is the Modern German form of the name. The spread of this name was undoubtedly helped by the widespread adoration of Rudolf Valentino (1895–1926), the American film star. Another American, the singer **Rudy** Vallee (1901–1986) made the pet form, found in Germany as **Rudi**, well known.

Rufus *m*
This is a Latin word meaning 'red-haired'. William Rufus was the second son of William the Conqueror and became King William II of England. It gained popularity as a given name during the 19th century.

Rupak *m*, Rupli *f*

An Indian name from a Sanskrit word meaning 'beautiful'. Other boys' names based on the same word are **Rupesh**, **Rupchand** ('as beautiful as the moon') and **Rupinder** ('of the greatest beauty'). Names for girls that have a basic meaning of 'beauty' include **Rupashi** and **Rupashri**.

Rupert *m*

This name has the same origin as ROBERT and means 'bright fame'. In Germany it became Rupprecht, and Rupert is an English form of this. Prince Rupert of the Rhine was the nephew of Charles I and a brilliant general. He came to England to support the Royalist cause during the Civil War and was much admired for his dashing bravery. It was because of him that the English form of the name was coined and became popular. For some reason the name has never caught on in the USA, where people seem to think of it a typically, and rather comically, English name.

Rupesh, Rupinder see RUPAK

Russell *m*

This is primarily a surname and is derived from the Old French *rousel*, which means 'little red(-haired) one'. It was a surname that came into use as a first name along with other family names in the 19th century. **Rus(s)** is a pet form.

Rusty *f* and *m*

This is most often found as a nickname referring to the person's hair colour or as a pet form of RUSSELL but is occasionally a given name, belonging with a set of names such as ROY, RUFUS and Russell, which all began as nicknames for the red-haired.

Ruth *f*

A biblical name that came into common use just after the Reformation on account of the Old Testament heroine who gave her name to the Book of Ruth. The name is also associated with the abstract noun, *ruth*, meaning 'sorrow' or 'pity'. **Ruthie** is a pet form.

Ryan *m*

A common Irish surname, perhaps meaning 'little king', now used as a first name. Its spread was greatly helped by the success of the film star Ryan O'Neal (b. 1941). It is also found as **Rian**. Popular worldwide for boys, it is now beginning to be used for girls, often in forms that are difficult to distinguish from developments of RHIANNON. As a surname its history is confused with that of **Regan** or **Reagan**, another Irish surname meaning 'little king', which, despite being the name of a deeply unpleasant character in Shakespeare's *King Lear*, is now being used in the USA as a girl's name, perhaps inspired by President Ronald Reagan.

Rylee, Ryleigh, Ryley see RILEY

S

Saagar see SAGAR

Sabah *f*
An Arabic name that means 'morning' or 'dawn'. The Lebanese singer of this name has made it well known in the Arab world. In India it is often **Saba**.

Sabina *f*
A Latin name meaning 'a Sabine woman'. It has been used in Ireland for the Irish **Sadhbh**, or **Sive** in its phonetic spelling, meaning 'sweet'. There is also a French form, **Sabine**.

Sabrina *f*
This is a very ancient name, used for the River Severn before the Romans came and probably the name of the goddess of the river. The poet John Milton (1608–1674) used it as the name of the nymph of the Severn in his masque *Comus*, and subsequent uses of it as a first name probably stem from this, although nowadays it is probably better known from the television series *Sabrina The Teenage Witch*.

Sacha *f* and *m*
A Russian short form of ALEXANDER. Although originally a man's name, the 'a' ending has led to its use for girls. **Sasha** is an alternative form.

Saddam *m*
This Arabic name means 'bulwark'

Sade *f*
Made famous by the British-Nigerian singer, Sade is a pet form of the Yoruba name **Falasade**, meaning 'honour bestows a crown'. Phonetic spellings such as **Shardai** or **Sharday** are also found.

Sadhbh see SABINA

Sadie see SARAH

Sa'eed *m*
Sa'eed or **Sa'id** is an Arabic name meaning 'happy, lucky'. From the same root come **Sa'd** (*m*) and **Sa'dia** (*f*), 'fortune, good luck'.

Saffron *f*
The name of the golden-yellow crocus pollen used as a spice that has come to be given as a first name in modern times.

Sagar *m*
An Indian name from the Sanskrit, meaning 'ocean'. The spelling **Saagar** is also used. **Sagarika** means 'wave' and is used for girls.

Sage *f* and *m*
This is one of the most recent plant names to come into fashion as a first name, its use boosted by several American entertainers choosing it for their children. The aromatic plant sage gets its name from the ancient reputation that tea made from its leaves had for boosting memory and wisdom. The spelling **Saige** is occasionally used.

Sahil *m*, **Sahila** *f*
An Indian name from the Sanskrit for 'guide'.

St John see JOHN

Sajan *m*
This Indian name comes from the Sanskrit for 'beloved'.

Sajjad *m*
This Muslim name refers to one who 'prostrates' himself, or worships God. The name is sometimes spelt **Sajad** or **Sajid**.

Salah *m*, **Saliha(h)** *f*
A popular Muslim name from the Arabic for 'goodness, righteousness'. The boy's name is sometimes spelt **Saleh**.

Salima *f*, **Salman** *m*
An Arabic name that means 'safe' or 'unharmed'. See also SALMA.

Sally *f*
Originally a pet name for SARAH but one that is nowadays used independently. It is shortened to **Sal**.

Salma *f*, **Salmon** *m*
From an Arabic word meaning 'peaceful'. The word for 'peace' is much used as a greeting in the Middle East, as in the Arabic *salaam* or the Hebrew *shalom*. The latter forms the basis of names like SALOME and SOLOMON, both of which mean 'peaceful'. **Salman** – see SALIMA – may sometimes be a variant.

Salome *f*
The Greek form of an Aramaic name meaning 'peace'. In the New Testament Salome was one of the women at Jesus' tomb on Easter Sunday. However, the name is better known from the story in St Mark's Gospel of the Salome who danced the dance of the seven veils and, at her mother's insistence, asked Herod for John the Baptist's head as a reward.

Sam, Sammy see SAMANTHA, SAMUEL

Samantha *f*
Probably an 18th-century coinage, meant to be a feminine version of SAMUEL. It first became popular in the 1950s when it appeared in the musical and film *High Society* and in the song *I Love You, Samantha*, and is well used once again. It shares the short forms **Sam** and **Sammy** with SAMUEL.

Samimah *f*
From the Arabic for 'true' or 'sincere'. The name is also spelt **Sameema** and **Sameemah**.

Samir *m*, **Samira(h)** *f*
An Arabic name that translates as 'one whose conversation in the evening or at night is lively', thus meaning an entertaining com-

panion. The spellings **Sameer, Samara, Sameera** and **Sameerah** are also used.

Samuel *m*

From the Hebrew meaning 'heard by God'. In the Old Testament the prophet Samuel was the leader of the Israelites who chose Saul and later David as their kings. In Scotland and Ireland it was for a long time used to transliterate the Gaelic **Somhairle**, a name anglicised as **Sorley**; this derives from the Old Norse term meaning 'summer wanderer', that is, 'Viking'. Currently a very popular choice, Samuel shares the short forms **Sam** and **Sammy** with SAMANTHA.

Sana *f*

This Arabic name means 'resplendence' or 'brilliance'. **Saniyya** has the same meaning.

Sanchia *f*

A Provençal and Spanish name derived from the Latin *sanctus*, meaning 'holy'. The name came to England in the 13th century when the Earl of Cornwall married Sanchia, daughter of the Count of Provence.

Sandip *f*

This Indian name means 'beautiful'.

Sandra *f*

This is a short form of Italian **Alessandra** (see ALEXANDRA), which is now used as a name in its own right. **Sandie** or **Sandy** (also used for CASSANDRA) are pet forms. It also appears as **Sondra**, and the designer **Zandra** Rhodes uses an unusual alternative form.

Sandy see ALEXANDER, SANDRA

Saniyya see SANA

Sanjay *m*

From a Sanskrit word that means 'triumphant' but referring specifically to the charioteer of King Dhritarashtra in classic Hindu epics. The name was made familiar by Sanjay Ghandi, son of the former Indian Prime Minister, Indira Ghandi, and, more recently, in the UK through a character in the television series *East Enders*.

Saoirse *f*
This is a relatively modern Irish girl's name, currently popular, which is based on the Irish for 'freedom'. It is perhaps best translated as **Liberty**, a name that has been used over the centuries in many countries, particularly at times of political turmoil. Saoirse is pronounced 'seer-she', with the stress on the first syllable.

Sapphire see RUBY

Sara(h) *f*
Sarah comes from the Hebrew, meaning 'princess', and was the name of Abraham's wife in the Old Testament. **Sara** is the Greek form found in the New Testament. SALLY, **Sal** and **Sadie** started life as pet forms. In Ireland Sarah has been used to render the Irish **Sorcha** ('sorr-ha', the 'h' as in Scottish 'loch'), meaning 'bright', and **Saraid** ('sahr-it'), meaning 'excellent'.

Sarika *f*
An Indian name that refers to the 'koel' or 'black cuckoo'.

Sasha see SACHA

Saskia *f*
This was the name of the wife of the Dutch artist Rembrandt (1606–1669) whose paintings of her introduced the name to this country. It may be connected with the word for Saxon.

Saul *m*
From the Hebrew, meaning 'asked for (child)'. The name occurs in the Old Testament as that of the first king of Israel and in the New Testament as St Paul's name before his conversion to Christianity. It was first used as a first name in Britain in the 17th century.

Savannah *f*
The name of a river and city in the state of Georgia, used mainly in

the USA. The name comes from the Spanish term *sabana*, meaning a treeless plain. It can appear with spellings such as **Savana** or **Savanna**.

Sayyid, Sayyida see SYED

Scarlett *f*
The use of Scarlett as a first name is entirely the result of the success of Margaret Mitchell's novel *Gone with the Wind* (1936) and the subsequent film. In the novel, Scarlett O'Hara is given her grandmother's maiden name as a middle name but is always called by it. **Scarlet** is also used.

Scott *m*
This is a surname, meaning 'a Scot', used as a first name. It is particularly popular in the UK.

Seamas *m*
This is an Irish form of JAMES. It is also spelt **Seamus**, and the Gaelic form is **Seumas** or **Seumus**. **Shamus** is a modern phonetic version of the name. See also HAMISH.

Sean *f* and ms
The Irish form of JOHN, developed from the French Jean. It is also spelt as it is pronounced, **Shaun** or **Shawn**. **Shane** is a variant form. Shawn and Sean are used now for girls, along with **Shawna** and **Shawndelle**. See also SHANAE.

Sebastian *m*
From the Latin *Sebastianus*, meaning 'man of Sebasta'. The name of this town in Asia Minor was derived from the Greek, meaning 'majestic' or 'venerable'. St Sebastian was executed by being shot with arrows, and his martyrdom was a particularly popular subject for paintings. The name took hold in Spain and in France, where it was shortened to **Bastien** (currently popular with French parents), and then taken by fishermen across the Channel from Brittany to the West Country, where the form **Bastian** took root. The name did not spread to the rest of Britain until modern times, but

Sebastian is now reasonably common, having the short forms **Seb** and **Sebbie**.

Seeta, Seetha see SITA

Sejal *f*
This Indian name means 'river' or 'water'.

Selina *f*
The etymology of this name is disputed. One possible derivation is from Selene, the Greek moon goddess; another is from the Latin name Coelina, from *caelum*, meaning 'heaven', through the French form **Céline**. **Celina** is also found, and **Selena** is currently the preferred spelling in the USA.

Selma *f*
Selma is the name of a castle in James Macpherson's 18th-century poems about Scottish legendary heroes. When the poems were translated into Swedish, the translator failed to make the meaning clear, and it was understood by many Swedish readers to be a personal name; some then used it for their children. Immigrants took the name to the USA, where it is still more common than in Britain. It is now sometimes spelt **Zelma**.

Seonaid see SHEENA

Serena *f*
This is a Latin word meaning 'calm, serene (woman)'. **Serenity** has also been used for girls.

Serge *m*
Sergius was a Roman family name, probably Etruscan in origin and therefore of unknown meaning. The name became used by Christians in honour of Saint Sergius, a 4th-century Roman officer martyred in Syria. In Russia St Sergius of Radonezh (*c*.1314–1392) became one of the country's most famous saints, which led to widespread use of the name **Sergei**. Russian emigrants, particularly White Russians fleeing communism at the beginning of the 20th

century, settled in France where the name was adapted to Serge and embraced with enthusiasm.

Seth *m*
This is a biblical name, meaning 'appointed', which was given to the third son of Adam and Eve.

Seumas, Seumus see SEAMAS

Seymour *m*
This, like names such as HOWARD and NEVILLE, is another aristo-cratic surname adopted as a boy's name. The surname comes from the town of Saint-Maur in Normandy, which in turn gets its name from the parish church, which is dedicated to St Maurus. Who this is is not known, but his name is simply the Latin for 'Moor', that is to say, a North African, the same word that gives us the name MAURICE.

Shahid *m*, **Shahida(h)** *f*
An Arabic name that means 'witness' or 'martyr'.

Shahin *m*
An Arabic name that means 'falcon'. **Shaheen** is a variant spelling.

Shaina *f*
From a Yiddish word meaning 'beautiful', Shaina is also found as **Shayna**, **Sheyna** or **Cheyna**.

Shakil *m*, **Shakila** *f*
These are Arabic names meaning 'beautiful, handsome'. They can also be spelt **Shakeel**, **Shakeela**, and among English speakers take forms such as **Shaquil(le)** and **Shaquilla(h)**. The basketball star Shaquille O'Neal made the name widely known in the USA.

Shakir *m*, **Shakira** *f*
This is an Arabic name meaning 'grateful'. The Colombian-Leba-nese singer Shakira has made the name widely known and use is increasing in the UK, although it is in decline in the USA. **Zshakira** is an unusual alternative form.

Sham see SHYAM

Shamina(h) *f*
An Arabic name from a word meaning 'scent' or 'flavour'.

Shamus see SEAMAS

Shanae *f*
A mainly African-American name, making use of the now fashionable prefix 'Sha-'. It seems to be an invented name of no special meaning, its sound being more important. It is also spelt **Shanay** and **Shanaye**.

Shane see JOHN, SEAN

Shanel(le), Shannel see CHANEL

Shani see SIAN

Shania *f*
Although this is regarded by some as a feminine form of SEAN, the singer Shania Twain, who has popularised the name, regards it as from the Native American Ojibwa language, meaning 'I'm on my way'. It has particularly attracted parents in Australia. **Shainya** is also found.

Shanice *f*
An African-American blend of the fashionable 'Sha-' prefix and JANICE. The name has been given publicity by the singer Shanice Wilson, who uses only her first name as her stage name. Spellings such as **Chaniece** or **Chanise** are also found. **Shaniqua** (**Shanika**) is a similar blend of Sha- and MONICA.

Shannon *f* and *m*
This is the Irish river and place name, meaning 'the old one', which has become a popular first name in recent years. It is less common for boys. **Shanna** can be seen as either a variant of this or of SEAN or SHANAE.

Shante, Shanti see ASHANTI

Shaquil(le), Shaquilla(h) see SHAKIL

Shantal see CHANTAL

Sharad *m*, **Sharada** *f*
From an Indian word for 'autumn'. An alternative feminine form is **Sharadini**. **Sharadchandra** (*m*) means 'autumn moon'. **Sharadindu**, also for boys, has a similar meaning.

Sharif *m*, **Sharifa(h)** *f*
This Arabic name means 'eminent' or 'honourable'. It is also used as a title for descendants of the Prophet Mohammed.

Shardai, Sharday see SADE

Sharlene see CHARLENE

Sharlott see CHARLOTTE

Sharmaine see CHARMAINE

Sharon *f*
In the Bible Sharon, which means 'the plain', is an area of rich natural beauty and to compare a woman to it came to be a great compliment. It has been widely used as a first name only since the 20th century, although there are earlier uses of it as a man's name. It is occasionally spelt **Sharron**. **Shari** is a pet form.

Shaun(a) see SEAN

Shaunti see ASHANTI

Shawndelle, Shawn see SEAN

Shay see SHEA

Shayla, Shaylee, Sheela see SHEILA

Shayna see SHAINA

Shea *f* and *m*
An Irish surname meaning 'descendant of the fortunate one' now used as a first name. **Shay**, brought to public attention in the UK by

the footballer Shay Given, can be a form of this name or a shortening of **Shamus** (see SEAMAS).

Sheba see BATHSHEBA

Sheena *f*
This is a phonetic form of **Sine**, the Gaelic for JANE. An alternative form of Jane is **Siubhan**, which in Irish becomes **Siobhan**, with phonetic spellings **Shevaun** and **Chevonne**. **Shona**, the Scottish form of JANET, comes from the same root and is a phonetic form of **Seonaid**, in Irish **Sinead** (shin-aid).

Sheila *f*
A phonetic spelling of **Sile**, the Irish form of CECILIA. It can also be spelt **Shelagh**, **Shiela** and **Sheela**. In the USA it has developed the forms **Shayla** and **Shaylee**.

Shelby *f*
An English place name and surname. The original meaning was probably 'settlement with willow trees'. Its use as a first name started in the USA and was sparked by a character in the 1989 film *Steel Magnolias*.

Shelley *f*
This is a pet form of MICHELLE and RACHEL as well as being a variant of the name SHIRLEY. From the 1940s the name was brought to public attention by the actress Shelley Winters.

Sheree, Sherrie, Sherry see CHERIE

Sheril, Sheryl see CHERYL

Shevaun see SHEENA

Sheyna see SHAINA

Shiela see SHEILA

Shirin *f*
The beautiful Shirin, whose name in Persian means 'charming,

sweet', is an important character in Middle Eastern legend. It is also found as **Shirrin** and **Shireen**.

Shirley *f*
This was originally a place name meaning 'shire meadow'. From this it became a surname in Yorkshire and elsewhere. It was primarily a boy's name until Charlotte Brontë started the fashion for it as a girl's name in her novel *Shirley* (1849). See also SHELLEY.

Shiva *m*
The name of the Hindu god, from the Sanskrit meaning 'benign'. Similar names are **Shivaji**, **Shivesh**, **Shivlal**, **Shivraj** and **Shivshankar**, which mean 'Lord Shiva'.

Shlomo see SOLOMON

Sholto *m*
This is an old Scottish name, traditionally used in the Douglas family. It is a form of the Gaelic name **Sìoltach**, which means 'sower', with the implied sense of 'fruitful'.

Shona see SHEENA

Shree, Shri see SRI

Shrikant see SRIKANT

Shyam *m*, **Shyama** *f*
From the Sanskrit for 'dark' but identified with KRISHNA. In some parts of India the male form becomes **Sham**. The feminine form, **Shyama**, is a name of the goddess DURGA. Similar names for girls, with a basic meaning of 'dusky', include **Shyamal**, **Shyamala**, **Shyamalendu**, **Shyamali**, **Shyamalika**, **Shyamalima**, **Shyamari** and **Shyamasri**.

Shyann see CHEYENNE

Sian *f*
This is the Welsh form of JANE, properly spelt **Siân**. **Siani(e)** is a pet form that may appear as **Shani**.

Sibyl, Sibylla see SYBIL

Sidney, Sydney f and m

This is a surname used as a first name from at least the beginning of the 18th century. The spelling **Sydney** did not appear until the 19th century, and the city in Australia was named after Viscount Sydney, who was then Secretary of State. The short form is **Sid**, and in the UK these are considered boys' names. In the 18th century girls were given surnames as first names more often than was usual until very recently, and Sydney as a girl's name dates from this. It has also been considered a form of the Latin name **Sidonia** ('woman of Sidon'), which became **Sidonie** in French and **Sidony** in English. In the USA Sydney is more common as a female name and can appear as **Sydnee** or **Sidni(e)**.

Sienna f

Like FLORENCE, this is the name of an Italian city that has come to be used as a first name in recent years. The Italian spelling, **Siena**, is also used.

Sierra f

The Spanish word for a mountain range used as a first name in the USA, although possibly, because of its association with automobiles, not destined to spread to the UK. The situation is complicated in the USA by the fact that **Ciara**, a feminine form of KIERAN, is a brand of perfume there which is also used as a first name and pronounced in the same way as Sierra. Spellings such as **Cierra** are also found.

Sigourney f

The actress Sigourney Weaver chose to call herself Sigourney while still a child, inspired by the character Sigourney Howard in Scott Fitzgerald's 1925 novel *The Great Gatsby*. Fitzgerald in turn is thought to have been inspired by the name of Lydia Huntley Sigourney (1791–1865), one of the earliest American women to earn her living by writing, although the name was already in use when Fitzgerald was writing, and it may be no coincidence that there was a prominent New York socialite at the time called Sigourney Thayer.

Silas see SILVESTER

Sile see SHEILA

Silvester, Sylvester *m*
The Latin for 'wood-dweller'. There have been three popes of this name, which was quite common in both forms in the Middle Ages. It has been shortened to **Sly**. The New Testament name **Silas** is probably a form of Silvester. Like so many names popular with the Puritans, Silas is showing signs of coming back into fashion. **Sylvestra** and **Sylvana** are rare female forms.

Silvia, Sylvia *f*
This is the Latin word meaning '(woman) of the wood'. Rhea Silvia was the mother of Romulus and Remus, the founders of Rome. This may have been the reason why the name was adopted during the Renaissance in Italy. Like other classical names, it came to England in Elizabethan times. Shakespeare used it in *Two Gentlemen of Verona*, and this probably gave rise to its use in Britain. The French **Silvie** or **Sylvie** is also used as a pet form.

Simon *m*, **Simone** *f*
This is the better-known English form of the New Testament **Simeon**, the name of the man who blessed the baby Jesus in the Temple. The popularity of Simon in the Middle Ages was because of Simon Peter, the Apostle, whose popularity was great at that period. The short form is **Sim**. **Simone** is the feminine form taken from the French.

Sine, Sinead, Siobhan see SHEENA

Sioltach see SHOLTO

Sion see JOHN

Siriol *f*
This is a Welsh name meaning 'friendly'. It is also found as **Sirol**.

Sis, Sisley, Sissy see CECILIA

Sita *f*
From the Sanskrit for 'furrow', the reference being to the goddess who personifies agriculture and is wife to Rama. **Seeta** and **Seetha** are other spellings of the name.

Siubhan see SHEENA

Sive see SABINA

Skye, Skyler *f* and *m*
Skye is the name of the Scottish island used as a fashionable name, comparable to the older use of IONA. It is currently well used in Scotlland for girls. The name's associations with the word 'sky' may have helped its rise, and it is sometimes found as **Sky**. The same sound may have helped make the Dutch surname **Skyler**, 'scholar', a popular first name in the USA, for it is often shortened to Sky. This, in the original Dutch form **Schuyler**, has been in use since at least the late 19th century. It is the surname of a family prominent in New York since the mid-17th century and was originally used in honour of Philip Schuyler (1733–1804), congressman, senator and hero of the American Revolution.

Sly see SILVESTER

Sneha(l) *f*, **Snehin** *m*
From a Sanskrit word that originally meant 'oil' but later came to mean 'friendly affection'. Snehal is the form with the meaning 'friendly'. The male form, Snehin, means 'friend'.

Sol see MARY

Solomon *m*
The Hebrew name **Shlomo**, borne by one of the most famous kings of Israel, became Solomon in the English translations of the Bible. The name means 'peaceful', so SALOME is the feminine equivalent. Solomon is being used increasingly in the USA and has short forms **Sol** and **Solly**. The Arabic forms of the name are under SALMA.

Somhairle see SAMUEL

Sonal *f*
An Indian name meaning 'golden'. **Sonali** and **Sonika** are variants.

Sondra see SANDRA

Sonia *f*
This is a Russian pet form of SOPHIA, and its use in Britain is 20th-century, perhaps a result of the novel of this name by Stephen McKenna, published in 1917. **Sonya** and **Sonja** are other spellings of the name.

Sonika see SONAL

Sophia, Sophie *f*
From the Greek, meaning 'wisdom'. Hagia Sophia ('Holy Wisdom') is a common dedication for Orthodox churches, as in the case of the great cathedral at Constantinople. This led to Sophia's use as a name in Greece. The name spread through Hungary to Germany and then to England when George I became king. Both his mother and his wife had the name. **Sophie** is the anglicised form that is currently the more popular in the UK and Australia, although **Sophia** is preferred in the USA. The forms **Sophy** and **Sofia** are also used. See SONIA.

Soraya *f*
This comes from the Persian for 'princess'.

Sorcha see SARAH

Sorley see SAMUEL

Spencer *m*
This name, originally a surname given to the steward of a great household, but later an aristocratic surname, was made famous by the actor Spencer Tracy.

Spring see AUTUMN

Sri *f*
This Indian name is from the Sanskrit, meaning 'light' or 'beauty', later developing into 'majesty' and used as a title as well as a name. Sri is one of the names of LAKSHMI, goddess of prosperity and beauty. **Shree**, **Shri** and **Sree** are variants.

Srikant *m*
From the Sanskrit words meaning 'beautiful throat', a name applied to the god Shiva. **Shrikant** is an alternative spelling.

Stacey, Stacy *f* and *m*
This is a pet form that has become popular as an independent name. For men it was a short form of EUSTACE; as a woman's name it was originally short for ANASTASIA. Currently, it is mostly given to girls, sometimes in the form of **Stacie**.

Stanley *m*
This was originally a surname derived from an old Anglo-Saxon place name meaning 'stony field'. It was used as a first name from the mid-19th century, partly because of its association with Sir Henry Morton Stanley, the famous explorer. It has the short form **Stan**.

Stefan, Steffan see STEPHEN

Stella *f*
This is the Latin word for 'star'. Use stems from its literary associations. An early example was in Sir Philip Sidney's *Astrophel and Stella* (1591). Then, in the early 18th century, Jonathan Swift used it as a pet name in letters to Esther Johnson. The French form **Estella** was popularised by Charles Dickens when he used it for the main female character in his novel *Great Expectations* (1861). **Estelle** is another French form. These share the short forms of ESTHER.

Stephen, Steven *m*, Stephanie *f*
From the Greek *stephanos*, meaning 'crown' or 'wreath'. The laurel wreath was the highest honour a man could attain in the classical

world. **Stephen** was a common personal name in Ancient Greece and was borne by the very first Christian martyr. **Steven** is the alternative spelling. **Steve** and **Stevie** are the modern pet forms. There is a Welsh form, **Steffan**, and also a Continental form, **Stefan**. The female form, **Stephanie**, has variants such as **Stefanie**, **Steffany** and the Italian **Stefania**.

Storm, Stormy *m* and *f*
This words have been used in recent years for both sexes, with Storm slightly more common for boys, Stormy for girls. **Cloudy** and **Cloudie** have also been recorded, although some cases could be pet forms of CLAUDIA.

Stuart *m*
From the Old English *sti weard*, an official who looked after animals kept for food. Although it has changed its meaning somewhat, it survives as 'steward' today. The co-founder of the Scottish royal house of Stewart or Stuart in the 14th century was William the Steward, who married the king's daughter and whose son later became king. **Stewart** is a common alternative, and **Stuert** is also used. The name is used most often by those of Scottish descent.

Suhayl *m*
An Arabic name that refers to a bright star, Canopus, in the southern constellation Carina. **Suhail** is a variant.

Sujan *m*
A Hindi name that means 'honest'.

Sumayyah *f*
A Muslim name of uncertain meaning, borne by the first martyr in the cause of Islam. It also occurs as **Sumaya**, **Sumayah** and **Sumayya**.

Summer see AUTUMN

Sunil *m*
This is a rather puzzling name, as it comes from an obscure, ancient Sanskrit word meaning 'very dark blue'. Its use as a first name is

modern. It has become a popular choice for parents in India and is sometimes interpreted as 'sapphire'. The form **Sunila** can be used for girls.

Sunita *f*

This name comes from the Sanskrit for 'of good conduct' or 'righteous' and was the name of a princess in epic poetry who was the daughter of the king of Bengal. **Suniti** is another form of the name.

Sunni see SURINDER

Suraj *m*

This Hindi name means 'the sun'.

Surinder *f* and *m*

This is a development of the name INDRA and can be interpreted as meaning 'mightiest of the gods'. It is also found in the form **Surendra**. It is less often used for girls than for boys, and as a boy's name can be shortened to **Sunni**.

Susan, Susanna(h) f

Shushannah is Hebrew for 'lily' and **Susanna(h)** was the earliest form of this name in England, occurring in the Middle Ages and becoming quite common after the Reformation. **Susan** was adopted in the 18th century. In the 20th century the French forms, **Suzanne** and **Suzette**, have also been used by English speakers, and spellings such as **Susana** and **Suzanna** have been found. **Sue**, **Sukey**, **Susie** and **Suzy** are pet forms.

Sven *m*

This is a Swedish name from the Old Norse for 'boy'.

Swan see RAVEN

Sybil *f*

In classical times the Sibyls were prophetesses, and some of them were supposed to have foretold the coming of Christ. Because of this, despite the pagan associations, **Sibylla** came to be used as a Christian name, the Normans bringing it with them to England.

Sybil or **Sibyl** had a revival in the second half of the 19th century after Benjamin Disraeli published his political novel of that name in 1845. The actress **Cybill** Shepherd has introduced another form of the name.

Sydney see SIDNEY

Syed *m*
This is a common way of spelling the Arabic name **Sayyid**, meaning 'noble' or 'master'. Its feminine form is **Sayyida**.

Sylvana, Sylvester, Sylvestra see SILVESTER

Sylvia, Sylvie see SILVIA

Syril see CYRIL

Tabitha *f*
This name derives from the Aramaic word for 'gazelle'. In the New Testament it is the name of a Christian woman of Joppa who showed great charity towards the poor and was raised from the dead by St Peter. The Greek translation of her name is **Dorcas**. **Tabatha** is a modern spelling of the name.

Tacey *f*
The Latin **Tacita**, 'quiet one', was chosen by religious parents in the past who wanted their daughters to conform to the medieval Church's injunction that women should be silent in church. This developed into various forms of the name, the most common of which is **Tacey**, but which includes **Taci**, **Tacie** and **Tacy**.

Tadhg see TIMOTHY

Taffy see DAVID

Tahir *m*
An Arabic name that means 'pure' and 'virtuous'.

Taja see ANASTASIA

Talia see NATALIE

Taliesin see CERIDWEN

Tallulah *f*
This name is well known from the American actress Tallulah Bankhead (1903–1968). She was named after her grandmother, who was in turn named after a place, Tallulah Falls in Georgia. The place name is said to come from a Native American word meaning 'leaping waters'. The name was given further publicity by a character in the 1976 film and musical *Bugsy Malone*.

Tally, Talya see NATALIE

Tam see THOMAS

Tamara *f*
Tamara is the Russian form of the biblical name **Tamar** (also found as **Thamar**), which is Hebrew for 'date palm'. Tamara was the name of a famous Russian queen and remains a popular name in Russia. A pet form is TAMMY.

Tammy f
A pet form of names such as TAMARA and TAMSIN, now used as an independent name. In 1957 a film called *Tammy* and a song of that name, which was the best-selling record in the USA, started a vogue for the name's use. It is also a Scottish form of Tommy (see THOMAS). **Tamia** (**Tamya**) is probably a blend of Tammy and TANYA, but **Tamika**, fashionable in the USA in the 1960s is a form of the Japanese name **Tamiko**, based on the word for 'people'.

Tamsin f
This is a West Country female form of THOMAS. It can also be found as **Tamsine, Tamzin** and **Tamzen**. It comes from **Thomasin** or **Thomasine**, which have been used since the Middle Ages. **Thomasina** is an old latinised version that was revived in the 19th century. TAMMY is a short form of these names.

Tanisha *f*
This name is used almost exclusively by African-Americans and seems to be a Hausa name from West Africa, meaning 'girl born on Monday'. It comes in a variety of forms, including **Taneisha, Tanesha, Taniesha, Tenecia, Tenesha** and **Tenisha**.

Tanith *f*
The name of a Phoenician goddess of love that has recently come into occasional use as a first name. It can also take the form **Tanit**.

Tanner *m*
A surname, from the job, used as a first name.

Tansy see ANASTASIA

Tanya *f*
Tanya or **Tania** is a pet form of **Tatiana**, which has been popular in Russia for many years, inspired by St Tatiana, a martyr revered by the Orthodox Church. **Tonya** is also found although, properly, this is the Russian pet form of ANTONIA.

Tara *f*
Tara is the name of the hill where the ancient High Kings of Ireland held court and which plays an important part in Irish legend. It has been used as a first name only since the end of the 19th century. It is occasionally used for boys. As an Indian name it means 'star'.

Taryn *f*, **Tarun** *m*
These are part of a group of names with varied origins. **Taryn**, as a girl's name, was coined by the actors Tyrone Power and Linda Christianson for their daughter, also an actor, Taryn Power, in 1953, and use spread after she started appearing in films in the 1970s. **Tarun** is an Indian boy's name, from the Sanskrit for 'young, tender'. In addition, the American author Lloyd Alexander coined the name **Taran** (probably based on TARA) for the hero of his Celtic fantasy novels, *The Chronicle of Prydain* (1964–1979), while **Torin** (*m*) comes from the Irish for 'chief'. Many other names with variants of these sounds have appeared in recent years.

Tasha see NATALIE

Tashan *m* and *f*, **Tashana** *f*
While Tashan is a common Turkish surname, as a first name these appear to be new creations, in use since about the 1970s. Tashan has been given publicity as the name of an American singer.

Tasia, Tassia see ANASTASIA

Tasnim *f*
An Arabic name meaning 'fountain of paradise'. It is also found as **Tasneem**.

Tatiana see TANYA

Tatum *f*
This name, which seems to have been coined for the actress Tatum O'Neal (b. 1963), comes from a surname that in turn comes from an Old English place name meaning 'homestead of a man named Tata'.

Tavia, Tavie, Tavian, Tavius see OCTAVIA

Taylor *f* and *m*
This English surname, indicating an ancestor who was a tailor, has been made familiar as a first name by the American author (Janet Miriam) Taylor Caldwell, who chose to use it as her pen name in order to obscure her gender. In the UK it is most likely to be found used for boys, but in North America and Australia, where the form **Tayla** is popular, it is now mostly used for girls. The more exotic spellings it takes shade into forms of TYLER.

Tea see TIA

Teagan see TEGAN

Tecla see THECLA

Ted, Teddy see EDMUND, EDWARD, THEODORE

Teena see TINA

Tegan *f*
This is an old Cornish name meaning 'lovely little thing' or 'ornament'. The name first got more general exposure in the 1980s in the television series *Dr Who*, when it was used for an Australian air hostess who became involved in the doctor's adventures. The name seems to have reappeared in the form **Tiegan** in the Australian soap opera *Home and Away*. Tegan is pronounced with a short 'e' sound, but Tiegan with the sound of 'tea', hence the common US spelling **Teagan**. The word *teg*, meaning 'pretty, fair', is found in Welsh as well as Cornish, for they are closely related, and there are

a number of Welsh names that use it, of which **Tegwen**, 'pretty and fair' (masculine **Tegwyn**), is the most common.

Tejal *f*
A Sanskrit name meaning 'lustrous'.

Tekla see THECLA

Tenecia, Tenesha, Tenisha see TANISHA

Terence *m*
This is from the Latin *Terentius*, the name of a famous Roman comic playwright. Short forms are **Terry** and **Tel**. It is now also found in the forms **Terance**, **Terrance**, **Terrence** and **Terrell** (although this could also be from the name of an American city). It is a comparatively modern name, having come from Ireland where it was used to transliterate the native **Turlough** ('tar-loch', pronounced as if Scottish), meaning 'instigator'. Terry as an independent name can also come from **Theodoric** (see DEREK).

Teresa, Theresa f
The meaning of this name is obscure. The first recorded **Theresa** was the wife of the 5th-century St Paulinus and was responsible for his conversion. The name was for a long time confined to Spain until the fame of St **Teresa** of Avila (1515–1582) spread the name to all Roman Catholic countries. It did not become common in the UK until the 18th century. It is often abbreviated to **Tess**, **Tessa** or **Tessie**. The form **Teri** or **Terry**, shared with some boys' names, is also found. A variant is TRACY. The French form, **Thérèse**, is also found occasionally.

Terrance, Terrel, Terrence see TERENCE

Tevin *m*
This recent name is probably a development of KEVIN, although some would link it to a French surname, Thevin, which comes from an old form of STEPHEN. The Texas-born singer Tevin Campbell has made the name widely known.

Thaddeau, Thady see TIMOTHY

Thamar see TAMARA

Thea see DOROTHY, THEODORA

Thecla *f*
St Thecla, whose name means 'God's glory', was the first female martyr, just as St STEPHEN was the first male one. The name was popular in the Middle Ages but is now an unusual choice. It can also be spelt **Tecla, Tekla** and **Thekla**.

Thelma *f*
Like MAVIS, this name was introduced in the 19th century as a character in a novel by the writer Marie Corelli and spread quickly throughout the country. There is a Greek word *thelema*, meaning 'will', which may have had some influence on its development.

Theodore *m*, **Theodora** *f*
From the Greek meaning 'gift of God'. There are 28 saints called Theodore in the Church calendar. In England the name did not become general until the 19th century, but in Wales it has long been used as a form of **Tudur** or **Tudor**, which in fact probably comes from a Celtic name. The usual abbreviation in North America is **Ted** or **Teddy**, as in the case of President Theodore Roosevelt who gave his name to the teddy bear. In England **Theo** (sometimes used as an independent name) is a more common abbreviation. The feminine form has been used since the 17th century. It is usually abbreviated to **Theo** (sometimes used as an independent name), **Thea** and **Dora**. The rarer **Theodosia** has a similar meaning.

Theodoric see DEREK

Theophania see TIFFANY

Theophilus see AMADEA

Theresa, Thérèse see TERESA

Thierry see DEREK

Thomas *m*
From the Aramaic nickname meaning 'twin'. It was first given by Jesus to an Apostle named Judas to distinguish him from Judas Iscariot. The abbreviation **Tom** appears in the Middle Ages. **Tam** and TAMMY are the Scottish pet forms. The use of **Tommy** as a nickname for a British private soldier goes back to the 19th century, when the enlistment form had on it the specimen signature 'Thomas Atkins'. Thomas has been one of the three top boys' names for some years in the UK and is widely popular elsewhere.

Thomasin, Thomasina, Thomasine see TAMSIN

Thora *f*
From the Norse, meaning 'Thor-battle'. Its earlier form was **Thyra**. Thor was the god of thunder in Norse mythology, and he also gave his name to 'Thursday'. It has a long history of use in Northern Britain, but Thora is now a rare name, although well known from the actress Dame Thora Hird (1913–2003).

Thurstan see DUSTIN

Thyra see THORA

Tia *f*
Tia is a Spanish word for 'auntie', but although its use in such contexts and the liqueur named Tia Maria may have helped its spread, it is probably best regarded as a pet or short form of such fashionable names as **Tiana** and **Tiara** (see KIARA, RUBY) or **Tierra**; or of names ending in '-tia'. It appears in numerous spellings, including **Téa** (which can also be a pet form of Teodora, an Italian form of THEODORA) and **Tya**. It has been used for some time in the USA, but has only come to be used fairly recently in the UK, although gaining popularity.

Tiara see KIARA, RUBY

Tiegan see TEGAN

Tierra see TIA

Tiesha see LETITIA

Tiffany *f*
Originally a pet form of the name **Theophania**, from the Greek, meaning 'the manifestation of God'. **Tifainé** was the Old French form, and this name was given to girls born at the time of the Epiphany, the words having the same meaning. The names were fairly rare until recently when Tiffany became popular, probably through the fame of the New York jeweller's, Tiffany's, and the success of the 1961 film *Breakfast at Tiffany's*.

Tilak *m*
An Indian name that refers to the *tika* or *tilak*, the red mark worn as a caste mark or decoration by Hindus. It is also placed as a blessing on the forehead of an honoured guest.

Tilda, Tilly see MATILDA

Timothy *m*
Timotheos is an old Greek name meaning 'honouring God'. Its use as a first name is because of Timothy, the companion of St Paul. It was not used widely until the 16th century when many classical and biblical names became much more common. **Tim** and **Timmy** are the abbreviations. **Timothea** is a rare female form. In Ireland Timothy has long been used as an equivalent for the native **Tadhg** ('tieg'), which means 'poet', although this also appears disguised as **Thaddeus** (from Aramaic 'praise') and its short form, **Thady**.

Tina *f*
Originally a short form for girls' names ending in '-tina', commonest of which is Christina (see CHRISTINE). It is now used in its own right. **Teena** is also used.

Titus *m*
This is a Latin name of unknown meaning. Two well-known holders of the name were a follower of St Paul and, in contrast, the infamous Titus Oates, an English conspirator and perjurer in the 17th

century. It is probably best known today as the name of the hero of
Mervyn Peake's *Gormenghast* books.

Toby *m*
Toby is the English form of the Greek **Tobias**, itself derived from the
Hebrew name that means 'the Lord is good'. The story of Tobias
and the Angel, which is told in the Apocrypha, was a favourite one
in the Middle Ages. Punch's dog Toby is named after the dog that
accompanied Tobias on his travels. Toby is increasingly used in the
UK.

Tod, Todd *m*
Originally a surname meaning 'fox', now used as a first name.

Toinette see ANTHONY

Tom, Tommy see THOMAS

Toni, Tonio, Tony see ANTHONY

Tonya see ANTONIA, TANYA

Torcall see TORQUIL

Tori, Toria, Torie see VICTORIA

Torin see TARYN

Tormod see NORMAN

Torquil *m*
This is the English rendering of the Norse name *Thorketill* ('Thor's
cauldron'). The first element is the name of the Norse thunder god,
Thor. The original became **Torcall** in Gaelic, which was anglicised
into Torquil. It is used in Scotland, especially in the Outer Hebrides
and among the Macleod family, and it has occasionally been given
in England.

Totty see CHARLOTTE

Toya(h) see LATOYA

Tracy *f* and *m*
This popular girl's name seems to have started life as a pet form of
TERESA. It is also found as **Tracey** and **Tracie**. Its beginnings as an
independent name were probably helped by the use of the surname Tracy (from a French place name) as a boy's name, particularly as at the time when it first became popular Spencer Tracy
(1900–1967) was a well-known film star. **Trace** is used as a boy's
name and as a pet form of the girl's.

Travis *m*
A surname, notably that of William B. Travis (1809–1836), US commander at the Battle of the Alamo, used as a first name. It comes
from the French word *traverser*, meaning 'to cross', and would have
been given originally to a toll-collector.

Trevor *m*
From the Welsh **Trefor**, meaning 'great homestead'. Trevor is the
English spelling. **Trev** is the short form.

Trey *m*
Trey is an old word for 'three' in card games and has been used,
particularly in the USA, as a pet name for the third bearer of the
same name, to distinguish him from his grandfather and father
(often called 'Junior'). More recently it has been used as a given
name, when it can also appear as **Tre** and (sometimes for girls) **Trea**.
Tricia, Trisha see PATRICIA

Trinity *f* and *m*
This vocabulary word has recently become popular as a girl's name
in the USA and is also found used for boys. **Trinidad**, which means
the same in Spanish, has a longer history of use. Both can be shortened to **Trini**.

Triss see BEATRICE

Tristan, Tristram *m*
This is a name of obscure origin, possibly Pictish. It appears as the
name of the noble hero of the medieval love stories of Tristram and

Isolda. When Tristram is escorting Isolda to be married to his uncle they unknowingly drink a magic love potion intended for the newly-weds and are doomed to adulterous love until their tragic deaths. **Tristran** is also found. It is currently well used in the USA, where it also appears as **Tristen, Tristian, Tristin, Triston** and **Trystan**. **Trixie** see Beatrice

Troy *m*
Troy was the ancient city in Asia Minor besieged by the Greeks for ten years. Its use as a first name was boosted in the 1960s by the actor Troy Donahue (1936–2001, given name Merle Johnson). It has been popular in Australia and is well used in the USA.

Tru, Trudi, Trudie, Trudy see Gertrude

Tudor, Tudur see Theodore

Tulsi *m*, Tulasi *f*
This Indian name is from the Sanskrit word meaning 'sacred basil', a plant that symbolises Vishnu. Tulasi, the girl's form, is also the name of a goddess based on the same word.

Turlough see Terence

Tya see Tia

Tyler *f* and *m*
A surname, from the job, used as a first name. It has been popular in the USA for some years and is now well used worldwide. It can be shortened to **Ty**. **Tyla** is a feminine form.

Tyrone m
The name of the Irish county, which means 'Eoghan's land', used as a first name. It was used in the past by the actor Tyrone Power (1913–1958) in the USA and by the British theatre director Sir Tyrone Guthrie (1900–1971). **Ty** is the short form, although Guthrie was known to his friends as Tony. **Tyree**, another Celtic district name, is also used. **Tyra** is used as a female equivalent. See also Taryn.

Ulick see ULYSSES, WILLIAM

Ulysses *m*
This is the Latin name for the Greek hero Odysseus, whose tale is told in Homer's *Odyssey*. Although little used in England, Scotland or Wales, it has been used in Ireland as an equivalent for **Ulick**, an Irish form of WILLIAM. In the USA, where it also appears as **Ulises**, use of the name probably comes from the fame of General Ulysses S. Grant (1822–1885), hero of the Battle of Appomattox and the 18th American president.

Uma *f*
A Sanskrit name of a goddess, meaning 'flax, turmeric', which has been made internationally famous by the actress Uma Thurman.

Umar see OMAR

Una *f*
The etymology of this ancient Irish name is obscure. It is found in the forms **Oonagh** or **Oona** (pronounced 'oo-na'), both of which are also found in Scotland. **Juno**, influenced by the name of the Roman queen of the gods, is another Irish form, best known from Sean O'Casey's play *Juno and the Paycock* (1924). The Elizabethan poet Edmund Spenser took the Irish name Una and gave it its Latin sense, 'one, unity', in his epic poem *The Faerie Queene*.

Unice see EUNICE

Unity *f*
This is one of the abstract virtue names that became quite common among Puritans after the Reformation. It is rarely found today.
Ursula *f*

From the Latin, meaning 'little she-bear'. The name was fairly common in the Middle Ages on account of St Ursula, a 5th-century Cornish princess who, along with her companions, was murdered near Cologne while on a pilgrimage. The name had a revival after Mrs Craik chose it for her heroine in her popular novel, *John Halifax, Gentleman* (1856).

Uthman *m*

A Muslim name from an Arabic word meaning 'baby bustard'. Uthman was the son-in-law of the Prophet Mohammed. The Turkish form of the name, **Usman**, is also much used, although often westernised as **Osman**. The name of the Ottoman Empire derived from this name's Latin and Italian plural form.

Val see Perceval, Valentine, Valerie

Valentine *f* and *m*
From the Latin *valens*, 'strong' or 'healthy'. St Valentine was a 3rd-century Roman priest martyred on 14 February, the eve of the celebrations of the pagan goddess Juno, when lots were drawn to choose lovers. The feast was absorbed into the Christian calendar. **Valentina** is an alternative girl's form, **Valentin** a Continental masculine form currently popular in France. **Val** is a common diminutive, shared with Valerie.

Valerie *f*
This is the French form of the Roman family name Valeria, and was taken into use in Britain in the late 19th century. It comes from a word meaning 'to be in good health'. It has the short form **Val**.

Vanda see Wanda

Vanessa *f*
A name invented in the early 18th century by the writer Jonathan Swift as a pet name for Esther Vanhomrigh. He took the first syllable of her surname and added Essa, which was probably a pet form of Esther. Short forms are **Es(sa)** and **Ness(a)**.

Vanna see Gianna

Vaughn, Vaughan *m*
From the Welsh *fychan*, meaning 'small one'.

Velma *f*
A name of unknown origin, first used in the 1880s in the United States. It may be a form of **Wilma**, which is also found as **Vilma** (see

WILLIAM). It has recently come to public attention via the character of Velma Kelley in the musical and film *Chicago*.

Venetia *f*

The Latin name for the Italian city of Venice used as a first name. It was previously thought to have a connection with **Venus**, the Roman goddess of love, which in turn is occasionally used as a first name, as in the case of the American tennis player Venus Williams.

Vera *f*

This name has two possible derivations. One source is the Russian for 'faith', another is the Latin word meaning 'true'. It was used in English literature in the 19th century and became popular in Britain at the beginning of the 20th century. It is sometimes used as an abbreviation of VERONICA. See also VERENA.

Verena *f*

The name of a rather obscure 3rd-century saint. Its meaning is not known but may well come from the same source as VERA. St Verena lived in Switzerland and her name is popular there, but its use among English speakers probably owes something to the name's prominence in Henry James's novel *The Bostonians* (1886).

Vergil see VIRGIL

Verity *f*

From the Old English word for 'truth'. It was first used by the Puritans in the 17th century and has been quite common ever since. The variant **Verily** ('truly') is also found occasionally.

Vernon m

Richard de Vernon was a companion of William the Conqueror. The surname comes from a French place name that means 'alder grove'. It was not used as a first name until the 19th century, when many such aristocratic names were taken into general use. The unusual name **Verna** can be seen as a feminine form of Vernon, as from the Latin for 'spring' or as a pet form of names such as VERENA and VERONICA.

Veronica *f*

Traditionally, this name is said to come from the Latin *vera icon*, meaning 'a true image'. St Veronica wiped the sweat from Christ's face on His way to Calvary, and a 'true image' of his face was said to have been left on the cloth. It is more likely, however, that the name is a form of BERENICE, 'bringer of victory'. **Véronique** has long been popular in France, and from there the name reached Scotland in the late 17th century. It does not appear much in England before the late 19th century (see also VERA). **Roni** or **Ronee** can be found as short forms.

Veva see GENEVIEVE

Victor *m*

This is the Latin for 'conqueror'. Although it occurs in medieval England it was not common until the 19th century when it was adopted as a boy's form of VICTORIA. The commonest short form is **Vic**.

Victoria *f*

From the Latin for 'victory'. This name was hardly used in Britain until the reign of Queen Victoria, who was named after her German mother, but during her long reign it spread widely. In the recent past the name has been very popular and is often found in one of its short forms, **Vicky**, **Vickie**, **Vikki** and **Tori**, **Torie** or **Toria**. **Vita** and **Viti** and the nickname QUEENIE are also found.

Vida see DAVIDA

Vijay *m*, **Vijaya** *f*

This Indian name is from a Sanskrit word meaning 'victory'. The feminine form, Vijaya, is also applied to the goddess DURGA, wife of Shiva.

Vikesh *m*

A Hindi name that means 'the moon'.

Vilma see WILLIAM

Vina see DAVIDA

Vinay *m*, **Vinaya** *f*
An Indian name that means 'educating to act in a proper way'. For Buddhists it suggests the modest behaviour appropriate to a monk.

Vincent *m*
From the Latin for 'conquering'. There was a 3rd-century Spanish martyr of this name, and it occurs in English records from the 13th century. But the 17th-century St Vincent de Paul popularised the name when he founded the Vincentian Order of the Sisters of Charity. It became quite common in the 19th century. Its usual short form is **Vince**. The Continental forms **Vincente** and **Vincenzo** are also found.

Viola, Violet *f*
Viola is Latin for 'violet'. Although it does occur in the Middle Ages, the modern use of this name comes from Shakespeare, who gave it to the heroine of *Twelfth Night*. **Violette** and **Violetta** have also been used.

Viral *m*
This Indian name comes from the Sanskrit for 'priceless, rare'.

Virgil *m*
The name of the great Roman poet. The original spelling of his name was **Vergil**. The name has been more used in the USA than in Britain.

Virginia *f*
Although there was a Roman family called Virginus, the modern use of this name dates only from 1587. Sir Walter Raleigh had called his newly founded colony in North America Virginia, after Elizabeth I, the 'Virgin Queen', and the name Virginia was given to the first child born to the settlers there. **Ginny**, **Gini** or **Jinny** is a common pet form.

Vishal *m*, **Vishala** *f*

An Indian name that means 'immense, spacious'. For girls **Vishalakshi** is also used, with the meaning 'wide-eyed'.

Vita, Viti see VICTORIA

Vitus see GUY

Vivian, Vivien *f* and *m*

From the Latin *vivianus*, which means 'lively'. **Vivian** is now used for both sexes but was originally the masculine form, with **Vivien**, **Vivyan** or **Vyvyan** mostly used for girls. The French **Vivienne** is always female, as is **Viviana**. **Viv** is used for short.

Vonda see WANDA

Wade *m*

Another old surname, now used as a first name, particularly in the USA, where it can also be **Waide**. The surname can either come from someone who once lived by a ford (sometimes called a wade in the past) or came from a place named after its ford; or it can come from the vocabulary word. In English folklore there are traces of a great hero called Wade, famous for his boat and for his strength and brave deeds, which included killing a dragon.

Waldo see WALTER

Wallace *m*

From the surname of Sir William Wallace, the great Scottish patriot of the 13th century. The use of his surname as a first name started in the later 19th century. The surname comes from the same root that gives us the word 'Welsh', but which was once used of the British in the north as well. Another spelling of the name is **Wallis**, found in North America where it is used for both sexes. The short forms, **Wal** and **Wally**, are shared with WALTER.

Walter *m*

From the Old German Waldhar, meaning 'army ruler'. The name was very popular among the Normans and quickly became established in England. Sir Walter Raleigh is a very well-known later example, and he used the short form **Wat** for his son. **Walt**, **Wal** and **Wally** are more popular short forms in use today, and Walt is used as an independent name in North America. **Waldo** is a pet form of a number of German names that begin with the same element for 'rule, ruler' that is found in Walter.

Wanda *f*
This is a Polish girl's name that is probably connected with the word 'vandal'. Its wider use may have started when a novel of the same name by Ouida was published in 1883. **Vanda** and **Vonda** are both variants.

Waqar *m*
This Arabic name means 'dignity' or 'soberness'.

Warren *m*
From the surname, which can either be from an old German tribe name, Varin, or from a Norman place name meaning 'a game re-serve'. The Normans introduced the forms Warin and Guarin to England, and these led to the surnames Warren, Waring and Gar-net.

Warwick *m*
The name of the English town, which means 'houses by the weir', used as a surname and then as a first name. **Warrie** is a pet form.

Wasim *m*, **Wasimah** *f*
An Arabic name that means 'handsome' or 'graceful'. The feminine form, **Wasimah**, also means 'pretty'.

Wat see WALTER

Wayne *m*
This is a surname meaning 'cart' or 'cart-maker'. Its use as a first name is mainly because of the popularity of actor John Wayne (1907–1979).

Wendy *f*
This name was first used by James Barrie in *Peter Pan* (1904). The name started as 'Friendy-Wendy', a pet name for Barrie used by a child friend of his, Margaret Henley. **Wenda** has been described as a variant of Wendy but is more probably a form of Gwenda (see GWEN).

Wenonah see WINONA

Wesley *m*
John and Charles Wesley were the founders of Methodism, and the name came to be used as a first name in their honour. As a surname it means 'west meadow'. **Wes** is a short form.

Whitney *f* and *m*
This name, made famous by the singer Whitney Houston, was originally a surname meaning '(living) at the white island'. Its use as a first name in the USA may be because of its being the surname of both a wealthy family prominent in national politics and arts, and of Josiah Dwight Whitney (1819–1896), geologist and surveyor, after whom the USA's highest mountain outside Alaska, Mount Whitney in southern California, is named. The similar-sounding **Whitley**, from a surname meaning 'white wood or clearing', had a brief fashion for girls in the late 1980s, early 1990s after it was used in the television comedy *A Different World*, which also introduced JALEESA.

Wilbur *m*
This name is used in North America but is practically unknown in Britain. The most famous example was Wilbur Wright, who, with his brother ORVILLE, made the first successful powered flight in 1903.

Wilfred, Wilfrid *m*
From the Old English Wilfrith, meaning 'desiring peace'. St Wilfrid was an important figure in the 7th century, and his name was particularly popular in Yorkshire where he preached and founded the bishoprics of Ripon and Hexham. The name did not survive the Norman Conquest but was revived by High-Church Anglicans in the 19th century. It has the pet form **Wilf**.

Will see WILLARD, WILLIAM

Willard *m*
The Old English name Wilheard, composed of elements meaning 'will, desire' and 'brave, hardy', died out but not before it became

a surname that was later re-used as a first name. It is well used in the USA but rare in the UK. It shares the short forms **Will** and **Willy** with WILLIAM.

William *m*, Wilma *f*

From the Old German, meaning 'desiring protection'. William was always a popular name with the Normans, who brought it to England, and, until the 13th century when it was ousted by JOHN, it was the commonest of all names in England. Today it is one of the most popular names throughout the English-speaking world. **Will** or **Willie**, **Bill** and BILLIE are short forms, with **Wills** well known as the pet name of Prince William, the elder son of the Prince of Wales. **Gwilym**, shortened to **Gwill**, is the Welsh form of the name, and LIAM a short form from Ireland; **Ulick** (see ULYSSES) is another Irish form. Feminine forms that have been used occasionally are **Wilhelmina** and **Wilma**. Their pet forms include **Willa** or **Vilma** (see also VELMA), **Minnie** and **Minna** and **Elma** (see ELMER). These feminine forms are more popular in America where German immigrants have spread their use.

Willow *f*

A recent plant name, usually used for girls but occasionally for boys. It is the name of a major character in the *Buffy the Vampire Slayer* television series.

Willy see WILLARD, WILLIAM

Wilma see VELMA, WILLIAM

Winifred *f*

From the Welsh feminine name **Gwenfrewi**, anglicised as Winifred and later confused with the Old English male name **Winfrith**, meaning 'friend of peace'. St Winifred, a 7th-century saint, is said to have been decapitated by a Welsh prince when she rejected his advances but was then miraculously restored to life. Although she was a popular saint in the Middle Ages, her name was not used much until the 16th century. It was a very popular name at the turn of the

19th-20th centuries. **Win**, **Winnie** and, less often, **Freda** are short forms. **Winifrid** is also used.

Winona *f*
This is a Sioux word meaning 'eldest daughter'. It is also the name of a city in Minnesota. The name occurs as **Wenonah** in Longfellow's poem *Hiawatha* (1855) and can also be found as **Wynon(n)a**.

Winston m
This is the name of a small village in Gloucestershire, which became a surname. The name has been used in the Churchill family since 1620, when Sir Winston Churchill, father of the 1st Duke of Marlborough, was born. His mother was Sarah Winston. It has come into use in honour of Sir Winston Churchill (1874–1965), to mark his contribution to world affairs.

Wyatt *m*
The use of this surname, from medieval pet forms of both Guy and William, as a first name is mainly restricted to the USA, where its popularity is growing. It is well known from Wyatt Earp (1848–1929), famous from the gunfight at the OK Corral.

Wyn, Wynfor, Wynne see GWYN

Wystan *m*
St Wystan, whose name comes from elements meaning 'battle' and 'stone', was a boy king of Mercia (central England) who was murdered by his regent in 849. He was buried in Repton, Derbyshire, where there is an important church dedicated to him. The most famous barer of the name was Wystan Hugh (W. H.) Auden, who seems to have been given the name because his father was born in Repton. Most modern uses are influenced by Auden.

Xan, Xander see ALEXANDER

Xanthe *f*
From the Greek meaning 'yellow'. It has occasionally been used in Britain.

Xara see ZAHRA

Xavier *m*
The surname of St Francis Xavier (1506–52) used as a first name. It is also occasionally spelt **Javier** or **Zavier**, and there are rare feminine forms, **Xavia, Zavia, Xaviera** and **Xaverine**. Use of Xavier is increasing in the USA, and this has been attributed, at least in part, to the prominence of the basketball player Xavier McDaniel.

Xenia *f*
The Greek word for 'hospitality' which in turn comes from 'stranger'. It is only occasionally found. **Xena** is also used (see also ZENA), but it is too soon to tell if the international success of the television series *Xena, Warrior Princess* will increase usage significantly.

Yasin *m*
A name formed by the names of Arabic letters from an important passage in the Koran. Yasin features in a well-known Egyptian tale fighting social injustice.

Yasmin, Yasmina, Yasmine see JASMINE

Yehudi see JUDE

Yekaterina see KATYA

Yessenia *f*
Still mainly restricted to the Americas, this name of unknown meaning became popular with Spanish speakers as that of the titular gypsy heroine of a Mexican film (1971), later made into a television series. It is also found as **Yesenia**.

Yolanda *f*
From the Greek, meaning 'violet flower'. The name of the Gilbert and Sullivan opera *Iolanthe* comes from the same root. **Yolande** is the French form.

Ysabel see ISABEL

Yseult(e), Ysolde see ISOLDA

Yusuf *m*
Yusuf or Yusif is a popular boy's name, the Arabic equivalent of JOSEPH.

Yves see IVO, IVOR, YVONNE

Yvonne, Yvette *f*
These are French names meaning 'yew'. They are female pet forms of the Breton boy's name, **Yves**. The boy's name has never been common, but the girls' versions are well known, if somewhat out of fashion.

Zachary *m*
The English form of **Zacharias**, the Greek for the Hebrew **Zachariah** or **Zechariah**, meaning 'the Lord has remembered'. Zachary was used occasionally in the Middle Ages but did not become at all common until the Puritans adopted it in the 17th century. It has variant forms, **Zachery** and **Zackery**, and the short form **Zac**, **Zak** or **Zack**. **Zacchaeus** and **Zakki** are other forms of the name. Zachary is popular in North America and Canada and growing in use in the UK.

Zahid *m*
An Arabic name that means 'abstinent'.

Zahra, Zara *f*
A Muslim name that means 'to flower' or 'to achieve splendour'. It was the family name of the Prophet's mother and is traditionally used in her honour. The English form came to the attention of the British public in 1981 when Princess Anne, the Princess Royal, used it as her daughter's name. It is occasionally found as **Xara** or **Zaria**.

Zainab see ZAYNAB

Zak see ISAAC, ZACHARY

Zake *m*, Zakiya *f*
An Arabic name meaning 'pure, chaste'. The feminine form can also be spelt **Zakiyah** and **Zakiyya**.

Zakki see ZACHARY

Zander see ALEXANDER

Zandra see SANDRA

Zane *m*
The American author Zane Grey (1872–1939, given name PEARL Grey) took his pen name from his home town of Zanesville, Ohio. The town was named after its founder, Ebenezer Zane; the meaning of his surname is not known. Thanks to him, the name is not uncommon in the USA.

Zara, Zaria see ZAHRA

Zavia, Zavier see XAVIER

Zaynab *f*
A popular Muslim name of uncertain meaning. Some scholars link it with a fragrant plant, and it was borne by several members of the Prophet Mohammed's family. It is frequently found as **Zainab**.

Zeb *m*
This can be a short form of such Hebrew names as **Zebulun** ('exaltation') or **Zebedee** ('my gift'), or can simply be an attempt by parents to find an unusual name. Similarly, **Zed** can be seen as a short form of **Zedekiah** ('justice of the Lord').

Zechariah see ZACHARY

Zed, Zedekiah see ZEB

Zeke see EZEKIEL

Zelda see GRISELDA

Zelma see SELMA

Zena *f*
One theory is that this name comes from a Persian word meaning 'woman'. Another makes it a pet form of various other names such as **Zinaida**, which comes from Zeus, the Greek king of the gods, and is the name of two Russian saints; and another a variation of XENIA. It is also found as **Zina**.

Zenobia *f*
This was the name of a great queen of Palmyra (modern Syria) in the 3rd century AD. She was seen as a threat to the Eastern Roman Empire, and her aggressive foreign policy forced the Emperor Aurelian to invade. This he did successfully and put an end to her power, although he spared her life. The name appears in Cornwall from the 16th century, but the reason for this is unknown.

Zeta see ZITA

Zillah *f*
From the Hebrew for 'shade'. The name occurs in the Old Testament (Genesis 4:19–23) for one of the two wives of Lamech, son of Methuselah and the first polygamist recorded in the Bible. Zillah was used occasionally after the Reformation.

Zina, Zinaida see ZENA

Zita *f*
The name of the last empress of Austria who, although deposed just after the end of the First World War, died only in 1989. It comes from an Italian word for 'little girl' and was the name of a humble but good maid who became the patron saint of domestic servants. It can also be found as **Zeta**.

Zoe, Zoë *f*
This is the Greek word for 'life'. The Alexandrian Jews used it to translate the Hebrew equivalent for EVE into Greek. The name spread throughout the Eastern Church but has been used in the West only in the last hundred years. It also appears as **Zoey** and **Zoie**.

Zorah *f*
An Arabic name meaning 'light of dawn', also found as **Zora**. It can also be understood as a Hebrew name, taken from a place name of unknown meaning found in the Bible.

Zshakira see SHAKIR

Zubaida *f*

An Arabic name, popular in India, meaning 'marigold'.

Zuleika *f*

From the Persian, meaning 'brilliant beauty'. The name is known from Max Beerbohm's satirical novel *Zuleika Dobson* (1911), whose heroine is so beautiful that all the young men at Oxford University kill themselves for love of her. The Arabic spelling is **Zulekha**.

Appendix 1

Websites

General sites

Oxygen Babynamer claims a database of 23,000 names, lets you compare different forms of the names and find similar-sounding names, as well as warning you of drawbacks and nicknames at http://tools.oxygen.com/babynamer/.

Behind the Name – the Etymology and History of First Names has a lot of useful background information on the history of names, is generally reliable and allows you to access lists of names by classes such as national origin at http://www.behindthename.com/.

Special sites for particular types of names

Indian Names and their Meanings has alphabetical lists of names used in India with brief meanings. There are separate lists for names from Sanskrit (generally Hindu or Sikh), Bengali names and Muslim names at http://www.ee.ualberta.ca/~naik/indnames. html.

Parents Pitara lists names from the Indian subcontinent alphabetically, giving meaning, gender and religion at http://www. parentspitara.com/toolbox/babynu/bn/.

Two sites with pages devoted to Sikh names are *Gateway to Sikhism* at http://allaboutsikhs.com/names/names.htm, which also has useful background information and *The Sikhism Home Page*, http://www.sikhs.org/names.htm.

There is a list of Muslim names *Islam – The Modern Religion* at http://www.themodernreligion.com/convert/names.htm.

Celtic Names of the British Isles is a rather erratic list arranged by Celtic language (including Breton). Not always entirely accurate, but with same rare names and information you are not likely to find elsewhere, at http://www.crosswinds.net/~daire/names/main. html.

Irish names are listed at *Irish Lane* at http://www.hylit.com/info/Names/index.html, which also gives some information on the popularity of names in Ireland.

National Statistics

For the USA there is extensive information on the popularity of names from 1880 onwards produced by the Social Security Administration at http://www.ssa.gov/OACT/babynames/index. html.

Statistics for English first names can be found on the Government Office of National Statistics site at http://www.statistics.gov. uk/cci/nugget.asp?id=184, from which links can be found for Scotland and Northern Ireland.

Lists of other sites devoted to names

The Babies Planet has an excellent list of sites on baby names at http://www.thebabiesplanet.com/bbnames.shtml.

For more serious research there is the *A Selective Bibliography of International Web Sites Relating to Toponyms, Anthroponyms and Miscellaneous Name Sites: For use in Conducting Onomastic Research* at http://www.wtsn.binghamton.edu/ANS/Hattendorf%20Bibliography.htm, where names for people are listed under Anthroponyms. Despite the daunting title of the site, some good and accessible sites are listed.

Appendix 2

Top 100 boys' and girls' names in England and Wales, 2002

	Boys		Girls		Boys		Girls
1	Jack	1	Chloe	35	Kieran	35	Millie
2	Joshua	2	Emily	36	Aaron	36	Anna
3	Thomas	3	Jessica	37	Brandon	37	Amber
4	James	4	Ellie	38	Bradley	38	Erin
5	Daniel	5	Sophie	39	Kyle	39	Sarah
6	Benjamin	6	Megan	40	Tyler	40	Phoebe
7	William	7	Charlotte	41	Louis	41	Abbie
8	Samuel	8	Lucy	42	Alex	42	Daisy
9	Joseph	9	Hannah	43	Jordan	43	Zoe
10	Oliver	10	Olivia	44	Reece	44	Rachel
11	Harry	11	Lauren	45	Edward	45	Laura
12	Matthew	12	Katie	46	Harvey	46	Nicole
13	Luke	13	Amy	47	Charles	47	Isabelle
14	Lewis	14	Molly	48	David	48	Maisy
15	George	15	Holly	49	Alfie	49	Paige
16	Callum	16	Ella	50	Robert	50	Isabella
17	Adam	17	Bethany	51	Henry	51	Freya
18	Ethan	18	Rebecca	52	Harrison	52	Natasha
19	Alexander	19	Grace	53	Joe	53	Isobel
20	Ryan	20	Mia	54	Rhys	54	Niamh
21	Ben	21	Georgia	55	Archie	55	Rosie
22	Mohammed	22	Abigail	56	Christopher	56	Alexandra
23	Liam	23	Caitlin	57	Sam	57	Imogen
24	Jake	24	Leah	58	Toby	58	Eve
25	Nathan	25	Amelia	59	Kai	59	Isabel
26	Connor	26	Eleanor	60	Morgan	60	Louise
27	Cameron	27	Emma	61	Muhammad	61	Alicia
28	Dylan	28	Jasmine	62	Jay	62	Alisha
29	Charlie	29	Lily	63	Andrew	63	Poppy
30	Jacob	30	Elizabeth	64	Isaac	64	Morgan
31	Owen	31	Shannon	65	John	65	Aimee
32	Jamie	32	Jade	66	Aidan	66	Ruby
33	Max	33	Alice	67	Joel	67	Tia
34	Michael	34	Courtney	68	Taylor	68	Jodie

	Boys		Girls		Boys		Girls
69	Kian	69	Mollie	85	Mason	85	Katherine
70	Mohammad	70	Hollie	86	Josh	86	Kayleigh
71	Oscar	71	Libby	87	Nicholas	87	Sophia
72	Lucas	72	Madeleine	88	Leo	88	Francesca
73	Leon	73	Jennifer	89	Declan	89	Gabrielle
74	Dominic	74	Georgina	90	Tom	90	Yasmin
75	Elliot	75	Harriet	91	Jason	91	Charlie
76	Sean	76	Lydia	92	Marcus	92	Aaliyah
77	Jonathan	77	Victoria	93	Finley	93	Stephanie
78	Scott	78	Samantha	94	Anthony	94	Elle
79	Finlay	79	Danielle	95	Sebastian	95	Eloise
80	Bailey	80	Chelsea	96	Ashley	96	Lara
81	Patrick	81	Kate	97	Zachary	97	Ellen
82	Billy	82	Madison	98	Kieron	98	Elise
83	Ewan	83	Evie	99	Peter	99	Gemma
84	Ellis	84	Melissa	100	Mark	100	Abby

Top 100 boys' and girls' names in Scotland, 2002

	Boys		Girls		Boys		Girls
1	Jack	1	Chloe	24	Thomas	24	Eilidh
2	Lewis	2	Sophie	25	David	25	Zoe
3	Cameron	3	Emma	26	Alexander	26	Leah
4	Ryan	4	Amy	27	Aaron	27	Jessica
5	James	5	Erin	28	Josh	28	Louise
6	Jamie	6	Ellie	29	Euan	29	Jennifer
7	Liam	7	Rachel	30	Sean	30	Eve
8	Matthew	8	Lauren	31	John	31	Molly
9	Ross	9	Megan	32	Luke	32	Aimee
10	Callum	10	Hannah	33	Calum	33	Courtney
11	Dylan	11	Rebecca	34	Jordan	34	Jade
12	Kyle	12	Emily	35	Ewan	35	Olivia
13	Ben	13	Caitlin	36	Robert	36	Kirsty
14	Connor	14	Lucy	37	Christopher	37	Charlotte
15	Adam	15	Holly	38	Mark	38	Rachael
16	Daniel	16	Katie	39	Jay	39	Laura
17	Andrew	17	Nicole	40	Craig	40	Bethany
18	Scott	18	Sarah	41	Finlay	41	Taylor
19	Kieran	19	Abbie	42	Fraser	42	Cara
20	Nathan	20	Morgan	43	Declan	43	Abby
21	Aidan	21	Anna	44	William	44	Abigail
22	Michael	22	Niamh	45	Robbie	45	Mia
23	Joshua	23	Shannon	46	Ethan	46	Samantha

Boys	Girls	Boys	Girls
47 Logan	47 Jodie	75 = Ciaran	75 = Eva
48 Reece	48 Kayleigh	= Darren	= Paige
49 Samuel	49 Heather	= Jason	
50 Joseph	50 Beth		77 Kate
51 Brandon	51 Stephanie	78 =Charlie	78 = Chelsea
52 Benjamin	52 Iona	= Jacob	= Kayla
53 Lee	53 = Georgia	= Marc	= Nicola
	= Isla	= Peter	= Ciara
54 Sam		82 Louis	82 = Alicia
55 Owen	55 Robyn		= Elizabeth
56 Rory	56 Melissa		= Rebekah
57 Harry	57 Brooke	83 Murray	
58 Paul	58 Grace	84 Conor	
59 Jake	59 Caitlyn	85 Tyler	85 = Alex
60 Shaun	60 Jenna		= Kara
61 Steven	61 Amber	86 Kian	
62 Rhys	62 Natasha	87 Gary	87 = Carly
63 Max	63 =Lisa		= Charlie
	= Skye	88 Mohammed	
64 Blair		89 = Charles	89 = Hollie
65 = Aiden	65 = Gemma	= Duncan	= Elle
= Taylor	= Hayley	91 = George	91 = Catriona
67 Oliver	67 = Freya	= Joe	= Kaitlyn
	= Kelsey	= Patrick	= Kiera
68 Gregor		94 = Arran	94 = Carla
69 Kai	69 Claire	= Bradley	= Fiona
70 Stuart	70 = Alice	= Finn	
	= Natalie		96 = Alexandra
71 Dean			= Ella
72 Stephen	72 = Catherine	97 Grant	
	= Danielle	98 = Alex	98 = Katherine
	= Demi	= Elliot	= Naomi
73 Jonathan		= Leon	= Rosie
74 Angus		= Mitchell	

Top 100 boys' and girls' names in the USA, 2001

Boys	Girls	Boys	Girls
1 Jacob	1 Emily	7 Andrew	7 Sarah
2 Michael	2 Madison	8 Joseph	8 Abigail
3 Matthew	3 Hannah	9 Daniel	9 Elizabeth
4 Joshua	4 Ashley	10 William	10 Jessica
5 Christopher	5 Alexis	11 Anthony	11 Olivia
6 Nicholas	6 Samantha	12 David	12 Taylor

	Boys		Girls		Boys		Girls
13	Tyler	13	Emma	57	Sean	57	Brooke
14	John	14	Alyssa	58	Charles	58	Sara
15	Ryan	15	Lauren	59	Evan	59	Michelle
16	Zachary	16	Grace	60	Jackson	60	Erin
17	Ethan	17	Kayla	61	Alex	61	Kimberly
18	Brandon	18	Brianna	62	Steven	62	Caroline
19	James	19	Anna	63	Jesus	63	Danielle
20	Alexander	20	Megan	64	Nathaniel	64	Zoe
21	Dylan	21	Victoria	65	Cody	65	Vanessa
22	Justin	22	Destiny	66	Bryan	66	Kaylee
23	Jonathan	23	Sydney	67	Jared	67	Trinity
24	Christian	24	Rachel	68	Timothy	68	Shelby
25	Austin	25	Jennifer	69	Ian	69	Bailey
26	Samuel	26	Jasmine	70	Seth	70	Jacqueline
27	Benjamin	27	Julia	71	Devin	71	Paige
28	Noah	28	Isabella	72	Richard	72	Courtney
29	Kevin	29	Morgan	73	Patrick	73	Autumn
30	José	30	Chloe	74	Cole	74	Melissa
31	Logan	31	Kaitlyn	75	Adrian	75	Jada
32	Robert	32	Natalie	76	Trevor	76	Angela
33	Nathan	33	Nicole	77	Blake	77	Mia
34	Thomas	34	Hailey	78	Sebastian	78	Alexa
35	Cameron	35	Haley	79	Gavin	79	Marissa
36	Hunter	36	Katherine	80	Chase	80	Catherine
37	Gabriel	37	Alexandre	81	Garrett	81	Christina
38	Caleb	38	Sophia	82	Julian	82	Claire
39	Jordan	39	Amanda	83	Lucas	83	Laura
40	Kyle	40	Maria	84	Miguel	84	Gabriella
41	Jason	41	Mackenzie	85	Alejandro	85	Leslie
42	Aaron	42	Stephanie	86	Antonio	86	Mariah
43	Eric	43	Savannah	87	Mark	87	Isabel
44	Luis	44	Allison	88	Aidan	88	Leah
45	Isaiah	45	Jenna	89	Jeremy	89	Ariana
46	Brian	46	Andrea	90	Jesse	90	Caitlin
47	Elijah	47	Rebecca	91	Jeremiah	91	Alexandria
48	Isaac	48	Jordan	92	Victor	92	Molly
49	Jack	49	Mary	93	Bryce	93	Kylie
50	Connor	50	Gabrielle	94	Kenneth	94	Breanna
51	Luke	51	Amber	95	Xavier	95	Angelina
52	Juan	52	Katelyn	96	Dakota	96	Aaliyah
53	Adam	53	Faith	97	Carson	97	Kathryn
54	Angel	54	Makayla	98	Dalton	98	Jade
55	Carlos	55	Madeline	99	Colby	99	Kelsey
56	Mason	56	Sierra	100	Jake	100	Briana